Urban Poverty in a
Cross-Cultural Context

Urban Poverty
in a
Cross-Cultural
Context

EDWIN EAMES
Bernard M. Baruch College,
CUNY
and

JUDITH GRANICH GOODE
Temple University

 The Free Press
New York

Collier Macmillan Publishers
London

The Free Press
A Division of Macmillan Publishing Co., Inc.
866 Third Avenue, New York, New York 10022

Collier-Macmillan Canada Ltd.

Library of Congress Catalog Card Number: 72-90545

printing number
1   2   3   4   5   6   7   8   9   10

We would like to express our appreciation to the authors as well as the publishers of the following works:

C. Coon (ed.), *A Reader in General Anthropology* (New York: Holt, Rinehart and Winston, Inc., 1948).

Oscar Lewis, "The Possessions of the Poor," in *Anthropological Essays* (New York: Random House, Inc., 1970).

David Simpson, "The Dimensions of World Poverty," *Scientific American*, Vol. 219, November 1968, pp. 27–35.

To our respective spouses,
Phyllis and Paul

Contents

Preface

Anthropology has traditionally been regarded as the study of exotic and little-known people. The general public as well as students, have at times been titillated by anthropological accounts of such strange institutions as infanticide, wife-exchanges, and the couvade. More recently, anthropologists have been concerned with the study of more complex communities and societies. An initial thrust was in the direction of studies of peasant or pre-industrial agrarian peoples.

When, in the early 1940s, anthropologists began studying peasant societies, the majority of the world's population could be classified as peasants. Studies of Chinese, East Indian, Mexican, Japanese and Guatemalan villages were conducted during this early period. There has been a continuing and increasing interest in this area of anthropological research.

At the present time, some cultural anthropologists have turned their attention to the study of large scale, complex, urban industrial societies. One reason for this shift in emphasis is the movement of formerly tribal or peasant peoples into large-scale social systems.

Both of the authors received their graduate training at Cornell University, which was itself caught up in this changing emphasis in the field. Both did their fieldwork in urbanizing societies, one studying rural-urban migration in India and the other an urban occupation in Colombia.

The authors started their teaching careers at an urban institution, Temple University. During the 1960s, the University, like many others in major urban centers, was focusing on urban studies. As teachers in this developing area, the authors were asked to develop a course designed to provide a broad framework for students who would be working with the urban poor, for example, teachers, social workers, judicial and law enforcement personnel, urban planners and administrators.

In developing the course, it soon became apparent that descriptive and analytical materials on poverty were very parochial and narrowly conceived. In addition, most of the better anthropological material was not readily available to the student. The need for a book on poverty which brought together the wide range of disparate materials and offered a broad perspective was recognized.

In the latter half of the 1960s, Oscar Lewis's work stimulated a great deal of discussion which transcended the limited field of anthropology. As anthropologists, the authors could not overlook the controversial issue of the "culture of poverty" and incorporated it into the development of the course and, later, the book. In treating this particular approach, it became obvious to the authors that there were many questions about urban poverty and the behavior of the urban poor which remained unanswered. A significant portion of this volume is their attempt to answer these questions or at least to narrow them down so they can be answered by future research. To do so has required a major search through the existing literature and the meaningful organization of the bits and pieces of material available.

While the volume does not claim to provide major innovative solutions to the problem of urban poverty, it does attempt to make the reader aware of the complex issues involved, the stereotypic oversimplifications frequently used and thus provide a vantage point for a realistic discussion of the issues.

Edwin Eames
Judith Granich Goode

Acknowledgments

It is difficult to list all those who have contributed to the completion of this volume, since any book of this type is a compendium of many ideas from many sources. We would, however, like to acknowledge the contributions of our colleagues in the Department of Anthropology at Temple University and the Department of Sociology and Anthropology at Baruch College (CUNY). In particular, we would like to thank Dr. Melvin Mednick, Dr. Gerald Obermeyer, Dr. William Schwab and Dr. Norman Storer for their conceptual and bibliographic suggestions. Dr. Eleanor Leacock was kind enough to provide us with some manuscripts which have subsequently been published in her volume: *The Culture of Poverty: A Critique.* Particular thanks are due to Dr. John Szwed, who as a former colleague and present co-director of the Center for Urban Ethnography provided stimulation and encouragement. The Center was instrumental in providing us with the opportunity to exchange ideas with other social scientists interested in the poverty issue.

The College of Education at Temple University, through its Primesite Program, stimulated the initial development of the course which led to the development of the present volume. Further stimulation in the development of the course was given by our colleagues and students in the Urban Studies Program at Temple. Dr. Belle Granich, School of Social Welfare, Fordham University, and her students have forced us to broaden our perspective and recognize the needs of practitioners directly involved with the poverty population. Dr. George Barnsby, a British historian, provided us with a detailed description of the English workhouse and also contributed to the development of the materials dealing with British welfare policy.

Maryanne Myers, a graduate student in anthropology at Temple University, was of great help in checking many of the bibliographic sources used in the volume. To our various patient typists: Maryanne Bonaquisti, Agnes Collins, Mona Eames, Alice Edelstein, and Margaret Peppelman, we extend our heartfelt thanks.

Our respective families, Mona, David and Lori; Larry, Andy and Josh, have been extremely patient during the various crises which appear to be normal in the writing of a book. Finally, we should like to thank the variety of students with whom segments of this volume have been shared. Their criticisms and suggestions have, we hope, made this a better volume.

Chapter 1

Introduction

POVERTY is a word which we now hear every day. We read about the plight of the poor in our newspapers and see television documentaries about the poor in America. Poverty and welfare policies have become major policy issues and are important items in political campaigns. Poverty is treated as one of the major components of the so-called "urban crisis." In almost all of these contexts, a very narrow view of the phenomenon is apparent. This volume is an attempt to broaden our perspective of poverty in America by making the reader more aware of the larger and more universal aspects of this problem.

Poverty and Society

General concern with the problem of poverty has varied during the last few decades. For most of the nineteeth century, poverty was considered to be a "natural" and inevitable phenomenon. Later in the century, however, as a result of social change, poverty increasingly came to be viewed as a problem which endangered the social system by producing antisocial behavior.[1] As productivity increased, poverty was seen as unnecessary; the result of social injustice which could and should be eliminated. Undoubtedly, one could find a high correlation between economic cycles and the concern with poverty; during periods of prosperity the problem has been ignored while periods of recession and depression have been characterized by social concern.

For at least a decade following World War II, it was assumed that American poverty would be eliminated through natural economic growth. However, in the 1960s a number of influential writers began to emphasize the fact that despite prosperity, large pockets of the poor remained in the United States. One indication of the early insignificance of poverty as an area of social science research can be seen in the topical listings of the *Social Science and Humanities Index.* If one goes to this source, no listing of "poverty" as a topic would be found until the middle of the sixties. Since then poverty has become a focal concern of social scientists and policy-makers and many "definitive" studies have been published. The middle sixties saw a proliferation of poverty work and 1965 was a particularly important year.[2] Almost all the articles and books of this time deal with the contemporary United States scene. A comparative study must take account of more than a few centuries of Western history, the era of capitalism and industrialism. To date, very little attempt has been made to lengthen the historical perspective or to broaden the cross-cultural.

In both popular and academic writing about poverty, two major areas are emphasized. One is the discussion of the causes of poverty. The other is the justification of the allocation of energy, money and man-power, to eradicate poverty, that is, the discussion of the importance of poverty as a social problem.

In the discussion of causes, two arguments have been heard. One suggests that the poor are responsible for their own condition (implying the need to change the poor as individuals) while the other sees the poor as victims of a larger social system over which they have little or no control (implying system-wide changes). Commitment to the elimination of poverty is justified in economic, ethical and political terms. Some see the poor essentially as receivers of welfare, non-producers and in-adequate consumers unable to contribute to economic growth. Others stress the ethical impropriety of the existence of poverty in one of the wealthiest nations of the world. Finally, there are those who view the poor as a basic threat—through crime, riots and revolution—to society at large.

Much of the literature dealing with the poor focuses on behavior which is considered typical. Such behavior is frequently described in pejorative terms and is viewed as dysfunctional, a barrier to upward mobility. High rates of crime, personal violence, drug addiction, alcohol-ism, mental illness, sexual promiscuity and illegitimacy are commonly attributed to the poor. Recently, social scientists have begun to question the validity of many of these attributions. Even where a correlation exists, the assumption that there are dysfunctional consequences for upward mobility is being questioned. A central issue in contemporary poverty research is the degree to which these behavioral patterns are, in fact, *adaptive* responses to an ecological setting.

The Anthropological Perspective

One of the social sciences most concerned with the actual description of human behavior in particular sociocultural settings is cultural anthropology. Most cultural anthropologists are involved in ethnographic fieldwork which focuses upon the collection of data by the direct observation of everyday activities. In addition, fieldwork involves participation in a variety of activities as well as intensive interviewing often related to the observed activities. Since the nature of the data collecting process involves the anthropologist in face-to-face contact with his informants he can rarely disregard the individual. In effect, what we are suggesting is that anthropologists are traditionally concerned with the humanistic description of real people based on first-hand observation.

A basic issue in anthropology is the analysis of such descriptions of behavior. Some anthropologists feel that the primary task is complete when they have described a society, emphasizing its unique aspects. Others suggest that the comparison of various cultural behaviors and lifestyles is the most important function. Anthropologists who claim that anthropology is a science suggest that comparison and explanation is the basis of their endeavor and must be their ultimate goal.

One result of the descriptive accounts compiled by anthropologists is the recognition of the tremendous variety of ways in which human beings have responded to the requirements of basic survival. Related to this is the core concept in anthropology, the concept of *culture*. A definition of culture which has been widely used by anthropologists is the following:

By culture we mean all those historically created designs for living, explicit and implicit, rational, irrational, and non-rational, which exist at any given time as potential guides for the behavior of men.[3]

The "designs for living" described by Kluckhohn and Kelly refer to the learned norms governing the behavior of people who live in a particular tradition.

Man is what biologists call a "generalized animal." Unlike other animals which have environmental niches for which they are especially adapted by such physical devices as coloration, locomotion or weaponry, man has no such distinctive characteristics. However, he is more than a "naked ape." His major adaptive mechanism is culture. Through the knowledge which his ancestors have gained and transmitted to him socially (non-genetically), he can cope with many different ecological settings.

The use of symbols is the most important technique involved in cultural transmission. The unique characteristic of man, and one which constitutes a qualitative difference between man and other animals, is his ability to symbolize.[4] A symbol is by definition something which stands for something else. Thus, all our language with the possible exception of pictographic writing, is symbolic. In addition to words, things or objects may have symbolic value or meaning. Our status in society is symbolized by the type of clothing and insignia we wear, the kinds of houses we live in, the titles we use and, in a polygynous society, the number of wives we have. Colors also have symbolic significance, for example "black is beautiful" and red, when it is in the form of a traffic light, means stop. The symbolic meaning of color can vary from culture to culture, for example, white is the color of mourning in India. Since symbolic meaning is not intrinsic in the object, the meaning can be changed, and the meanings are limitless.

In describing the infinite variety of designs for living found around the world, anthropologists attempt to find those aspects of behavior which are universal and may truly be said to relate to "human nature" as well as those which are variable. The two themes of cultural universals and differences permeate the analytical discussions in the field. In order to document both the similarities and the differences, the mission of the discipline has been the study of man *in all times and all places,* that is, historically and cross-culturally.

One result of this comparative perspective has been the growing awareness of cultural relativity. Simply stated, cultural relativism suggests that every cultural system must be studied in and of itself without introducing any judgmental bias. Cultural systems cannot be comparatively evaluated, that is, called better or worse than others. This position is the reverse of *ethnocentrism* in which one considers his own values and culture to be the best, the right or the most advanced and developed. While cultures must be understood in their own terms and cannot be rated qualitatively, there are some aspects of cultural complexity which can be quantitatively compared (in terms of measurable indices, more or less, rather than better or worse). Thus, Coon states:

One rule which this discipline has taught us is to avoid value comparisons between cultures. As members of the anthropological profession, we in America believe both in the rights of individuals to live at peace with each other within societies, and in the rights of separate societies and cultures to coexist in the world. . . .

In expression of this belief the Executive Board of the American Anthropological Association has recently sent a *Statement on Human Rights* to the Commission on Human Rights of the United Nations. The essence of this communication lies in Principle Two: "Respect for differences between cultures is validated by the scientific fact that no technique of qualitatively evaluating cultures has been discovered."

In this declaration and in its purpose I am in complete agreement with my fellow members. Strongly as I endorse our stand, I feel equally strongly that we should back the statement quoted above with positive as well as negative validation. In my opinion one profitable way to seek this positive evidence is to study *quantitative* differences between cultures, a far different thing from the pursuit of value judgments. The fact that one category of differences has fallen into disfavor does not mean that we should avoid the study of all other categories. To the contrary, by the quantitative method we may be able to help discover both how and why cultures differ, a basic step in the formulation of those codes of international behavior with which the United Nations Commission is concerned.

I also believe that the study of the quantitative method is profitable because it is the method of systematic science which has proved fruitful in all other fields of learning in which it has been used. The essence of the quantitative approach in cultural anthropology lies in the thesis that the main stream or streams of human culture must proceed from simpler to more complex. The evidence of archaeology and of history supports this thesis, which in turn accords with all that we know of life in general. It must be equally apparent that the living cultures of the world vary in degrees of complexity, and that whole cultures can be listed and studied with greatest profit on the basis of such a progressive scheme.[5]

There still exists considerable controversy about the precise definition of anthropology and some of its major concepts. However, from the above discussion it can be suggested that the essence of the anthropological framework is the descriptive, humanistic approach, the emphasis on historical and cross-cultural comparison, the use of the culture concept and the relativist position.

Anthropology and Poverty

When poverty emerged as a central issue in the popular and social science literature, some anthropologists responded. Anthropological writing, particularly the work of Lewis, Liebow, Hannerz and Valentine, can be viewed as a major component in the social science discussion of the behavior of the poor. However, the concern with poverty did not have a major impact on the field of anthropology.

In a growing, diversified field undergoing increased division of labor and subspecialization, one issue could not be expected to capture the attention of most anthropologists. Many still prefer the traditional analysis of small-scale tribal groups or small peasant communities to the attempt to decipher the sociocultural complexity of an urban industrial system.

Most of those who have studied non-Western societies entering the urban industrial phase have attempted to *avoid* a social problems concern. As humanistic observers of other cultures, they have striven to point out the positive capacities of their subjects for coping with stress and they ignore areas which reveal problems. Thus, they have concentrated on the adjustment of migrants to urban life and other aspects of the transitional process. Inventiveness and the use of traditional culture to cushion the stress of change are emphasized. In an attempt to show that the materialistic values of the West are not inevitable or necessary for progress, these anthropologists have de-emphasized the impact of material deprivation and long-term unemployment.[6]

Anthropologists who became interested in poverty are those who in recent years have come to focus on their own society, primarily because of a concern with problems requiring political solutions. Thus, poverty has become an area of research for those committed anthropologists interested in eradicating social injustice in their own system. In the parochial concentration on the contemporary American poor, the traditional historical and cross-cultural emphasis is missing and we are faced with a limited time perspective of two hundred years and the limited cross-cultural focus which extends only to ethnic groups in the United States as in comparisons of poor blacks, poor whites and poor Chicanos.[7]

Much of the work in this area followed the traditional anthropological concern with humanistic, first-hand observation. These anthropologists lived with the poor or interacted with them frequently and intimately and described what they saw. They provide accounts of the poor as real people. Since the descriptions were of conditions of life which were deplorable, the humanistic element in their work led to a compassionate desire to improve the lot of the people they were studying, especially since the people were segments of their own society.

One significant exception to the emphasis on the American poor is the work of Oscar Lewis who studied poverty outside the United States. His work attempts to generalize about modern man's response to the conditions of poverty. Lewis's approach alienated many anthropologists interested in American poverty because the policy implications which he and others drew from his work were antithetical to theirs. His approach was generally ignored by those studying the non-Western world because it emphasized problem and despair. Such reactions to Lewis's work effectively hampered the development of a cross-cultural study of poverty.[8]

The Work of Oscar Lewis

Oscar Lewis's first fieldwork among rural Mexican peasants was in the tradition of peasant studies.[9] In the process of fieldwork, he found evidence of migration from the village to Mexico City, and later followed migrants into the city to examine their experiences in an urban setting. Since most of these migrants had few marketable skills in the urban economic system, they entered the lowest stratum of urban society and Lewis began to do fieldwork in Mexico City slums. As Lewis became more concerned with urban poverty groups, he recognized that these were people whose everyday activities had been neglected by traditional social science.

During field experience in slums in Mexico City, San Juan, Puerto Rico and among Puerto Ricans in New York City, Lewis began to conceptualize the culture of poverty.[10] Briefly stated, Lewis asserted the belief that in an urban industrial setting, the behavior of people who are materially deprived is a response to their circumstances. He called this behavioral response the "culture of poverty."

Among the behavioral responses of the poor identified by Lewis as part of this "culture" were some characteristics of the individual such as weak ego structure and oral fixation; some family characteristics such as the female-based household and unstable consensual unions; some community variables such as lack of organization as well as some variables affecting integration with the larger society such as apathy, withdrawal, hostility, dependence and other, often mutually inconsistent attributes.

The poor are also pictured as provincial, rooted in the present and fatalistic.

Lewis has been criticized for his use of pejorative and value-laden terms in his description of the poor. In spite of Lewis's anthropological training and extensive fieldwork, much of the description of the culture of poverty is lacking in the relativity and objectivity which by now are an integral part of the dogma of anthropology. Among those characteristics which Lewis cites as definitive attributes are the mother-centered family, and psychological maladies and the idea that "the poverty of culture is one of the most crucial aspects of the culture of poverty." [11] The emphasis on the mother-centered family described from the point of view of the middle-class American family seems peculiar indeed in the light of the anthropologists' experience with a wide variety of family systems in human groups. Furthermore, much of Lewis's characterization of those in poverty uses such terms as weak ego structure, maternal deprivation and orality. There seems to be undue stress on psychological rather than cultural variables. Moreover, these variables are developed from the point of view of a supposedly "healthy" Western middle-class ego. Anthropologists rarely take the position of characterizing a culture as "thin" or "inadequate" even when they recognize that change is desirable, yet Lewis does not hesitate to use these adjectives.

Lewis has also been attacked for sloppy conceptualization. In at least three sources, Lewis has mentioned over seventy characteristics which he has delineated as definitive.[12] In a careful reading of these sources, no more than fifty-five characteristics have been obtained by the authors. In many cases, these fifty-five items were hardly discrete. What is probably most disturbing about them is the total lack of weighting or relative significance given to the various characteristics. It appears absurd to place in the same order of significance the non-use of banks and the preponderance of female-centered household units. There is very little effort in Lewis's work to distinguish those elements which are central to the culture of poverty from those which are peripheral. Leeds has recently done a systematic analysis of the "traits" listed by Lewis indicating many conceptual and logical inconsistencies. He points out how Lewis has assumed his miscellany of traits to be a well-integrated system of parts without making an effort to describe the structure or logic of their relationship. Leeds says: "He [Lewis] fails to give us either the dynamics, *in natura* of how these traits are linked or the logic at the meta-language level of assuming their linkage." [13]

Many of the characteristics which Lewis mentions have been challenged as empirically invalid by other anthropologists using Lewis's own data as well as their own. Thus, Valentine using material from Lewis's own work suggests that the Rios family in *La Vida* are by no means "parochial" and have considerable knowledge about politics and the social system in which they live.[14] He similarly challenges the notion that the poor are apathetic and withdrawn. Mangin and Leeds have pointed to the high levels of organization in several Latin American slum communities to refute Lewis's suggestion with new data.[15] The ethnographic fieldwork of the Valentines in Blackston (pseudonym for a black urban community) also refutes many of Lewis's notions.[16]

Methodological criticisms have also been leveled at Lewis. In working with individual families in each of his studies, Lewis is called to task for generalizing about community functioning and organization which he had little chance to observe. Furthermore, in not using any systematic device to sample his families he has been cavalier in his selection of subjects. It becomes essential to know on what basis the families were selected and how representative they are of the poor. Despite the criticisms of Lewis's methodology, many anthropologists recognize the family-centered ethnography as an important contribution.[17] By concentrating upon the family as a unit, Lewis has provided humanistic, first-hand descriptions of the everyday life of the poor.

The Culture Issue

One of the most devastating criticisms of Lewis's culture of poverty concept and one which goes beyond Lewis's specific work, is the use of the culture concept. In using the word culture, Lewis was claiming that the behavioral responses of the poor were systematically related and passed down from generation to generation. Thus the behaviors took on a regenerative power of their own, recapitulating themselves and becoming independent of material circumstances. Poverty begat poverty culture and induced behavior which interfered with upward mobility, further perpetuating poverty conditions. This view can easily be misread to reinforce the already strong American belief that the poor are to blame for their own poverty because of their impulsive, immoral and indolent behavior.

The concept of culture which we have previously noted as a key concept in anthropology has been under attack by many contemporary cultural anthropologists. Many of those who focus upon urban industrial society suggest that the concept has very little utility and in many ways confuses basic issues in the description of human behavior in complex systems. Viewing culture as "designs for living" raises numerous questions in a multi-ethnic, class-stratified and large-scale social system.

As it is commonly understood by social scientists, culture is a set of beliefs and behaviors learned early in life which are strongly internalized and resistant to change. Lewis uncritically accepts this view as can be seen in the following statement about the culture of poverty:

> By the time slum children are 6 or 7 they have usually absorbed the basic attitudes and values of their subculture. Thereafter they are psychologically unready to take full advantage of changing conditions or improving opportunities that may develop in their lifetime.[18]

In an urban industrial society characterized by high rates of social and geographical mobility and continuous socialization throughout the life cycle, this emphasis on early and intensive culture learning is misplaced. Where the number of social strata and possible status combinations is so great, to talk about *a* set of learned behavioral guides is questionable. Lewis has done little to justify his use of the culture concept.

A number of anthropologists have suggested that the "behavioral guide" approach to culture tells us little about the lifestyles of individuals. They prefer a behaviorally descriptive approach (an emphasis on *overt* rather than *covert* behavior). One attempt to modify the culture concept and reintroduce it in the study of complex societies is to focus upon subcultures and view the total culture as a complex mosaic of diverse subcultural units. Lewis actually does use the term subculture interchangeably with culture, but he does not conceptually distinguish the two.

W. B. Miller is one anthropologist who is trying to refine the subculture concept. He has begun to develop a mapping of status categories in the United States which can be grouped into empirically discovered combinations which he calls subcultures and attempts to describe.[19] However, his scheme imputes strong internalization and commitment to the behavioral guides he discovers and is not useful to discussions of change. Hannerz, on the other hand, has tried to develop a definition of "soft" culture as opposed to the traditional "hard" concept which implied lack of flexibility and change. He also develops the notion of *cultural repertoire* which implies that individuals possess a wide range of alternative behavioral guides which they use in appropriate interaction situations and to which they feel differentially committed.[20] Gans has also pointed out that not all culturally learned behavior is internalized to the same degree and thus some behavior is easier to change than other types.[21]

One of the reasons why the culture issue is central to anthropological discussions of poverty is that the emphasis on cultural maintenance and continuity has had important implications for policy formulations. If one views the behavior of the poor as forming an autonomous, cohesive system which perpetuates itself, this implies that the only way to eradicate poverty is to change the behavior of the poor. Such a notion fits in well with the social science notions of "cultural deprivation" and "cultural pathology." Cultural deprivation implies that the poor are unsocialized and have *no* culture. Obvious implications of this view are that the separation of children from their parents at an early age, as in compensatory preschool programs, would compensate for lack of socialization. Cultural pathology implies that the poor have been improperly socialized producing a twisted, deviant version of the culture of society at large and implies the necessity of resocialization. Lewis's approach states that the poor have been socialized *differently* in order to help them adapt to an environment poor in resources. However, the political implication of this view is much the same: change the behavior of the poor.

In many ways, the culture issue may be related to the two basic questions which permeate the historical and contemporary writings about poverty. These two questions relate to the *causes* of poverty and the *justification* for its eradication. Both questions are intimately related to the behavior of the poor since such behavior has long been seen as a cause of, not a response to, poverty. Moreover, its antisocial nature has long been used as a major justification for the eradication of poverty without consideration of the economic and moral factors. Contemporary use of the culture concept as in Lewis's work serves merely to dress up the earlier more simplistic views of the behavior of the poor.

A shift away from the uncritical use of the culture concept has led to a much more detailed description of the behavior of the poor as a *response* to the resource-poor environment in which they live. This approach can be related to the anthropological interest in ecological adaptation. Where the term culture is used in ecological studies, it is only one aspect of the larger ecosystem, and one which is malleable when the total system changes.

In the ecological approach in anthropology, we can see that anthropologists are interested in exploring the ways in which different cultures adapt to similar sets of resources. They ask such questions as:

What do desert hunters and gatherers have in common? What do Arctic hunters and gatherers have in common? What do tropical forest agriculturalists have in common?, and so on. They fully recognize, of course, that the style and content of Amazonian tropical forest culture will be different from that of Southeast Asia. There is nevertheless an awareness of ecologically related similarities.

A contemporary ecological approach to poverty would emphasize the man-made nature of the social and physical environment to which the poor must adapt. Shannon makes the point about the nature of adaptation (in this case of urban migrants) in an urban industrial system:

> Primitive migrants lived within an eco-system in which the main problem was to cope with the challenge of their physical environment, the flora and fauna of their geographical location. Modern-day migrants are part of a system within which people must learn to cope with a pleasant or unpleasant, facilitating or unfacilitating social and organizational environment in which the most powerful determinants are neither vegetative, nor animal nor meteorological.[22]

While some of the aspects of the behavior of the poor can be explained in purely ecological terms, other aspects may be the result of different forces. Amongst these complex forces we find not only behavior which is adaptive to resource-poorness, but ethnic behaviors (the carryovers of older traditions), and behavior influenced by community dynamics, age-sets and peer groups. It is the failure to delineate the different influences on specific behaviors which has caused considerable confusion in the literature of poverty. This confusion can be seen in the careless equation of "poverty culture," black culture, teen-age gang culture, and so forth.

In the rest of this volume we will attempt to describe the ramifications of material deprivation in man's history and to compare the Western industrial world to the contemporary developing nations. Some of the important questions to be discussed are: What has been the extent of material deprivation in mankind's total experience? How has the extent changed with each technological breakthrough? Moreover, how has poverty been socially recognized, defined and evaluated during man's history? What have been the behavioral responses to material deprivation at different times? What are the independent effects of material deprivation as opposed to other forms of deprivation in other societies? Are there differences in the way non-Western contemporary peoples perceive and react to poverty? Are there similarities in such perception and response? Can similarities be linked to a specific stage of sociocultural evolution? Does the use of the culture concept help to explain similarities in the behavior of the poor?

To briefly recapitulate the relationship between anthropology and the study of poverty, it can be suggested that despite the maintenance of the descriptive and humanistic tradition, most studies have been lacking in a cross-cultural and historical perspective. The use of the culture concept in relation to the behavior of the poor has also been a frequent source of confusion. Recent studies have either bypassed the concept or attempted to redefine it for use in a complex society.

The Present Approach

The American social scientists (including anthropologists) working in poverty studies have been extremely parochial in their views. Their self-imposed national boundaries have limited their perspective on material deprivation and its implications. In reviewing the literature, it becomes apparent that the only reason mention is made of other periods or other nations is to express the magnitude of the problem elsewhere so as to minimize the problem in the United States. To us, a global perspective seems imperative for any long-term goal of poverty elimination. One of the goals of this volume is to reintroduce a longer time perspective and a broader cross-cultural orientation to contemporary studies of the American poor.

By focusing upon actual descriptions of the everyday life of the poor, we hope to sensitize the readers to the fact that these are real people living real lives rather than a statistical category. However, our focus upon the particular will not negate the search for large-scale generalizations.

One of the basic difficulties with much of the social science literature dealing with American poverty is the confusion of three basic forms of deprivation associated with low social position. These three characteristics are material deprivation, powerlessness and social worthlessness or prestige deprivation. To a very large extent, we follow the work of Max Weber in making these distinctions. In our society, these three characteristics tend to occur together. However, as we shall see, at many times in recorded history and in different cultures of the world, it is possible to see less correlation between types of deprivation. The most important semantic component of "poverty" is material deprivation and yet many social consequences allegedly related to poverty in our society may stem from power or prestige deprivation rather than material deprivation. This is especially true of certain psychological variables and attitudes which when discussed in the poverty literature are implicitly and incorrectly related to material deprivation. In this volume, we will focus as much as possible on material deprivation alone and its effects on behavior. The historical and cross-cultural data which form the basis of the rest of this volume force us to recognize the independent effects of the different types of deprivation.

In the ensuing discussion, we will be using a fourfold typology of social systems which includes primitive society, traditional agrarian society, transitional society and urban industrial society.

Notes

1. F. F. Piven and R. A. Cloward, "The Relief of Welfare," *Transaction,* vol. 8, May 1971, pp. 31–39, 52–53.

2. For example: Louis A. Ferman et al. (eds.), *Poverty in America* (Ann Arbor: University of Michigan Press, 1965); Margaret S. Gordon (ed.), *Poverty in America* (San Francisco: Chandler, 1965); Ben B. Seligman (ed.), *Poverty as a Public Issue* (New York: The Free Press, 1965); Burton Weisbrod (ed.), *The Economics of Poverty: An American Paradox* (Englewood Cliffs, N.J.: Prentice-Hall, Inc., 1965); Robert E. Will and H. G. Vatter (eds.), *Poverty in Affluence* (New York: Harcourt, Brace & World, Inc., 1965).

3. C. Kluckhohn and W. Kelly, "The Concept of Culture," in R. Linton (ed.), *The Science of Man in the World Crisis* (New York: Columbia University Press, 1945), pp. 78–105.

4. L. White, *The Science of Culture* (New York: Grove Press, Inc., 1949), pp. 22–39.

5. C. Coon (ed.), *A Reader in General Anthropology* (New York: Henry Holt and Co., 1948), p. vii.

6. A few exceptions to this besides the work of Oscar Lewis are: P. C. W. Gutkind, "The Poor in Urban Africa: A Prologue to Modernization, Conflict and the Unfinished Revolution," and William Mangin, "Poverty and Politics in the Latin American City," both in W. Bloomberg and H. J. Schmandt (eds.), *Power, Poverty and Urban Policy,* Urban Affairs Annual Review, vol. 2, 1970.

7. Some examples of this type of research are: Lola Irelan et al., "Ethnicity, Poverty and Selected Attitudes: A Test of the Culture of

Poverty Hypotheses," *Social Forces*, vol. 47, 1969, pp. 405–443; N. Johnson and P. Sanday, "Subcultural Variations in an Urban Poor Population," *American Anthropologist*, vol. 73, 1971, pp. 128–144, and the preliminary findings of research by Hugh P. O'Brien, at the Center for the Study of Man in Contemporary Society of the University of Notre Dame, as reported in *The Catholic Virginian*, April 12, 1968.

 8. C. Valentine, *Culture and Poverty: A Critique and Counterproposals* (Chicago: University of Chicago Press, 1968); Review article of Valentine, *Current Anthropology*, vol 10, 1969, pp. 181–201; and E. B. Leacock (ed.), *The Culture of Poverty: A Critique* (New York: Simon & Schuster, Inc., 1971). Lengthy anthropological discussions can also be found in the introduction to W. Mangin (ed.), *Peasants in Cities* (Boston: Houghton Mifflin Company, 1970), and U. Hannerz, *Soulside* (New York: Columbia University Press, 1970, pp. 177–200).

 9. Oscar Lewis, *Life in a Mexican Village: Tepoztlan Revisited* (Urbana: University of Illinois Press, 1951).

10. Lewis, *Five Families: Mexican Studies in the Culture of Poverty* (New York: Basic Books, Inc., Publishers, 1959); *Children of Sanchez* (New York: Random House, Inc., 1961); *La Vida: A Puerto Rican Family in the Culture of Poverty* (New York: Random House, Inc., Vintage Edition, 1968).

11. Lewis, *La Vida*.

12. Lewis, "The Culture of Poverty," in J. TePaske and S. Fischer (eds.), *Explosive Forces in Latin America* (Columbus: Ohio State University Press, 1964, pp. 149–174); Introduction to *La Vida*, pp. xlii–lii; "The Culture of Poverty," *Scientific American*, CCXV, 1966, pp. 19–25.

13. Anthony Leeds, "The Concept of the 'Culture of Poverty': Conceptual, Logical and Empirical Problems with Perspectives from Brazil and Peru," in E. B. Leacock (ed.), *The Culture of Poverty* (New York: Simon and Schuster, Inc., 1971, p. 244).

14. Valentine, *Culture and Poverty*.

15. Mangin, *op. cit.,* and Leeds, *op. cit.*

16. C. Valentine and B. L. Valentine, "Making the Scene, Digging the Action and Telling It Like It Is: Anthropologists at Work in a Dark Ghetto," in N. Whitten and J. Szwed (ed.), *Afro-American Anthropology: Contemporary Perspectives* (New York: The Free Press, 1970), pp. 403–429.

17. Many positive comments on the humanism of these techniques can be found in the lengthy "Review of Lewis's Work," *Current Anthropology*, vol. 8, 1967, pp. 480–500.

18. Lewis, *La Vida*, p. 21.

19. Walter B. Miller, "Subculture, Social Reform and the 'Culture of Poverty,'" *Human Organization*, vol. 30, 1971, pp. 111–125.

20. Hannerz, *op. cit.,* pp. 177–200.

21. H. Gans, "Culture and Class in the Study of Poverty," in Daniel

Moynihan (ed.), *On Understanding Poverty* (New York: Basic Books, Inc., Publishers, 1968).

22. L. W. Shannon, "The Economic Absorption and Cultural Integration of Immigrant Workers," *American Behavioral Scientist,* vol. 13, 1969, p. 37.

Chapter 2

Material Deprivation: An Historical View

Definitions

THE term poverty has been used in various ways by different analysts. Basically, a distinction should be made between a set of measurable *objective* conditions of material deprivation and a set of *subjective* attitudes and beliefs related to material deprivation.

For any meaningful discussion of material deprivation, recognition of the economic factors of *production* and *distribution* is essential. The total productivity of a system is a result of the resources available and the level of technology. If one focuses on the total social system, aggregate productivity may be determined. In order to discover if the *system as a whole is poor*, the total population can be divided into the aggregate to determine a *per capita level of production*. Where the per capita production figure is very close to minimal survival needs for the perpetuation of life in the society, the total system can be called poor. It is very difficult actually to determine the total productivity of a socio-economic system since the techniques for measuring Gross National Product are useful only in monetized economies and even there fail to include all goods and services. However, for the purpose of the ensuing discussion we shall assume that total productivity can be measured accurately and leave it to our economist colleagues to develop the actual techniques. It is also difficult to measure the survival level or minimal goods and services necessary for group survival since requirements for food, clothing and shelter vary depending on climate and energy needs for different work tasks. It is likely that certain measurable indices such as rate of mortality (particularly among infants) and length of life span could be considered rough measures of the survival capacity of a system. Such indices usually reflect the level of nutrition, caloric intake, medical knowledge and protection from natural forces.

Even where the system is not poor, that is, where per capita production is well above survival needs, there may still exist large numbers of individuals and families who are "poor." This is a function of the *distribution system* rather than production. Therefore, per capita indices of productivity by no means reflect the real distribution of goods and services among individuals, nor the number of materially deprived.

OBJECTIVE CONDITIONS OF MATERIAL DEPRIVATION

By objective conditions we mean those which can be *measured,* although precise measures may not be available at the present time. These conditions may be different in particular societies. They may vary during different times in one society's history as well as between different societies existing at the same point in time. A society which cannot produce goods and services sufficient for survival (due to a lack of resources or technological capacity) will not be able to perpetuate itself. On the other hand, the capacity to decrease infant mortality and increase life expectancy roughly indicates the degree to which a society has moved above minimal survival needs. In those societies characterized by inequitable distribution, even when productivity is great, high mortality and short life spans may be characteristic of large materially deprived segments of the population without endangering the survival of the total system.

As one moves away from systems which are vulnerably near the survival level, an additional factor must be considered; this will be referred to as the *comfort level.* Disregarding distribution for the moment it can be suggested that throughout man's history, as production expands, additional goods and services which influence material comfort come to be defined as necessary, as well as desirable. As an illustration of this we cite housing. Multi-room housing with easy access to light and ventilation and facilities to control climate was not available early in man's history. As such housing amenities became available the demand for them increased. One could argue that such houses did not directly provide increments in survival potential. In fact, the recent introduction of amenities such as central heating and air-conditioning have indirect negative effects on survival through increasing pollution and waste of resources. Throughout man's history, however, where such material comforts became available, they have been defined as highly desirable and necessary for survival. As cultural relativists we must accept any people's perception of the necessity of such material comforts. It is the rare case indeed when large segments of a population are willing to forgo these comforts to live the "good and simple" life.

The direction in which human society is moving is definitely toward greater material consumption and higher levels of material comfort even though to some modern ecologists this is not necessarily "progress." Once one moves beyond societies which existed at or near the survival level, *material deprivation* is no longer measured absolutely in terms of survival but can be *relatively* measured against the *material comfort standard* of the system. Thus, in the contemporary economic analysis of American poverty, a distinction is made between *survival* budgets and *adequacy* budgets. The latter is an attempt to define a standardized and minimum *comfort level* for the American population. Recent statements of the rights of man declare that freedom from want is not to be understood as merely the right to survival but as the right to a *decent standard of living* relative to the standard of comfort existing in the system.

Societies can also be compared on the basis of the degree to which their comfort standard is removed from the mere survival level. Since most of the societies we shall be discussing in the rest of this volume have per capita productivity which is above the survival level, the concept of material deprivation is related to the comfort level of these societies as well as the survival level. Thus, *the materially deprived or poverty segment of the population consists of those who are significantly below the comfort level as well as those living very close to the survival level.*

Subjective Views of Poverty

Shifting to poverty as it is subjectively viewed by individuals or in the ideologies of total systems, we would suggest that in many societies which could be characterized as materially deprived systems (that is, having low per capita production, and comfort standards equal to mere survival) there is a lack of *social recognition of poverty.* As we shall see, many primitive societies did not perceive poverty as a condition nor did they recognize a social aggregate called the "poor." In traditional agrarian states, poverty was conceptualized, but the state of being poor was seen as the result of unalterable conditions and was not necessarily a negatively valued phenomenon.

In the case of these stratified societies, regardless of the view of poverty which existed in the value system, a new phenomenon, that of perceived *relative deprivation,* emerged. Individuals and groups could perceive themselves as materially deprived when they compared themselves to a more affluent group. Even if they lived well above the survival level and close to the standardized comfort level, the existence of groups with a greater share of material benefits could make them perceive themselves as, relatively, materially deprived. This subjective feeling of relative deprivation can have an impact on one's behavior, which is totally independent of any condition of objective material deprivation. Feelings of relative deprivation can affect the near-elite in agrarian societies as well as the middle class in industrial society and has little to do with the actual conditions of material poverty.

It is unfortunate that much of the poverty literature deals with the behavioral and ideological results of subjectively perceived relative deprivation rather than objective material deprivation. In this volume, we are primarily concerned with the effects of material deprivation and not the psychological consequences of perceived relative deprivation.

What we are suggesting is that the existence of objective material deprivation does not always lead to social recognition of this state. This is true not only of primitive societies, but can be seen in post-World War II America where objective material deprivation still existed, but because of the optimistic belief system of society was largely ignored.[1] Moreover, individuals who are not objectively poor in relation to survival or comfort levels can see themselves as relatively deprived. The distinction between the incidence of material deprivation in the objective sense and the perception of deprivation in the subjective sense must be kept in mind throughout the remaining chapters.

Primitive Society

Primitive societies, sometimes referred to as pre-literate or tribal societies, are social systems which are small, relatively isolated, homogeneous and simply organized. They are not part of extensive state systems involving large-scale political and economic institutions.

If we focus upon the productive activities of primitives, those dependent upon extractive activities, that is, hunting and gathering, can be considered as a single type. In such systems, production consists of processes through which man obtains from nature that which already exists. Man exerts little control over natural forces. The amount of goods obtained is usually limited and the comfort level is kept close to the survival level. Mortality rates are high, life expectancy is short and entire systems are extremely vulnerable to radical changes in the natural environment (that is, climate and the supply of flora and fauna). Many primitive societies described by anthropologists have what is recognized as a well-balanced man/land relationship, in which the population and resources are evenly matched. Such groups are frequently forced to be mobile in order to cover areas extensive enough to provide food and other resources. When flora and fauna are depleted in one area, the group is forced to move on. Such nomadism on a daily or periodic basis allows group survival while high mortality rates and short life expectancies keep the population from expanding and threatening the balance. Nomadism precludes the possibility of raising the comfort level through the development of complex storage facilities, constant water or food surpluses, more substantial housing or inventories of other material goods which would contribute to physical comfort.

However, it should be noted that despite the low comfort level in hunting and gathering bands, life in such societies frequently had a vitality and sense of meaning which stemmed from rich social relationships and belief systems. Such richness is not always found in the more comfortable segments of complex society. Recent descriptions of simpler social systems have emphasized the meaningful uses of leisure time. Men sitting in groups while they fix or prepare their weapons discuss topics of common concern. These informal groups talk about events of the past in such a way as to reinforce the basic values of the society. Stories are told and embellished as a rich oral literature is transmitted.

Moreover, the picture of the starving nomad never ceasing in his pursuit of game is not accurate for all hunting and gathering societies. While early man during his first several million years was forced to eke out a meager existence, frequently succumbing to starvation, for the last 50,000 years hunting and gathering groups in many of the more hospitable resource areas of the world have developed sophisticated techniques designed to get the most from their particular resource cluster. This has enabled them to live in relative security. Thus the salmon fishers of North America, with their specialized fishing and woodworking stone tools, lived in circumstances of relatively high per capita productivity and comfort.

That many primitives today are vulnerable to material deprivation is frequently the result of the fact that these groups have been forced to live in marginal resource areas as a result of direct political intervention (for example, American Indians and Australian aborigines on reserved lands). In some cases, indirect population pressure resulting from the expansionist migrations of other groups forces a people into new areas (for example, the Bushmen in South Africa and the Siriono of Bolivia). Such marginalized primitives are forced to live in minimal survival conditions with low comfort levels either because resources are scarce or technology is not suited for the new environment.

As examples of societies in which the resource base is limited we might cite the very different environmental sets of the Eskimos inhabiting the Arctic and the Bushmen inhabiting the Kalahari desert region of southern Africa. Although most anthropologists who have studied the Eskimo express great admiration for their inventiveness in developing such items as the kayak, whaling boat, harpoon, various spears and a complex inventory of fishing gear and techniques, the limits set by the environment were so great that little surplus could be accumulated and death was a constant threat. For much of the year food was so scarce that even the small bands had to disband and small family units became the functioning elements of the group. In addition to scarcity of food, many Eskimo groups were faced with limited fuel and building materials. Freezing temperatures which dominate the climatic conditions for much of the year resulted in massive ice flows and made hunting and fishing a hazardous and precarious source of food. A very different set of environmental conditions is to be found among the Bushmen of the Kalahari, who were pushed into this arid area by waves of Bantu migrations. Hot temperatures and the lack of water resulted in a precarious level of existence which was analogous to that of the Eskimo. Small bands lived in temporary settlements which were frequently abandoned. Conditions of life for the Eskimo are depicted in the classic documentary filmed by Flaherty, *Nanook of the North,* and the ethnographic film, *The Hunters,* is a graphic account of life in the Kalahari.

As examples of tribal peoples who live in more hospitable environments but are at a technological disadvantage we have the cases of the Great Basin Shoshone and the Siriono of Eastern Bolivia. Although the Shoshone of the Basin-Plateau region of native North America had accumulated vast knowledge about the edible plants and berries growing in the area which they inhabited, their only tool was the digging stick.

This lack of technological development limited their hunting ability in a region which had plentiful supplies of game.[2] Because of the limited technology, the Shoshone were only able to hunt small game, for example, rabbits, and expended vast amounts of collective energy in hunting these animals. In contrast, the Siriono live in the heavily-forested region of a tropical rain belt area. They are believed to have been pushed here by population pressures indirectly related to the Spanish conquest. In the move, they seem to have lost the knowledge of firemaking and are forced to carry fires with them from place to place. Moreover, their unusually large bow and arrow is cumbersome in their new jungle environment and the Siriono are frequently in a state of near starvation. Lacking the poisoning technique used for fishing by their neighbors, they use the bow inefficiently for this activity too. Holmberg's description of monkey hunting among the Siriono is an indication of the human effort needed to obtain a relatively small increment to the food supply.[3] For both of these tribes a minimal level of community organization exists and the size of the community is quite small.

Simple food-producing societies are those which use relatively simple gardening or animal-domestication techniques to produce their own food. However, since these societies are technologically unable to control soil nutrients, water and other strategic resources, nature again sets obvious limits on production. These societies are also compelled to rely on extractive techniques to supplement their production. In a food-producing society there is going to be, in general, a greater degree of control over food resources and a greater regularity in their availability. If we look at the gardening peoples of the world, it is obvious that most are more sedentary than the extractors. Gardening provides the opportunity for sedentary life for relatively long periods of time. However, since soil nutrients are depleted after several growing seasons periodic moves are made. Food is produced and available on a cyclical basis; seeds are planted and gardens are weeded before crops are harvested, but sedentarism allows groups to develop storage techniques to keep food and make it available during those times of the year when food crops are not harvested. Such control over the food supply is also evident in the food producing technique of breeding and raising livestock.

While food extractors as a class are more prone to conditions of minimal survival and low comfort levels than food producers, there are many exceptions in both types of societies. Food collectors living in savannah areas with large game, forest areas and coastal or riverine systems had higher comfort levels than some simple food producers. In any event, both kinds of techniques yielded lower aggregate production than either advanced agrarian states or urban industrial states.

When we look at distribution systems in such societies we must first look at stratification. In simple societies, there was little social differentiation other than through distinctions based upon sex, age or kin-group membership. Most people engaged in the same daily work activities as others of their sex. Aside from some part-time political, religious or medical specialists there was no occupational specialization. Frequently the cultural values of such groups placed heavy emphasis on generosity and sharing. Often explicit rules existed to distribute equally that which was produced (that is, rules existed for dividing up a large game animal, distributing a collectively produced harvest or for ceremonial redistribution such as sharing food at life cycle rituals). There were no explicit norms designed actively to keep large segments of the population from getting their share.

One can overstate the egalitarianism of primitive society, and thus ignore the fact that some individuals were better hunters or gardeners or curers than others and achieved wealth differences which were not altogether offset by sharing. Moreover, achieved wealth often gave the individual prestige or political influence. In the systems with greater per capita productivity, institutionalized ranking systems developed based on age, number of wives, prestige-ranked kin groups and even birth order. Finally, in some primitive groups where there is keen competition for goods and services in spite of low productivity there is not much equality. An example here is the Kapauku, a group of quasi-capitalistic pig farmers in Papua. However, in none of these cases does private wealth produce an hereditary capitalist class.

In general, the cultural ideology of primitive societies which are based on egalitarian distribution systems does not recognize material deprivation as important. Since little economic differentiation occurs, there is no group perception of a social category called "the poor" nor much individual feeling of relative deprivation. In spite of the relatively high level of material deprivation, poverty, the poor and relative deprivation are irrelevant concepts in primitive society.

Traditional Agrarian States

Traditional agrarian societies are characterized by a higher rate of per capita productivity than primitive societies. Moreover, there is a complex system of social differentiation in such societies necessitating integrative, centralized economic and political institutions. Greater productivity releases part of the population from food-producing activities and a full-time occupational specialization develops. Closely related is development of true social classes; hereditary groups with differential access to wealth, prestige and power. Cities often develop as central points for administering large-scale marketing, taxation and other functions. Writing develops as a means of record-keeping. However, most of the population remains distributed in agricultural villages. When compared to the geographic units in urban industrial society, such villages are relatively self-sufficient in the economic and political sense.

Compared with primitive societies, agrarian states have much greater productive capacity. Where water is a problem, some form of irrigation is frequently found. Where leeching of the soil is a problem, some ameliorative fertilization measures are utilized. As a result of the different techniques used by peasants to produce food and other goods, there is a higher rate of production per capita and therefore a greater inventory of material wealth than in primitive societies.

However, such systems have less control over the environment than urban industrial societies and they are still vulnerable to catastrophic events such as floods, drought, locusts, epidemics, and so on. This is partly because of technological limitations on the physical distribution of goods from one area to another in times of disaster (that is, transportation and communication technology).

Whereas primitives live in relatively stable ecological balance, the population/resource balance of agrarian states is cyclically unstable. Technological success breeds population growth which often makes the man/resource ratio precarious. In other words, technological sophistication is great enough to ensure the relative safety of the system (in comparison with a primitive system) but a very large number of people in agrarian societies are often at risk. In general, the total amount produced in such societies and the per capita production, when contrasted with urban industrial societies, is still limited. Thus while productivity has increased, the margin of survival and the comfort level are not as great as in industrialized systems.

Moreover, the inequities of the distribution system geared to an ascribed (birthright) stratification system meant that a large proportion of production was siphoned off by the higher strata. This makes it likely that some segments of the population live at relatively high comfort levels while a very large proportion live at a marginal survival level. In fact, it is safe to say that while the total social system in agrarian states is less vulnerable than primitive systems, large numbers of people in these states are probably materially worse off than many individuals in primitive groups.

THE BASIS OF STRATIFICATION

In agrarian states where large-scale, intensive agriculture is practiced and people do not move in search of natural resources or to facilitate shifting simple agriculture, a different orientation to land and land ownership emerges. The control of rights to land becomes the basic source of wealth and it is such control which creates the basic distinction in the system between elites and non-elites. The most numerous group in the system is still the non-elite agrarian population living in rural villages. However, as a result of the possibility of full-time specialists who are not agrarian, other occupational groups emerge. These may be based in the village, or else they may be found exclusively in urban areas. In fact, one of the basic characteristics of the urban area is that it is a constellation of non-agricultural occupations. It is in these centers that we find the merchants, the bureaucrats and rulers, the skilled artisans, and the intellectual and religious elite, as well as household servants and menial laborers.

Furthermore, within the non-elite, the relationship between the economic function of an occupational activity and the social rank, wealth and power rewards of such activity seem to be generally correlated. However, there are some occupations which are economically important yet yield few rewards. In these cases, such as waste removers and butchers, it seems as if the symbolic beliefs of the society rather than the economic system determines rank. The most important fact is that the material basis of the occupational ranking-system is not the *ideologically recognized* basis for stratification; it is spiritual and non-material. This affects the subjective perception of "poverty" and the "poor."

In contrast to urban industrial societies, where stratification is socially recognized as based primarily on wealth, factors other than wealth are given primacy in ideologies of agrarian societies. This is a result of the (relatively) less productive systems and the lack of total wealth available. Such considerations as the quality of work done, the use of leisure, intellectual achievement, religious purity and the hereditary exclusive right to certain luxury goods (sumptuary laws) are as important as wealth differences in evaluating strata.

One basis used in the ranking of occupations is the amount of direct manipulation of worldly elements (matter, money, people) involved in one's work as opposed to the purer manipulation of ideas and symbols. Obviously, the further removed a man is from manual labor, the higher his rank, but jobs involving the manipulation of money or direct interaction with the masses are also less highly esteemed. Those activities which confer the highest rank involve only the manipulation of ideas. Such activities involve the formulation and reworking of religious scriptures, laws and military strategies. From the elite-born, some are recruited into the controlling positions of the political, intellectual, military and clerical bureaucracies. The status of these individuals has previously been validated by birth and family position and they work not out of necessity (to earn a livelihood) but out of a sense of social obligation. Physical activity is permissible only in leisure time activities which are not directly productive of goods and services. Some members of the elite do not work at all but devote the major part of their life to the acquisition of sacred and secular knowledge. These individuals are the purveyors of the Great Tradition or codified world view of the society. Peasants who work the land, artisans who manipulate matter, merchants who manipulate money and lesser bureaucrats who work directly with the people are considered to be doing work of a less pure nature.

At this point, the reader must be cautioned not to confuse the elites we have been describing in traditional agrarian states with the elite in developing nations today. While the elite enjoyed higher levels of comfort in earlier times, technological limitations precluded their comfort level and life expectancy from being as high as even that of the middle class in urban industrial society. The capacity to produce certain goods or services such as central heating or immunology simply did not exist. The elite in feudal England lived in dark, drafty, poorly ventilated dwellings. Journeys were long, dangerous and uncomfortable. Elizabeth I almost died of smallpox. Today, however, prestigious elites in developing countries who legally control most of their nation's wealth have access to air-conditioning, airplanes, medical technology, and so on. The gap between the top and bottom in *material terms* is thus much greater than in preindustrial states and distributional inequities are more striking.

As part of the world view in most peasant societies, there is a belief in the inherent, qualitative difference between people. These differences are based upon birth and fix one's position in the social hierarchy. Thus, position is determined by birth. The stratified social order is usually believed to be divinely created. The tremendous emphasis given to the inherent and unchangeable qualities of the individual results in a relatively static system. Where elite status, or pariah status, is based upon birth, and it is further believed that one's fate is deserved, social mobility is minimal.

SOCIETAL RECOGNITION OF POVERTY

In primitive society where productivity and comfort levels are low and where, in many cases, we find an emphasis on sharing and generosity, no attention is given to the question of poverty. As we have indicated before, in these societies, there is no subjectively defined category of people who are called "the poor" and no socially perceived condition called poverty. It is otherwise in most agrarian states. The elite begin to make a basic distinction between themselves and all others, calling the masses "the poor." Overall, poverty is viewed as a condition, but there is no specific definition of the poverty group. People are not categorized in terms of their income level at all, but in terms of their occupation. Monetary rewards are not the basic evaluative medium in agrarian systems.

SUBJECTIVE RELATIVE DEPRIVATION

Feelings of relative deprivation in agrarian society are possible because a system of stratification exists and individuals may begin to use the system as the basis for evaluating their own particular efforts and place within the society. Thus, a small peasant landowner may see himself as materially and socially better off than the agricultural laborer while also seeing himself worse off than the high urban official. People who feel relatively deprived are not necessarily objectively deprived. They may live in above-average comfort and well above the survival line, but still feel deprived. Since we have previously mentioned the ascriptive sources of stratification in a peasant society, it would seem to follow that feelings of relative deprivation would not be as prevalent there as in urban industrial societies where individual achievement and potential mobility are emphasized. Sacred justification of poverty and promises of future rewards to the poor also help to ease the feelings of deprivation. Therefore, it should not surprise us that in the United States where material deprivation exists today, but only in a small section of society (estimated to be about 20 percent), that subjective feelings of deprivation are widespread among those with comparatively low standards of living.

THE RELATIONSHIP OF THE UNDERCLASS, THE DISLOCATED AND THE POOR

From a contemporary Western point of view, there might be a tendency to confuse two social categories in agrarian society with what we think of as the poor. These two groups are the underclass and the dislocated. In all occupational systems, certain tasks are considered to be so degrading to the individual who performs them (although, perhaps, essential to the system) that these individuals are considered to be pariahs and collectively they form an underclass. This category of the population, although usually materially deprived, should not be viewed as a segment of the population socially defined as poor, since they are differentiated on the basis of occupation and lifestyle, not wealth. Examples of such groups are "the untouchables" of India, the *eta* of Japan and and slaves, wherever slavery has occurred in history.

Agricultural villages are normally able to produce enough material goods and food to take care of their internal needs as well as provide a surplus for ceremonial activities and an additional surplus to be siphoned off by the State or landowner. However, natural disasters can and do periodically disturb this balance. When floods, droughts, epidemics or attacks of crop-destroying pests take place, large numbers of people die or are forced to leave the land. It should be noted that when such regional catastrophes occur, even the local elite are adversely affected, although they are able to use their powers of expropriation to mitigate the effects.

One response to such calamities is to move away from the affected area. Thus, displaced farmers leave their region when war, famine and plague strike. Similarly urban residents flee beleaguered cities. Movement means dislocation from the group in which one is known and has a stable social place. Elites in most systems have the advantage of dual residence (landed estate and town dwelling) and can escape by moving to another part of their own domain. However, the number of non-elite from integrated villages or urban occupational guilds forced to move out is expanded during these times. The dislocated become defined in low status terms as vagrants and vagabonds.

However, these people do not fit into a stable social category called "the poor." If they remain *geographically* stable, their low-class condition is temporary and not hereditary. If they leave the region of their birth, they are frequently recruited into underclass groups where they are socially devaluated in moral and spiritual but not material terms. The most explicit references to the poor in peasant societies list widows, orphans, the disabled and the "needy." Poorness is an attribute of individuals rather than corporate groups and the condition is usually regarded as temporary rather than permanent.

THE GREAT TRADITIONS

Since the elite controls the formal systems of knowledge and monopolize literacy, they are the purveyors of the written Great Traditions. We can expect to find some references to the conditions of deprivation, including material deprivation in their written ideologies. Furthermore, such coded ideologies could be expected to explain the condition of poverty so that the elite's superior position could be justified. This we could expect to be done by emphasizing either the good qualities of being poor or the fitness of this condition for those in it. These explanations provide a codification of the society's subjective view of poverty.

We have previously mentioned, without attempting to define, the term Great Tradition in reference to peasant societies. At this time, we should like to define the term and indicate its implications for a study of poverty which takes cognizance of the cross-cultural dimensions of this phenomenon and its historical depth. The term Great Tradition was used by Redfield in discussing peasant societies, since he considered the study of such societies which focused exclusively upon the local village community to be incomplete. Redfield stated:

The culture of a peasant community, on the other hand, is not autonomous. It is an aspect or dimension of the civilization of which it is a part. As the peasant society is a half-society, so the peasant culture is a half-culture. When we study such a culture we find two things to be true that are not true when we study an isolated primitive band or tribe. First, we discover that to maintain itself peasant culture requires continual communication to the local community of thought originating outside of it. The intellectual and often the religious and moral life of the peasant village is perpetually incomplete; the student needs also to know something of what goes on in the minds of remote teachers, priests, or philosophers whose thinking affects and perhaps is affected by the peasantry.[4]

A major function of the Great Tradition is to give continuity and cohesiveness to the basic postulates about man, nature and the universe for a geographically dispersed population. For small-scale societies, this can be done through an oral tradition which can be maintained by a small group of part-time specialists such as storytellers and shamans (religious practitioners and healers) as well as the general population. In peasant societies, where a literary tradition exists, full-time specialists, usually priests and scholars, perform the same function. By maintaining a virtual monopoly of learning, this section of the elite helps maintain the superior position of the elite as a whole. In addition, by determining the content of the tradition, they become the models of correct behavior for other elements in the social system.

It should be recognized that the Great Tradition does not summarize a totality of the world view of the society; this totality can more realistically be seen as the result of the interplay of the Great Tradition with a Little Tradition. In many cases, a distinction is made between, on the one hand, classical music, dance, literature, art and, on the other, folk music, dance, oral literature and art. In effect, this is parallel to the distinction between the Great and Little Traditions. Little Traditions are established by the peasants who need models which more nearly approximate life in their village environment. In many areas the Little Tradition is a way of maintaining aspects of a world view which has been held by the village population before they came under the domination of the elite with their Great Tradition. One aspect of tradition in which this interplay is readily seen is that of folklore and mythology where we find many of the same characters and themes in both traditions and where it is impossible to cite either as the major source because of the long-term relationship between the two. Redfield, who has worked most extensively with this concept, states:

In a civilization there is a great tradition of the reflective few, and there is a little tradition of the largely unreflective many. The great tradition is cultivated in schools or temples; the little tradition works itself out and keeps itself going in the lives of the unlettered in their village communities. The tradition of the philosopher, theologian, and literary man is a tradition consciously cultivated and handed down; that of the little people is for the most part taken for granted and not submitted to much scrutiny or considered refinement and improvement.[5]

One aspect of a Great Tradition deals with a supernatural explanation of the creation of the world including man and his stratified society.

Since minimally there is a distinction between elites and non-elites in peasant societies, the sacred component of these traditions contains explanations and justifications for this distinction. This literature also says something above man's relations with and obligations to his fellow man, particularly those relations based on superordinate and subordinate positions. Other elements of the Great Tradition deal with such questions as spiritual purity and the afterlife. There is not always a direct relationship between one's position in this life and one's eventual position in the afterlife.

In all Great Traditions, there are, in addition to the sacred literature which either describes the next world, or presents an idealized view of this world, historical traditions created and transmitted in the secular literature which specifically deal with society as it actually exists or has existed. Sometimes, these traditions may be in direct conflict with the sacred literature, but in all cases, they provide a picture of the real world.

In discussing Great Traditions, we shall deal with historical sources and commentaries as well as the sacred texts which are the major source of these traditions. Since we are primarily concerned with poverty, we are interested principally in those aspects of the Great Traditions which are relevant: descriptions of the ideal and real social stratification system and the rational for this system, problems of those who are dislocated in the social system, and attitudes toward worldly possessions and the significance of charity.

Medieval Islam in the Middle East. One source of the sacred Great Tradition in the Islamic Middle East is the Koran. It is considered to be a revealed text and where it is specific, no questioning of the text is possible. However, many commentaries and discussions of the implications of the Koran are also part of this tradition.

In the Koran, we find a hierarchical order based on supernaturally-related values, such as kinship to the prophet, date of conversion and piety (fulfillment of the five pillars or necessary ritual actions of Islam). Aside from these distinctions, the Koran specifically states that all believers in Islam are equal in the eyes of God. It should be noted, at this point, that Islam spread rapidly throughout many societies, some of which were more hierarchically organized than others. The secular tradition of Islam derives from an immense body of writings by Islamic geographers, historians, chroniclers and philosophers. However, secular literature, both before and after the time of Mohammed, indicates a strong hierarchical tradition, based on worldly social distinctions, in most societies where Islam became the major religion.

One author recognizes several interesecting hierarchies based on sacred and secular characteristics, sometimes complementary, sometimes contradictory, which fixed the individual in the social system.[6] It should be recognized that the descriptions of these hierarchies were done by members of the elite and therefore are much more concerned with specifying the relative position of segments of the elite to each other, than with describing the lower orders of the hierarchy. As an example of this kind of order, we have the following description:

1. Rulers
2. Visirs (advisers), distinguished by wisdom and discrimination
3. high placed, whom wealth has placed aloft
4. the middle class (attached to others by culture)
5. mere scum, who know but food and sleep [7]

The theme of an hierarchical social order permeates the descriptions of society. There are several criteria which appear to be important in the secular stratification system. In the upper ranks, birth, education, bureaucratic control, military power, political influence and wealth are the bases of an individual's rank in the system. There is a great deal of discussion concerning the merits of different kinds of civil servants; however, occupation is only one of the ways in which an individual's elite status may be evaluated. For the non-elite, occupation is the basic determinant of status with extrinsic factors operating only to rank individuals in terms of a specific occupation.

The merchants and craftsmen are never defined as an elite by the elite. These are probably the "middle-class attached to others by culture" referred to above. In addition, there seems to be much ambivalence in the attitude of scholars to merchants. The merchants and craftsmen are classed with the scum of humanity by many of the intellectual and bureaucratic aristocracy, but there are indications that this is a residue of pre-Islamic social tradition and that Islam granted higher status to merchant and craft activities. The importance of mercantilism in Mecca and the tradesman origins of Mohammed tended to give commerce and crafts a more favorable position in Islam. The merchant who treated trade as a social obligation was praised. "The markets are God's table and whoever visits them will receive from them." [8] The position of the merchant was even favored by some as being freer than the scholar or bureaucrat who was forced to be a cringing subordinate of the ruler. The Islamic merchant was probably given higher status than merchants in the other traditions which we shall discuss.

Craftsmen were organized into craft guilds whose membership became more and more hereditary. Craftsmen were ranked according to such criteria as the presumed social value of the material they worked on, the social value of the product made, the basic social need for the product and the skills involved. Even the lowly bathkeeper and scavenger were valued for the useful service they performed. Farmers were valued for providing a necessary product (food), but they were considered along with other artisans and, despite their number, not given separate treatment. This is probably the result of the urban orientation of Islam which places disproportionate emphasis on urban occupations such as mercantilism and crafts.

Work was considered a worthwhile activity by and for everyone but the scholar and official. The Koran justifies work—especially as a craftsman or merchant—as an aid and tool for acquisition of life everlasting. Thus the ruling ideology gave the non-elite rationalizations for their humble position, which allowed them to view their efforts as a contribution to society. In many cases the non-elite categories were organized in formal guilds which were entitled to special dress and insignia and which occupied a formally delineated residential community. Rich or poor in these groups were viewed in terms of their occupation and, within the group, wealth was a secondary consideration.

Below these "middle classes" were the scum "who knew but food and sleep." This marginal group consisted of outsiders and outcasts who were *not* in any specific social category by fixed ascription, but had become dislocated from their social and occupational place and were forced to live by their wits. This group contained people identified as beggars, jugglers, vagrants, rogues and swindlers. (Even if they sometimes hired out their labor on a temporary basis, they were still regarded as part of the disreputable group.) It is this group which comprises those dislocated people in peasant societies whom we described as poor. Even here they were often classified by occupation and other descriptive labels rather than being defined as a social category which might be called "the poor." Individuals in this group were condemned for their deceitful and lazy ways and therefore their position at the bottom was justified. This condemnation of their activities did not take into account the fact that the sources of dislocation were beyond their control.

Below this group were slaves who were conquered non-believers and as such were considered too lowly to be regarded as part of humanity. However there was a tradition that slaves could move into the general population through concubinage and legitimization of offspring. In addition, slaves could buy freedom. In fact, the material impoverishment of some members of this group was not necessarily greater than the material impoverishment of some individuals who were in trade or industry. It was their social definition, that is, their perceived societal contributions and consequent worth, which made them different.[9]

In the Koran, or sacred text, we find mention of the poor and needy as a social category. However, this is a very vague and unspecific category and it exists merely to give meaning to Zakhat, the compulsory almsgiving which is one of the five pillars of Islam. The rules specifying the conditions under which alms should be given and the amount to be given are explicit. In part, this almsgiving, known as the poor-due, was related to the notion that property belonged to the community rather than the individual. The individual was only a temporary holder of wealth. Through Zakhat, some of this wealth was redistributed throughout the community. Among the recipients of Zakhat specifically listed are: the poor, the needy, widows and orphans. This is part of what the Koran has to say about almsgiving:

It is not righteousness that ye turn your faces to the East and the West; but righteous is he who believeth in Allah and the Last Day and the angels and the Scripture and the Prophets; and giveth his wealth, for love of Him, to kinsfolk and to orphans and the needy and the wayfarer and to those who ask, and to set slaves free; and observeth proper worship and payeth the poor-due.[10]

Lo! those who believe and do good works and establish worship and pay the poor-due, their reward is with their Lord and there shall no fear come upon them neither shall they grieve.[11]

Alms could be given in three ways: (1) directly to the recipient, (2) to the mosque which would then distribute it, and (3) to the state for distribution. In addition, alms had to be given publicly so that all would see one's compliance with the law. Further recognition of the importance of almsgiving can be seen in the fact that those who withhold the alms are classed with idolaters. Another category of almsgiving was voluntary and personal. We still find a commitment to these principles in present-day Islamic society which allows the maintenance of a large number of beggars. In some contemporary Islamic societies, an attempt is being made to convert the notion of Zakhat to that of state-supported social welfare programs. However, indications are that the general population is unwilling to accept this interpretation. An interesting addendum to this is one which indicates the social need for beggars. Beggars in Pakistan have gone on strike several times in recent years to demand a stated minimum donation according to the degree of deference shown by the beggar to the individuals solicited.[12]

No specific definition of the poor appears in Islamic tradition and they remain a vague category. The poor exist only to allow the non-poor to fulfill social obligations and to achieve spiritual grace.

A later development in the Islamic tradition is the emergence of Sufism. One aspect of this movement is its emphasis on asceticism, or the denial of the value of worldly goods. As in many other peasant societies, moralists have always depreciated money. The following is a quotation from a Sufic text:

> For this world has neither worth nor weight with God, so slight it is . . . It was offered to our Prophet, with all its keys and treasures . . . but he refused to accept it, and nothing prevented him from accepting it—for there is naught that can lessen him in God's sight—but he disdained to love what his Creator hated, and to exalt what his Sovereign had debased. As for Muhammed, he bound a stone upon his belly when he was hungry. . . .[13]

A later sage of Sufism is quoted as saying:

> A certain man was constantly bewailing his condition and complaining of his poverty. Ibrahim ibn Adham said to him: "My son, perhaps you paid but little for your poverty?" "You are talking nonsense," said the man, "you should be ashamed of yourself. Does anyone buy poverty?" Ibrahim replied: "For my part, I chose it of my own free will: nay, more; I bought it at the price of this world's sovereignty, and I would buy one instant of this poverty again with a hundred worlds, for every moment it becomes worth yet more to me . . . Without any doubt, I know the value of poverty, while you remain in ignorance of it. I give thanks for it, while you are ungrateful.[14]

This celebration of the higher value of spiritual well-being and the ennobling nature of poverty is to be found in many Great Traditions. In fact, some of the general beggar population included adherents of Sufic conventicles. Almsgiving was seen as benefiting the giver who would be repaid by the intercession of the Sufi in the next world.[15]

Classical Hinduism in India. The Great Tradition of Hinduism can be traced through a large number of sources, beginning with the *Rig Veda* supposedly composed in the second millenium B.C. and continuing through the present time. It is generally recognized that these texts have been written by the *Brahmins* (priests) after first having been transmitted through oral means. These texts give an idealized version of all aspects of human behavior, man's relationship to the cosmos, other men and nature. Secular aspects of the Great Tradition are found in historical writings, plays, stories and parables (for example, the *Ramayana* and *Mahabharata*).

Hierarchy as the basis of Hindu society appears continually throughout all writings, both secular and sacred. It is generally assumed that the stratification system, know as the caste system, originated with the Aryans who invaded the area around 1500 B.C. and developed this system which maintained control over the conquered peoples. A four-fold system is usually described: (1) *Brahmins* (priests and scholars), (2) *Kshatriya* (warriors and rulers), (3) *Vaisya* (merchants), and (4) *Sudra* (servants). These four categories of society are presently referred to by the term *varnas,* to distinguish them from the large number of functional and endogamous occupational groups referred to as *jatis.* Members of the first three *varnas* are referred to in sacred literature as the twice-born. In effect, this means that only members of these three groups may wear the symbolic representation of high status called the sacred thread (*jenu*) which is conferred upon men during an initiation ceremony marking a second birth. The inferior position of the *Sudra* is constantly mentioned and it is assumed that the conquered peoples were recruited into this category of the population. As an extreme example of their inferior status, we find statements to the effect that a *Brahmin* may kill a *Sudra* with impunity. Position in this system is totally ascribed and upward mobility is, ideally, conditional upon a rebirth cycle.[16]

An article of faith which reinforces the system is the emphasis on duty (*dharma*) which requires each individual to perform the traditional duties of his position to the best of his ability. It is possible through following one's *dharma* to move up in the next life. The goal of the whole rebirth cycle, and life itself, is to reach a state in which one joins the godhead and ceases the rebirth cycle. Good deeds, performance of one's duty, devotion and knowledge, are all ways in which this state of being, which the Buddhists later called Nirvana, may be attained. If one violates one's *dharma,* then it is possible to be reborn in some lower form of life, even a non-human one. It is possible for one of lowly status to bypass the cycle of rebirths through extreme devotion or piety. Thus Hinduism, in common with most of the other Great Traditions, is an ideology which is based on the assumption that, if one behaves correctly in this life, one's lot in the next one will be greatly improved. Such dogma makes for acceptance of the status quo and helps society maintain control of the behavior of its members. The entire stratification system is ultimately justified in a myth describing the creation of man.

Once again, despite their relatively small number, elites are given most attention in the classification system and in textual discussions of it. Careful distinctions are made between categories of *Brahmins,* such as temple priest, household priest, the priest with much sacred knowledge and the priest with little sacred knowledge. Not all of those born into the priestly classes could follow this profession, but if they did not, the sacred texts carefully delineated which occupations they could enter.

There appears to have been constant tension between the priests and rulers. Although the sacred texts written by *Brahmins* are unequivocal about the higher status of priests, other writings indicate that rulers were unwilling to accept this position. Since *Brahmins* were directly dependent upon the *Kshatriya* for their livelihood, their claim to dominance in the system could be, and was, effectively challenged at different times. It is not surprising, therefore, that the two major reform religions which emerged in India, that is, Buddhism and Jainism, were both founded by members of the ruling group (*Kshatriya*) and were specifically anti-Brahminical.

Although merchants are considered part of the twice-born group, their relative position vis-à-vis both the other twice-born categories is quite low, since there is a general feeling of disdain for those who engage in trade. A general term used for the merchant-money-lender is *baniya* which, traditionally, has negative connotations. According to Basham,

In Vedic times, the *Vaisya* or mercantile class, though entitled to the services of the priesthood and to the sacred thread of initiation, was but a poor third to the *Brahmans* and *Kshatriyas.* In the *Aitareya Brahmana* . . . the *Vaisya* is described as "paying tribute to another, to be lived on by another, to be oppressed at will." [17]

Other adjectives applied to him are "wretched" and "downtrodden." In reality, merchants frequently lived in great luxury and were organized into powerful guilds, but they were viewed with great ambivalence. [18] Within the large *varna* of *Vaisyas,* numerous corporate groups which we have referred to as *jatis* emerged. Among the merchants, clearcut *jati* distinctions can be observed between bankers, wholesale and retail merchants, textile merchants, and so on. Each of these is an endogamous group with its own subculture and its own rank in the hierarchy.

Since the original Aryans were primarily warriors and pastoralists, very little attention was paid to farmers in the ranking system although the nature of the economy became such that they were the largest and most essential element. Although farming was not specifically prohibited to the *Brahmins,* certain activities, like plowing and harvesting, were prohibited. The sacred justification was that plowing was a form of "raping the earth" and harvesting was killing some form of life. However, we may see these prohibitions as a way of denying the value of manual labor for this elite group. For all other groups in the system, farming became a viable alternative occupation which would not lead to the degradation of the *jati* or individual. All of the land being cultivated within the realm of a given ruler ultimately belonged to him. He would in turn distribute the land to petty nobles of the same *varna* (*Kshatriya*) who in turn rented the land to other cultivators. It was not unusual for a ruler to give a large land grant to a major warrior who had successfully led his army in battle. Members of craft groups living in villages and unable to support themselves completely through their crafts would become part-time cultivators. In addition, at the local level, *jatis* which performed services or produced goods for the landlords (*Kshatriya*) were rewarded in part by being given sections of land to cultivate.

At the lowest rung of the *varna* scheme were the *Sudras* whose major function in life was to provide services for the rest of the population. As in most pyramidal stratification systems, this category, the broad base, represented the largest section of the population. *Sudra* groups are, typically, domestic servants, litter bearers, water carriers, and others.

A fifth category of the population, not mentioned in·the sacred texts and therefore having no corresponding *varna,* is that which has been referred to as "the untouchables" or more recently "scheduled castes." The history of recruitment into this category is unclear, although some authors suggest that the conquered people whose style of life was repugnant to established Hindu society formed the basis of this group. In addition, the sacred texts make considerable mention of those individuals who do not perform the *dharma* of their groups and are as a result ostracized by their *jati.* This process, called outcasting, should not be confused with the phenomenon of untouchability, but historically, outcastes might have formed the nucleus of untouchable groups. At the present time, outcastes are unacceptable to any untouchable group and must either go to a different community and maintain themselves there as best they can, or remain within the community cut off from friends and kin and attempt to be readmitted through repentance and restitution.

Untouchable groups are generally considered to be unclean or defiled by the nature of their traditional occupations. Sometimes they are referred to as unclean *Sudras,* at other times they are referred to as simply unclean (*achut*). In all cases of untouchability, the traditional occupation of a particular *jati* is defined as ritually defiling. Thus, the washerman who comes in contact with dirty clothing, the leatherworker who comes in contact with dead animals, the sweeper who comes in contact with all kinds of dirt, particularly human feces, are all ritually unclean.

In the Indian stratification system, we find explicit descriptions of what is considered proper behavior for various *varna* within the system. Many of the behavioral characteristics imputed to the untouchables violate these normative proscriptions. Untouchables permit widow remarriage and are believed to eat meat, particularly beef. Specific references to the physical distances which untouchables had to maintain between themselves and higher *varnas* in some areas of South India, led to the development of a system in which the untouchable would announce his approach which warned members of higher groups to leave the area. Emphasis is also placed upon the prohibition of higher groups from accepting food and water from those of lower groups. In some areas of India, the length of one's loincloth was an indication of status; the longer the loincloth, the higher the status.

The higher status *varnas* had legal rights superior to their less prestigious counterparts. A *Brahmin* could murder a *Sudra* with impunity, but a *Sudra* was liable to extreme penalties for a lesser crime against a member of a higher category.[19]

Lack of prestige and spiritual deprivation is the rationale for low status in this system rather than material deprivation. An untouchable could be wealthier than a clean *Sudra* but there would be no way to improve his position or prestige. However, in general, wealth tends to follow higher social status. In addition, all those who are materially deprived in this system are not primarily socially classified as poor, but their basic identity comes from the corporate occupational group into which they are born. Specific attempts at *jati* mobility (that is, when a *jati* is attempting to claim higher status in the larger system) are not made through material wealth, but through claiming direct descent from one of the high-ranked groups and by emulating the ideal behavior of the *Brahmins*.

The nature of the *jati* system in India usually means that any individual is incorporated into a group. In some cases, these corporate groups may, as a traditional occupation, engage in activities which are anti-social. Examples of such *jatis* are the various criminal groups in India which maintain themselves through theft and robbery. Another roving corporate group is that of the entertainers (acrobats and jugglers).

In a very different category are groups of roving bandits or robbers called *dacoits* who are usually recruited from local communities and who are dislocated as a result of catastrophe or outcasting. They prey upon villagers and travelers. Other types of groups which recruit from the dislocated element are prostitutes and beggars. In ancient Hindu texts, the harlot and gambler are classified with the thief and blackmailer as disreputable and anti-social. These groups, while not true *jatis,* have some degree of organization and recruit internally through reproduction. As in the other instances they are still primarily identified by labels, usually occupational, rather than classified as the poor.

A strong other-worldly tradition exists in the Hindu world view. Commitment to worldly goods and property is given a negative value within this tradition. This can most directly be seen in the four stages of life prescribed for all Hindus. After a householder has had sons who can take over his responsibilities, he should renounce all worldly goods and possessions including family and *jati* and become a hermit or a wandering mendicant. When he does this, his survival is dependent upon the largess of others. Although very few Hindus take this step, it is still an ideal and at any moment of time, large numbers of these individuals can be observed at religious festivals or sacred places. These holy beggars can be distinguished from the previously mentioned beggars by dress and physical appearance. Both groups of beggars are rarely by-passed by other Hindus without some donation, nor are they turned away from any door without food. Almsgiving of this nature is considered to be an act of piety and devotion. Maimed beggars are considered to be afflicted through divine intervention and therefore deserving of support. The religious beggar is seeking divine enlightenment and should be aided in his quest. Thus, Gore states:

The Indian who gave alms or gave in charity did so not to meet the needs of the person who was being helped but to meet his own need for accumulating religious merit or doing atonement for his sinful deeds.[20]

Perhaps the most striking form of asceticism combined with religious wandering is demonstrated in the group of naked holy men called *nagas* who wander about unclothed as an indication of complete lack of concern with worldly goods.

Imperial China.   The Chinese Great Tradition has the longest continuous history of any of the traditions under discussion. Two major intertwining strands make up this tradition. These are the influence of Confucianism as an ethical and secular tradition and the impact of Buddhism which spread from India through Southeast Asia to China. Major sources of the tradition are the writings of Confucius and his followers, Buddhist texts, and indigenous historical studies of the development of Chinese society.

On a very broad basis, the society was ideologically divided into two categories, the elite and the non-elite, frequently referred to as the rulers and the ruled. In much of the ancient writing about Chinese society a distinction is made between the great man, *chun-tzu,* and the small man, *hsiao-jen.* This system of stratification is explicated in the writings of Confucius, a member of the bureaucracy, who codified the precepts of the system and clearly delineated the mutual rights and privileges, on the one hand, and responsibilities and duties on the other, of sets of relationships. Yen-kung, a philosopher, says: "The great men devote themselves to governing and the small men devote themselves to labor." [21] According to Quo: "The commoners, the artisans, and merchants, each attend to their professions to support their superiors." [22]

Among the great people, we find hereditary nobility, the bureaucrats and the local gentry who were a leisure class which eschewed manual labor. Of these three prestigious groups, the bureaucrats monopolized power, and they were largely recruited from the gentry. One of the features of this system which has attracted wide attention, is the composition of the bureaucracy. Individuals were recruited into this category through competitive examinations based primarily upon scholarly attainment in such areas as poetry and interpretation of the Confucian ethic. Although most of those recruited into the bureaucracy were from the gentry, it was not impossible for individuals from the other groups to enter the system. Movement within the bureaucracy depended upon performance on the job and performance in examinations. Thus, the basis of the intricate stratification within the bureaucracy depended primarily upon the individual's ability to perform in progressively more difficult examinations. Passing an examination earned promotion in rank, and increased prestige, power and financial rewards. Overt manifestation of rank could be seen in clothing and scholar buttons (insignias). It is estimated that there were 40,000 positions established in this system and many ranks. The lowest ranks were set aside for district administrators and the highest were located in the urban center.

The other main social category, that of the small man (*hsiao-jen*), consisted of merchants, craftsmen, farmers and those who provided services. Amongst the farmers we find small landholders who tilled their soil themselves and landless agricultural laborers who worked on the land of the local gentry but who were socially respectable. Sometimes the small peasant proprietors were able to single out a particular kinsman who could be prepared through formal education for entry into the bureaucracy. The successful applicant was a source of prestige for the kin group.

The merchants and artisans were primarily urban. Once again, mercantile activities were a source of great wealth, but limited prestige. As in most peasant societies, the elite did not trust merchants. During different periods of Chinese history, merchants were specifically denied access to such sumptuary items as silk clothing and the ownership of riding horses. Since they were low in the social scale, wealthy merchants tried to leave the class by supporting their son's education, through buying land, or through the purchase of titles. However, at certain times, this class was prohibited from participation in the examination system.

Artisans were organized into local, regional and provincial guilds in order to restrict competition, promote fair dealings and provide mutual security. As a group, artisans had fewer restrictions placed upon them than did merchants, but their potential wealth was more limited. Some of the respectable service occupations were those of gatekeeper, innkeeper and night watchman.

Although most studies of the Chinese stratification system concentrate upon the distinction between the great people and the common people, there was a third group, an underclass, referred to as the "mean" people. Prostitutes, slaves, entertainers and government runners (messengers) were relegated to this class on a system-wide basis, and in various regions groups such as boatmen, "lazy" people and permanent servants belonged to this category. An intriguing group which has been improperly referred to as beggars falls into this disreputable category in some areas. These individuals performed ceremonial services at weddings and funerals from which they derived their livelihood. Unlike the permanent servants attached to particular households, these people were attached to the life-cycle events of birth, marriage, and death, and had little security.

Perhaps the greatest disability of this underclass was its ineligibility to participate in the civil service examination system. Marriage upward outside this stratum was also socially and legally forbidden. In certain regions the "mean" people were required to wear clothing which specifically identified them as members of this class. Finally, under the law if a "mean" person committed some offense against a common person, or in the more extreme case, a great person, the punishment was greater than if he committed the same offense against one of his own class. Once again we have a social category in which prestige deprivation is basic and material deprivation is less correlated to social rank. If anything, material deprivation follows from low prestige and does not lead to it. This aspect of stratification is summed up by a follower of Confucius, Hsun-tzu, who states, "One's rank must correspond to his virtue and his salary must correspond to his rank." [23] Thus the "mean" people were viewed as low in rank due to lack of virtue and they were poor as a result of low status.[24]

Throughout Chinese history, there have been times when population growth, subdivision of landholdings, and/or expropriation of land by despotic rulers have made conditions for the peasant intolerable. Added to this were major catastrophic events, such as droughts, floods, and epidemics, which have further burdened rural populations.

As Loewe states:

For much of the Han period, he (the peasant) existed in a state of uncertainty often in conditions of distress or penury. For he lived at the mercy of nature. As often as not the victim of flood or drought, which could destroy his livelihood at a blow . . . Small wonder that many of the peasants were forced by economic stress to take to a life of the wilds, living as vagabonds or beggars, as starvelings or robbers. These were the men who could easily be attracted to join the ranks of a rebel or bandit leader. . . .[25]

When these conditions prevailed, mass war and revolution were frequently the order of the day. Some ideological justifications for these disturbances were found in the Confucian ethic which counsels the people to remove despotic leaders by force. The Chinese themselves recognized that such disorder led to poverty. According to Hsun-tzu, "When there is contention, there will be disorder; where there is disorder, then there will be poverty." [26]

In these times of turmoil, widespread banditry was common. It would seem that these bandit hordes were largely recruited from the dislocated peasantry. In addition, the military, which directly subsisted upon forced levies of material goods from the peasant population, were considered quasi-bandits. Occasional mention of roving beggars are also found. Thus, another instance is found where regional calamities cause large-scale social dislocation and roving groups of people with no stable means of livelihood. The ubiquity of this phenomenon is attested to by the fact that all Chinese cities were walled to protect the inhabitants from such roving bands of bandits as well as foreign invaders. Loewe refers to ". . . armed bandits or beggars, displaced from their homes by stress of natural calamity or war." [27] In such circumstances the Chinese clan served as a mutual aid support for its members as did the *jati* in India. The clan was often of regional scale and extremely cohesive.[28] It served as a buffer between the family and the larger social system. Through the establishment of charitable trusts, educational funds and the pooling of common resources, regional segments of the clan or individuals, provided aid in times of illness, crop failure and the untimely death of a head of family. Although clan systems are found in other peasant societies, they are larger, stronger and more meaningful units in China. The artisan guilds mentioned above were also sources of mutual aid, but not on the scale of the clan.

One of the characteristics of traditional Chinese philosophy generally agreed upon by students of Chinese life is the emphasis on worldly rationalism. There is uncertainty about the Confucian attitude to the supernatural, but it can be stated that the overriding emphasis of the doctrine is on the affairs of this world. When Buddhism entered China, it did not make much headway in shifting this emphasis. Much of the monastic and ascetic emphasis of Buddhism has never been accepted in China. As we have already observed, most of the other traditions stress the possibility of improving oneself in the afterlife or a new incarnation; despite the wide acceptance of Buddhism in China, this orientation is rare. On the other hand, although there were limits to individual mobility, the social ideal of achievement, primarily through scholarship, was that it should be rewarded in terms of upward mobility. In addition, the barriers between the upper ranks, the merchants and the peasants were more permeable than in other societies. In theory, all but the "mean" people who took on another occupation would be eligible for the examination system in three generations. Of course, in practice the high ranks of the bureaucracy tended to be filled from the elite and gentry, and at times merchants and artisans were excluded from taking the examinations.[29]

Because of the lack of asceticism and concern with spiritual grace, there is no belief in almsgiving as a means to divine redemption. Beggars as a class are largely ignored. The few references to beggars portray them as predatory and in no sense glorified. With the exception of descriptions of society during periods of political turmoil, little attention is given in Chinese literature to the dislocated, such as beggars and vagabonds. However, archeological excavation of early cities and foreign descriptions of later cities indicate the existence of slums. According to Loewe:

> We can only assume, on the basis of conditions which existed in Chinese cities in later ages, that the population included a high proportion of vagabonds and beggars, and that many of the inhabitants spent their lives in conditions of filth and squalor, disease and misery.[30]

Catholicism in Feudal England. One major source of the sacred tradition of Catholicism is the New Testament and the commentaries on it. The burden of intellectual activity was borne by theologians who discoursed on man's relationship to God and his obligations to his fellow man. Christians consider all men equal in the eyes of God. However, this belief has not infrequently coexisted with a secular stratification system based upon inequities. In Christian terms, the division of labor was a divine arrangement adapted to the needs of a fallen humanity.

A major distinction in the stratification system is made between manual and mental labor. As in most peasant societies, intellectual activity is considered to be the prerogative of the elite. Transcendental contemplation is a basic activity of the priest-scholar group. However, manual labor is considered to be good and proper for those who are destined by birth to participate in such activities. Social mobility is rare because of the ascriptive nature of the system.

The stratification system was a minutely graded system of estates and corporations. At the apex of the stratification system in feudal England were hereditary ruler-warriors and a clerical elite. Control of land and population was the basic source of wealth and rank within the landed, military and clerical hierarchies. It should be noted that celibacy was a basic characteristic of the priestly class and therefore the clerical hierarchy was recruited from the landed aristocracy.

The secular system was based on a hierarchical chain of personal contracts based on oaths of loyalty which carefully specified the duties and obligations of those in the system to their superordinates and subordinates. In general, superior ranks provided their subordinates with rights to use land in return for military service. The elite provided counsel to subordinates and goods and services were obtained from the non-elite. The basic tenet of the system was that "a man's wealth is proportionate to the number of people for whom he is responsible, and (that) power and position or prestige are dependent upon the possession of land and tenants." [31] At the top of the secular hierarchy was a king who held ultimate title to all land. A large proportion of the realm was made over through oaths of fealty to the barons who inhabited fortified castles. The baronial land was distributed again through oaths of loyalty to mercenary knights who occupied the manor houses.

Parallel to this secular hierarchy was a clerical hierarchy. Each manorial community had a local cleric as did each barony. The king's court, however, was the locus of the largest and most powerful group of churchmen. The church as an organization was in its own right a major holder of wealth and power through the land.

This feudal social system was basically rural in orientation with urban centers only gradually developing in importance. Titles with greater prestige and other perquisites were held by courtiers, both religious and secular, who spent part of their time at the central court and less time in the domain. The central court and its ruler were in the topmost social ranks. Once again we see careful distinctions made within the elite category and reflected in the titles, privileges, wealth and power of the various ranks.

At the other end of the social hierarchy were those who worked the soil. The rural agricultural community was a small village of a few dozen families which owed rents in produce as well as labor service to the manor house. At the peasant level, a basic social distinction was made between the freedman and the serf. Most peasants were serfs who were bound to the soil and owed rent and service obligations to the manor house. However, it was possible for a serf to achieve freedman status through purchase. In this instance he often became an independent small landowner. A serf could also become a freedman by entering the priesthood with his lord's permission. This occurred when intellectual aptitude was recognized and access to formal education provided. Finally, a serf who ran to the city for a year and a day achieved freedman status. In the city he would have to acquire a mercantile or artisan occupation or live by "his wits." Freedman status was hereditary.

Mercantile activities were never highly valued in this tradition. While they were recognized as necessary to the fabric of society, enrichment of oneself at the cost of others was contrary to Christian teaching. Thus, strict regulation of profits by the Church, the banning of usury (stemming from the defiling nature of making money with money), as well as the prohibition of monopolies and other attempts to speculate on and manipulate the market system limited the merchant's ability to acquire wealth, power and high rank. In the Christian ethic, mercantilism was considered

. . . the most reactionary form of earning a living, ethically lower in the scale than agriculture and manual labour, and it was safeguarded by the precautionary regulation that in fixing the price all that might be asked was the costs of production plus the additional amount necessary for a moderate profit.[32]

This is another example of the lack of esteem for merchants and their control by elites in traditional agrarian societies.

Craft groups tended to become organized and hereditary over time with the introduction of a guild system. Guilds were in effect closed corporate groups with their own legal system. They developed residential locations as well as insignias of identification. The ranking of crafts depended upon the items made and the level of skills required. Moreover, the manufacture of luxury items for the elite carried more prestige than those producing goods for the common man.[33]

Unlike some of the other traditions which we have previously described no specified underclass existed. Some elements of an underclass can be found among the roving groups of the countryside and in urban areas. Groups such as bandits and entertainers outside the city and beggars and thieves within the city could be placed in this category. Groups which were singled out for extreme penalties in legal statutes and those poorly reputed in folk literature can be considered an underclass. In England during the early feudal period, organized bands of brigands referred to as "Wastours, Roberdesmen, and Drawlatches" were so singled out.[34] Prostitutes were segregated in "stewhouses" which were located outside the city proper. They wore certain styles and materials so that their dress might distinguish them from other women.[35] Parallel to the Hindu system, butchers are negatively viewed, but in this case explicitly for secular reasons as major polluters of the environment because of their disposal problems (blood, entrails and other by-products of the slaughter of animals).[36] They were also considered disreputable as a group who deviously overcharged the public.[37] Streetcleaning or dirt removal was also considered particularly defiling.[38] These groups tended to become organized over time as they had in many other peasant societies.

While life was predominantly rural, the manor offered security to all its members except in times of regional catastrophe when all conditions of men were affected. In the cities, the guilds of merchants and artisans performed these same social security functions for their members. However, as the process of urbanization accelerated, the number of dislocated people increased. An indication of this phenomenon is the increase in the number of references made to those called "vagabonds" through history. Jusserand describes the fourteenth century in feudal England as a period in which several factors, in particular the great plague of 1349 known as the Black Death, upset the stable relationships between groups and swelled the number of roving people such as beggars and robber bands.[39]

One major strand of the Christian ethic is the ascetic one. Possession of wealth and worldly goods was viewed in a dual framework. Where such possessions enabled the individual to divorce himself from worldly activities they were viewed as good. However, the accumulation of wealth for its own sake was depreciated. Otherworldliness was central to Christian teaching and attachment to worldly goods was held to interfere with the salvation of one's soul.

As a result, the renunciation of possessions was a matter for praise. The development of monastic orders is consistent with Christian doctrine which regarded poverty as a blessed state. Troeltsch says, "Poverty is still highly honored as a method by which we reach the knowledge of God; indeed it is often voluntarily induced by giving away all of one's possessions." [40] Recently, Pope Paul VI has reiterated the same theme:

Poverty purifies the Church; poverty teaches it to avoid putting its heart and trust in the goods of this world. It withdraws the Christian from all thievery and administrative dishonesty, from every illegal and often obsessive absorption in affairs. It sensitizes minds to needs and injustices that oppress so many lowly people.[41]

At the same time he also said, "Poverty is the best condition for entering the kingdom of God."

It would seem that a distinction is implicitly made between voluntary and involuntary poverty. Those who voluntarily divest themselves of worldly goods are blessed without qualification. On the other hand, those who are born into this condition may be blessed if their lives demonstrate piety. Since birth into this condition was viewed as a result of a fall from grace which was used to justify the entire stratification system, the involuntarily poor were viewed as tainted in some way.

A corollary of Christian asceticism is the central position given to charity in the Christian ethic. For those desirous of attaining a state of grace, contemplation without charity was considered to be inadequate. Charity was not viewed as a cure for material deprivation but as a means for the giver to attain further divine revelation and the awakening of the spirit of Christian love. The necessity for the existence of a socially recognized category of the poor is indicated in the following statement from Troeltsch:

> The charity of the Church, particularly that of the Religious Orders, was mainly needed for the service of the déclassés, the sick, and the abnormal. On the other hand, the presence of such needy folk was considered normal and desirable, since they provided an opportunity for the exercise of charity; far from being hindered and set aside by a rational social policy they formed a normal Christian "class" of their own, which was regarded as necessary for the whole.[42]

The déclassés mentioned in this statement are the dislocated, those who have lost their place in the social hierarchy through the deliberate or accidental breaking of the personal contract which bound them.

Initially, medieval charity was based upon spontaneous, sporadic giving of alms by wealthy individuals directly to the needy. Such alms-giving was particularly noted during religious holidays. As vagabonds increased, almsgiving was institutionalized through the monastic orders. Funds for disbursement by the orders were received through bequests from the wealthy. However, the distribution of charity by this means was inefficient and funds were not sufficient to care for the increasing number of the destitute population. Charity was always considered to be more beneficial to the giver than to the receiver. However, the institutionalization of charity within the ethic created a semi-permanent class of alms recipients.

Tokugawa Japan. The Great Tradition of Japan provides us with some of the best descriptions of the lowest levels (outcasts) of a traditional agrarian stratification system. There are many similarities between this and other agrarian systems. Feudal Japan was characterized by a social stratification system of legally defined hereditary classes. The *daimyo* or landed elite and their *samurai* (warrior) supporters constituted the elite. Intellectual activities dealing with the ideological bases of the society were restricted to this elite for whom *gakumon* or scholarship was very important. Bellah notes the basically ascetic lifestyle of the *samurai* warrior which was necessary for the achievement of selfless devotion which the religious ideology of Japan viewed as the ultimate fulfillment of sacred goals.[43] He also notes the existence of medicant monks and the negative attitude toward luxury.

Below the elite were the *ryomin* or "good people" consisting of merchants, farmers and craftsmen. Merchants were residentially segregated within the city and were required to wear demeaning modes of dress. According to Hagen: ". . . no matter how great their wealth, they (merchants) were officially declared to be the lowest (respectable) social class, and (this) entailed restrictions on their dress, behavior, and relationships to other classes." [44] A specific class of merchant, the moneylender, was particularly vulnerable since debts incurred by the nobility could be legally repudiated and his wealth was frequently expropriated. He was also frequently criticized for his excessive luxury.

Farmers were recognized as a separate social category and ranked next to the elite. Craftsmen were organized in guilds which formed a strong corporate group for those involved in craft activities.

According to Price, the bottom of the stratification system consisted of *senmin* (lowly people), an hereditary group, and *gomune,* a non-hereditary class. The former group consisted of several named subgroups, among them the *hinin* (non-people) and *eta* (full of filth). *Gomune* status might have evolved from lowly *chonin* (merchant) status, but later in history these occupations revolved around begging. As beggars the *gomune* were controlled, taxed and licensed either by the government or by outcast chiefs who were their superordinates. Begging usually involved entertaining such as "singing, dancing . . . rope tricks, magic, story telling, imitating bird cries and animal barking." [45] These beggars were allotted exclusive areas.

There were also illegal beggars ("straw mat beggars") who were organized and formed a "somewhat distinct subculture." They did not entertain but stood in front of the houses of the wealthy.

The *eta* were divided into occupational groups similar to those of Hindu untouchables, for example, shoemakers, butchers, and others who work with carcasses. The *hinin* activities are described as follows:

The *Hinin* took care of prisoners, their execution and burial. . . . The private enterprises of *Hinin* in Edo (Tokyo) centered around begging, scavenging, and professional celebrating or mourning (at childbirth, marriage and death). A Hinin with a prosperous merchant in his area who was celebrating a special occasion would put on his best clothes, go to the house, and with extreme politeness offer appropriate salutations and then protect the merchant's house by keeping the other beggars away.[46]

For this work he was paid and given special privileges.

It is obvious that such outcast position was very different from the modern status of "the poor." There was an extremely complex classification system of outcast groups (although as in China it varied in different localities). In addition, the groups were strictly organized with chiefs, an autonomous system of taxes and social control, and territoriality. Finally, the material wealth of the group was not significantly lower than that of the *ryomin* (good people), and it varied greatly within the group since the chiefs had different lifestyles from the ordinary population. The chiefs lived in great mansions and were surrounded by servants. The groups, however, were viewed as homogeneous by the larger society.[47]

COMPARATIVE STRATIFICATION

In the Great Traditions which we have discussed—medieval Middle East, classical India, Imperial China, feudal England, and Tokugawa Japan—some strikingly similar characteristics can be seen. We shall attempt to delineate these parallels in the following discussion which will center upon the stratification systems and poverty.

One major theme which pervades the social perception and justification of the stratification system is that high or low position is interrelated with prestige and power to a much larger degree than with wealth and comfort.

Elites. In all four societies, there is a marked difference between the elite and the non-elite. In the Middle East, Islam emphasizes the equality of all, but the social system which existed prior to Islam and which continued to exist alongside it was based on inequality. Much the same can be said of the Catholic tradition. Among those classified as elites in all of these cultures, we find high-level religious practitioners, sacred and secular philosophers, rulers and high-level bureaucrats. Within this segment of the population, a miniature stratification system existed in which positions were ranked from low to high, depending upon the necessary duties and attendant rewards. Both within the elite stratum, and in distinguishing the elite from the non-elite, differences of lifestyle were significant. Such items as insignias, clothing, housing and food distinguished subsections of the elite from one another, and the elite from the non-elite. In some cases, these different consumption patterns were regulated by law rather than an open market. This reflects the idea that the difference in status was one of inborn essence rather than something one could achieve by accumulating wealth. It should be emphasized that the perceived distinctions within the stratification system were not based on monetary rewards or wealth display. The elite was rewarded with wealth because of the *qualitative* superiority which it was assumed they possessed.

Common to all of the Great Traditions is an anti-materialist bias. In part, this is based upon an other-worldly emphasis or an emphasis on intellectual attainments.[48] Manipulation of ideas rather than material objects was basic to elite positions in the stratification system. A further indication of the anti-materialist bias in some of these traditions can be seen in the high value placed upon asceticism which is the renunciation of worldly goods. It is this bias which relegates the merchant to a non-elite stratum in spite of his material wealth. His wealth, as a potential source of power, was suspect. Thus, his inferior status was maintained by law, or at the very least, his position in society was ambivalent and his relationship with the elite was a source of tension.

For the elite, the poor existed as a vague category. In some traditions, the existence of the poor was necessary to assure the attainment of spiritual grace by the elite. Since most of these stratification systems had supernatural sanctions, the validity of various strata could not be questioned. Mobility was seen as something which occurred either in the afterlife or in a reincarnated life to those who fulfilled their roles on earth.

Respectable Non-Elites. Although manual labor was depreciated in the elite ideology, it was recognized that agricultural and craft occupations were necessary to the social system. Occasionally, specific references are made to the worthwhile nature of these activities. Members of this category of the population tended to form corporate occupational groups in the urban areas. In rural areas, the village was regarded, in some cases, as a corporate group, while in others, sub-village groupings such as clans, joint families and *jatis* served a similar purpose. Such groups, as well as the feudal oaths of fealty, gave the individual a basic sense of security, real mutual aid, and a source of social identity. Therefore these groups were never socially classified as "the poor," in spite of their possible material deprivation.

The Disreputable Underclass. All traditional stratification systems included an underclass such as the untouchables of India, the "mean" people of China, the scum of Islam and the outcasts of Japan. In each case, the kind of work done is viewed as the determinant of low rank. Spiritual and moral deprivation are seen as crucial. Material deprivation is common but not necessarily associated with such positions. Poverty is thus merely incidental but not a primary attribute of the group. Moreover, the effects of deprivation are mitigated by the corporate organization and mutual aid mechanisms.

Those work activities commonly allocated to an underclass position are activities which involve contact with dirt, human excrement and dead carcasses. Mobile occupational groups such as entertainers, petty ceremonialists and beggars are also included. Another segment comprises participants in illicit or immoral occupations, such as thieves and prostitutes. Other groups classified in this way are those in dependent status such as slaves and permanent servants.

Those who follow such demeaning occupations are thought of as following immoral and depraved lifestyles. They are usually considered dirty, sexually immoral and promiscuous, excessive drinkers and violent. These behavioral attributes are believed to result from inherent spiritual and moral deprivation.

The Poor. Although the poor are not described in great detail within any of these Great Traditions, some references do occur and we shall attempt to derive certain general patterns of extent and evaluations of poverty from the preceding discussion.

COMPARATIVE MATERIAL DEPRIVATION

None of the sources cited attempt to estimate the proportion of the total population which could be classified as materially deprived. However, it can be assumed that the hierarchical nature of the social systems and the limited productive capacity of the economic systems must have meant widespread material deprivation. Among the underclass groups who were not defined in terms of poverty, that is, Indian untouchables,

Chinese "mean" people, Islamic scum and Japanese outcasts, there were probably a significant number of people who faced a resource scarce environment. The impact of catastrophe, particularly noted in China where security mechanisms such as the clan existed, can only be interpreted as an indication of the marginal nature of subsistence for large segments of the total population.

In comparing primitive and agrarian societies we have observed a number of basic points. First, in primitive societies, total productivity (aggregate production) was lower and the total system was threatened by catastrophic events. In traditional agrarian society, where total productivity was greater, the *system* was not so vulnerable to catstrophic events. Despite low productivity in primitive society, a more equitable distribution system and a lack of formal stratification resulted in minimal differences in the comfort levels of individuals and groups. In contrast, in traditional agrarian society, institutionalized inequality reflected in the distribution system led to great differences in material possessions and comfort level. This meant that in spite of greater productivity a large proportion of the total population remained materially deprived and it is likely that more people were more deprived than in primitive society.

COMPARATIVE SOCIAL DEFINITION OF THE POOR

In primitive socities there is usually to be found no definition of a segment of the population known as the poor. However, in traditional agrarian societies such a social segment is recognized, although it is not very clearly delineated. A basic distinction is found between the "needy" and the "disreputable." For the former, some institutionalized charity exists, while the latter are defined in terms of their defiling nature and left on their own. Any material deprivation they suffer is accepted as incidental to their low morality and fitting to their nature. It should also be noted that frequently the "disreputable" were not as materially deprived as other segments of the population and unlike the dislocated they maintained their mutual aid mechanisms.

In the case of the "needy" poor two major sets of circumstances are recognized factors leading to this condition: personal and economic catastrophe. Personal catastrophes consisted of events such as the death of the head of the household (leading to widowhood and dependent-orphan status), accident and illness. Economic catastrophes were such events as crop failures and natural events which dislocated large segments of the population. In both cases the catastrophes were viewed as the result of divine intervention and were considered a temporary condition which those involved must overcome. The poor were not a permanent category in the social system.

COMPARATIVE EVALUATION OF POVERTY

In several of the Great Traditions which we have been describing poverty exists as a means for the elite to achieve spiritual grace. Supporting those in poverty through the giving of alms is viewed as a spiritual and sacred duty. In addition, a distinction is made between voluntary and involuntary poverty, with the former condition receiving spiritual sanctions. In part this is related to the anti-materialist bias of many of these traditions and a corresponding emphasis upon asceticism. For those who do not choose poverty but have it thrust upon them, a basic ambivalence can be seen, but certainly they are not singled out for pejorative treatment as are the poor in urban industrial society. Such despicability is reserved for the spiritually deprived underclass. In general, the poor are seen as spiritually pure and, more importantly, they are promised easier access than the non-poor to the rewards of the next world or next life.

BELIEFS ABOUT THE BEHAVIOR OF THE POOR

The "needy" poor are considered to behave in the same way as the other members of their ascribed corporate groups. A peasant, rich or poor, behaves like a peasant. A merchant has all the behavioral attributes of a merchant regardless of wealth. Lifestyles are based on one's ascribed occupational group, not one's income level.

Underclass groups, however, follow a way of life which is more distinctive. Their behavior is frequently viewed as immoral and they are segregated by dress and residence. Here too, it is the inherent impurity of the group which is believed to affect behavior and lifestyle, not the degree of material deprivation. Poverty is socially perceived and defined more concretely than it is in primitive society. It should also be obvious that the existence of poverty was rationalized and justified in the ideologies of such societies and was not viewed as a social problem of major proportions. Poverty was not seen as violating the canons of social justice nor as producing threatening anti-social behavior.

Notes

1. Michael Harrington, *The Other America: Poverty in the United States* (Baltimore: Penguin Books, Inc., 1962), p. 12.

2. Julian Steward, *Theory of Culture Change: The Methodology of Multilinear Evolution* (Urbana: University of Illinois Press, 1955).

3. Alan Holmberg, *Nomads of the Long Bow*, Smithsonian Institution, Washington, Institute of Social Anthropology, Publication no. 10, 1950.

4. R. Redfield, *Peasant Society and Culture* (Chicago: University of Chicago Press, 1956), Phoenix edition, p. 41.

5. *Ibid.*, p. 42.

6. M. G. S. Hodgson, *Introduction to Islamic Civilization* (Chicago: University of Chicago Press, 1958), p. 103.

7. *Ibid.*, p. 103.

8. *Ibid.*, p. 135.

9. G. E. von Grunebaum, *Medieval Islam* (Chicago: University of Chicago Press, 1953), pp. 170–220.

10. M. M. Pickthall, *The Meaning of the Glorious Koran* (New York: The New American Library, Inc., 1961), *Surah* ii, no. 177, p. 48.

11. *Ibid.*, *Surah* ii, no. 277, p. 59; for a lengthy discussion of Zakhat see K. Cragg, *The Call of the Minaret* (New York: Oxford University Press, Inc., 1964), pp. 150–157.

12. *The New York Times*, April 17, 1969, p. 3.

13. J. A. Williams, *Islam* (New York: George Braziller, Inc., 1962), pp. 139–140.

14. *Ibid.*, p. 141.

15. *Ibid.*, pp. 136–144.

16. For a general discussion of classical Hinduism in India, see A. L. Basham, *The Wonder That Was India* (New York: Grove Press, Inc., 1954), chap. 7. For discussion of social stratification, see Basham, *ibid.*, chap. 5, and M. Singer (ed.), *Traditional India* (Philadelphia: American Folklore Society, 1959). See also articles in Myron Wiener (ed.), *Introduction to the Civilization of India: Changing Dimensions of Indian Society and Culture* (Chicago: University of Chicago Press, 1957).

17. Basham, *op. cit.*, p. 142.

18. *Ibid.*, pp. 142–143.

19. *Ibid.*, p. 144.

20. M. S. Gore, "Society and the Beggar," *Sociological Bulletin*, vol. 7, 1958, pp. 23–48.

21. T'ung-Tsu Ch'u, "Chinese Class Structure and Its Ideology," in J. Fairbank (ed.), *Chinese Thought and Institutions* (Chicago: University of Chicago Press, 1957), p. 236.

22. *Ibid.,* p. 236.

23. *Ibid.,* p. 238.

24. Michael Loewe, *Everyday Life in Imperial China* (New York: Harper & Row, Publishers, 1968), pp. 33, 40.

25. *Ibid.,* pp. 235–250.

26. *Ibid.,* p. 236.

27. Michael Loewe, *Imperial China* (New York: Praeger Publishers, Inc., 1966), p. 149.

28. *Ibid.,* p. 149.

29. For a general discussion of dislocation, see Loewe, *Everyday Life;* for a discussion of asceticism, see C. K. Yang, "The Functional Relationship between Confucian Thought and Chinese Religion," in Fairbank (ed.), *op. cit.,* pp. 269–290.

30. Loewe, *Everyday Life,* p. 231.

31. E. Troeltsch, *The Social Teaching of the Christian Churches* (New York: Harper & Row, Publishers, 1960), vol. 1, p. 252.

32. *Ibid.,* p. 128.

33. F. Stenton, *The First Century of English Feudalism* (Oxford: Clarendon Press, 1961).

34. J. J. Jusserand, *English Wayfaring Life in the Middle Ages* (first published 1889) (London: Ernest Benn Ltd., 1950), p. 142.

35. G. T. Salusbury, *Street Life in Medieval England* (Oxford: Pen-in-Hand, 1948), pp. 153–154.

36. *Ibid.,* p. 91.

37. D. M. Stenton, *English Society in the Early Middle Ages (1066–1307)* (Harmondsworth, Middlesex, England: Penguin Books Ltd., 1951), p. 183.

38. Salusbury, *op. cit.*

39. Jusserand, *op. cit.,* pp. 146–148.

40. Troeltsch, *op. cit.,* p. 227.

41. Words spoken at his weekly audience by Pope Paul VI, October 2, 1968.

42. Troeltsch, *op. cit.,* p. 253.

43. R. N. Bellah, *Tokugawa Religion: The Values of Preindustrial Japan* (New York: The Free Press, 1957).

44. E. Hagen, *On the Theory of Social Change* (Homewood, Illinois: Dorsey Press, 1962), p. 334.

45. John Price, "A History of the Outcast: Untouchability in Japan," in G. De Vos and H. Wagatsuma (eds.), *Japan's Invisible Race* (Berkeley and Los Angeles: University of California Press, 1966), p. 25.

46. *Ibid.*, p. 27.

47. For a general description of the outcasts in agrarian Japan, see the article cited above (pp. 6–30) as well as John Price, "The Economic Organization of the Outcasts of Feudal Tokyo," *Anthropological Quarterly,* vol. 41, 1968, pp. 209–217.

48. For a general discussion of "otherworldliness" as a major ideological component in agrarian societies, see James Peacock and Thomas Kirsch, *The Human Direction* (New York: Appleton-Century-Crofts, 1970), pp. 169–193.

Chapter 3

The Transition to Urban Industrial Society: The Western Case

IN the previous chapter we have described certain aspects of traditional peasant and primitive societies in order to put the entire question of objective material deprivation and socially-defined poverty in perspective. In this chapter we shall discuss the transition to urban industrial society in Western Europe, and in particular, the transformation of English society, the implications of which were of major importance to the rest of the world. Our purpose is to demonstrate the impact of social and economic changes of magnitude upon the conceptualization of the poor and the conditions which make for poverty.

Urban Industrial Societies

The effects of the industrial revolution in Western Europe and the United States and more recently in other parts of the world can easily be summarized. The greatest effect from our point of view was that a system of technology was developed which resulted in tremendous growth in productivity. This meant that a relatively closed economic system became an open one. There was no longer a recognized limit on the amount of material goods and food which could be produced. We would argue that this in turn caused a real shift in world view, particularly in relation to the stratification system. The opening up of the system of production made the closed view of the social system which emphasized an individual's fixed position no longer tenable.

One of the immediate effects of the industrial revolution was that large numbers of people, many of them moving from rural villages to urban centers, were uprooted and placed in a new social and economic condition. In some areas this was stimulated by government policy, while in other areas it occurred without official sanction. The changing technology resulted in the growth of new, primarily urban occupations. This, in conjunction with large-scale agricultural unemployment and underemployment as a result of population growth and the concentration of large landholdings, led to a massive rural-urban migration. To a large extent, population growth was itself an ancillary effect of the industrial revolution; it resulted from greater control over disease which went hand in hand with technological innovation in the productive sphere. Another aspect of the industrial revolution which also aided in this movement was the improvement in communication and transportation techniques. These massive changes undermined local stability and the ascriptive basis of the existing stratification system.

Corporate occupational groups both in the village and urban area were undermined by the growth of new occupational specializations. Many of the goods produced by artisans in craft guilds (where traditional teaching of skills required years) could now be produced by less skilled workers who could learn to utilize the new machinery in a matter of days. Since occupational skill was no longer important for many productive jobs, there was a basic change of criteria for evaluating social rank. Money now became the major criterion.

One significant development was the shift in the definition of occupation or job. In peasant societies, occupation was linked to familial traditions and was conceived of as a way of life. In the new social system, work was viewed as a part of one's life activity, not as a summation of one's social place. For the peasant, the distinction between work and leisure is frequently hard to draw; for the industrial laborer, this distinction can readily be made. As the definition of job changed, the concept of unemployment replaced the concept of dislocation from a stable social position.

With the shift away from a primarily self-sufficient village community to residence in urban areas and the assumption of new occupations, there was increasing dependence on markets and money as the medium of exchange. In this way, individuals became enmeshed in a market-money system over which they had little control and of which they had little understanding. Fluctuation in supply and demand in the increasingly important world market had a tremendous impact upon these new recruits to the emerging industrial system. The capitalists who became the new elite had a much better view of the system than the peasant and were in a better position to manipulate the marketplace.

In this emergent social system, a new perspective on the poor emerged. No longer looked upon as an amorphous category nor a category of people existing for the spiritual good of others, the poor were now viewed as those who were materially deprived (with cash as a reference) either because of their unwillingness to participate in the new system or their inability to adapt to it. In the past, those who were materially deprived and yet members of stable corporate groups were viewed primarily as members of these groups, not as the poor, and they were protected by whatever mutual aid system the group provided. Those who were materially deprived as a result of dislocation were not highly visible due to their mobility; now they became permanent settlers in urban areas and were eminently visible. Many were not members of disreputable occupational groups but were unemployed job-seekers.

Another basic shift which occurred was from a sacred to a secular explanation of the human condition. The pursuit of otherworldly goals was largely replaced by the pursuit of the good life in this world. Asceticism played little part in the new value system. Mercantile activities which had previously been either downgraded or viewed with ambivalence now were considered worthwhile. Traditional elites whose worth was based upon spiritual purity and sacred scholarship were replaced by money elites and scholars who followed a secular-scientific trend.

The Transformation of England

We have selected England as an example of a society which has become industrialized because the transformation occurred early, had far-reaching effects, is well documented and is probably familiar to our readers. The actual development took a long time from our contemporary perspective: it involved more than basic changes in the techniques of production. Basic shifts in the organization of society and changes in many of the underlying values occurred at much the same time.

England remained until the beginning of the sixteenth century essentially a traditional agrarian society based upon the feudal system. It should be recognized that the changes which took place in England did not occur in isolation. To a very large extent, the stimulus to English commercial activity can be seen in the changing patterns of trade and colonial activity in the rest of Europe. The religious writings of Luther in Germany and Calvin in Switzerland and agricultural innovations in Holland and Northern Europe were also important elements. It is difficult to give primacy to any single factor in the transformation of English society. The process was a complex interplay of economic and ideological changes.

English commercial activity can be seen as part of a commercial revolution which swept Western Europe in the sixteenth and seventeenth centuries. During an earlier period, from the thirteenth to the fifteenth century, commercial activities in Europe had been dominated by the Italian city-states. However, as knowledge of the world expanded through the exploration efforts of Spain, Portugal, France, Holland and England, the trade activities of these nations were stimulated. New trade routes were established and new sources of wealth were discovered. Most of the trade was based upon the use of ships and the capital outlay for ship-building and outfitting was very large. In many cases these expenditures were beyond an individual's capability and the risk of investment in a single voyage was great. Eventually joint stock companies were established to pool large amounts of capital and to spread risk. Another development which stimulated these capitalist ventures was the interest of governments in acquiring wealth which led to the granting of monopolies to companies of private entrepreneurs. One such enterprise was the British East India Company established in 1600 which eventually dominated the Indian subcontinent. As part of this commercial and capitalistic expansion, a change occurred in the attitude toward banking and the manipulation of money. According to McNeill: ". . . the social stigma which had been attached to the taking of interest in the Middle Ages lost its basis in economic fact." [1]

A fundamental change resulting from the commercial revolution was the growing use of money as the basic and generalized medium of exchange. Although money had existed for millenia and had been used as a means of exchange and payment and a way of setting standard values, its use was greatly expanded. The use of money in establishing standard measures of value is particularly important for us. In addition, money, which had been previously used for payment and exchange, in a limited sphere (not part of everyday transactions) was used to pay for a much greater inventory of goods and services. Payment in kind or mutual exchange of labor was replaced by money payments for labor and basic subsistence goods.

England became caught up in the world competition for wealth in specie. Internal consequences of the shift to money can be seen in the declining self-sufficiency of the village-manor community and the production of agricultural goods for a cash market. An example of such cash production was the expansion of sheepherding which was a response to a rising demand for wool, which in turn was based upon changing technology.[2] The use of money had previously been restricted to a narrow range of goods and services in feudal society. Land, the right to which was traditionally inalienable, was the status-giving economic good. However, with the commercial revolution, the use of money was expanded until it became capable of purchasing all social goods, power, prestige, health and spiritual purity.[3]

Paralleling the commercial revolution was a long process of change in the agricultural sphere. Prior to the eighteenth century some small-scale enclosures occurred in which landlords forced peasant villagers off the land and established relatively large-scale enclosed farms which were based upon cash-producing sheepherding rather than grain production. In the eighteenth century such technological innovations as crop rotation, new crops, metal plows and horse-drawn cultivators made large-scale agricultural enterprises even more desirable and increased the rate of enclosure and population dislocation. This was further stimulated by governmental action which established the legality of this movement. Agricultural expansion was also a response to the growth of urban markets and improvements in transportation. The two significant results of agricultural changes for our purposes were the intensification of cash-cropping as opposed to subsistence farming and even more significant, the dislocation of large numbers of peasant villagers who began to migrate to urban centers.

The commercial revolution did not affect manufacturing at first because of the tight control of production by urban craft guilds. Such control, however, was not possible when large-scale manufacturing enterprises began to develop toward the end of the eighteenth century. In England, the two major industries first influenced by technological innovation were mining and textile production. In both cases, the basic innovation was the steam engine which replaced human and animal energy by mechanical sources. After the development of the steam engine in the 1760s the scale and organization of production enterprises increased tremendously.

The earlier development of capitalism and banking which occurred during the commercial revolution was easily transposed into the industrial sphere. To a certain extent, commercial and industrial activities became mutually reinforcing elements in the transformation of British society. Even in the early stages of the commercial revolution, certain items produced in England had to be used in trade with their colonies and other non-European areas of the world. Once the industrial revolution became established in England, the need for large-scale markets and sources of raw materials increased. Since England had already developed commercial markets outside Europe during the commercial revolution, these existing markets now gave greater impetus to the developing industrial activities.

Displacement of the rural population by the earlier enclosure activities resulted in movement to urban centers. This movement away from the land was reinforced in the latter part of the eighteenth and throughout the nineteenth century by the increasing economic opportunities available in the cities. With the shift in geographic locus of the population came a change in the occupational structure of society. Both the shift of population from rural to urban areas and the increasing importance of commerce and industry in urban areas led to a monetary revolution in which cash became necessary for the acquisition of all goods and services.

A concomitant of technological change was the devaluation of skilled labor and the decline in craftsmanship. Many of the industrial machines were designed so that an individual with relatively little skill or training could operate them. Thus skill adhered to the machine, not to the worker. The availability of a large labor force of unskilled workers recently displaced from the rural economy acted as an additional stimulant. Perhaps the hardest hit traditional craft was that of weaving; men who had been master craftsmen could no longer find work in this craft. In effect, we have an early case of the process of technological unemployment which has been a source of dislocation since that time. As late as the 1840s Mayhew noted the recruitment of weavers into the "London Poor," with many of them finding employment as dockworkers.[4]

Accompanying these changes in production, a related shift occurred in the market system which had far-reaching implications for poverty. During earlier times, craftsmen produced goods on a made-to-order basis for a limited market in which prices were more or less fixed. Now goods were produced to meet an anticipated demand in an expanding mass market where prices followed the law of supply and demand. These emergent conditions led to extreme fluctuations in the business cycle which were not really under the control of the entrepreneur and affected all the occupations related to production and distribution. These new man-made forces now replaced natural forces which traditionally had been regarded as the prime generators of poverty.

Man's inability to understand the forces creating massive material deprivation in the early days of the industrial revolution was reinforced by the ideology of laissez-faire or non-intervention in the market system. This ideology enabled the capitalists, who were the new elite, to exploit the masses without their actions being viewed as immoral or unethical.

In other areas of ideology, the otherworldly orientation was replaced by one emphasizing action, manipulation and control of the universe. In the feudal period, emphasis was placed on the manipulation of symbols as the only truly non-defiling activity. Now it was legitimate to manipulate matter as well as money to control the world and accumulate wealth. Commerce and pragmatic scientific activity became acceptable. Control of one's destiny was now to be achieved only by control of material forces. A new view of the social order emerged in which one could achieve wealth and prestige through one's own efforts. A derivative ideological commitment emerged which emphasized controlled change and planning for the future.

CHANGES IN MATERIAL DEPRIVATION

We tend to assume that as man gained greater control over his environment by harnessing inanimate sources of energy to the productive process, the proportion of the population, although not the absolute number, which could be characterized as materially deprived declined. In addition, it would seem fair to assume that the threshold of material deprivation changed as the increased productive capacity of the society raised the standard of living. More elaborate shelter and items such as transportation services came to be regarded as necessary for survival. We are, of course, looking at trends over long periods of time. One of the difficulties with the emerging industrial system in England is that it was under the direct influence of market conditions which caused periodic fluctuations in both supply and demand. When demand diminished, when supply far exceeded demand, or when political conditions caused a disruption in the market, large numbers of the working population became jobless which resulted in a relatively high incidence of material deprivation. Since the jobless were highly visible in dense clusters in the urban center, it seemed that material deprivation had increased.

As the feudal system in England disintegrated and the personal contracts of this system were replaced by the impersonal contracts of the marketplace, insecurity and misery became widespread and commonplace. The peasant in traditional society had an extremely low level of material wealth, but he did have, barring natural catastrophe, relative security. The wage contract system enabled the employer to utilize the services of his employee only when his labor was needed. The shift to a wage system also allowed the employer to freeze the wage level of his workers in a period when food and other prices were increasing. In this period of capital formation, labor was the factor of production most easily manipulated. In addition, the trend toward large-scale sheep farms later replaced by large-scale cash crop-oriented grain and vegetable farms, led to the displacement of a growing number of rural workers who frequently went to the city to obtain whatever jobs were available there. Closely related to the displacement of tenant farmers by the enclosure movement was the tendency of major landowners to take the common lands which belonged to the village community and maintain them as private farms. Traditionally, the English villager has had access to the "commons" where he could forage for fuel, graze sheep and hunt game. The usurpation of these lands by the wealthy caused further difficulties in the rural areas.

However, disruption of life in the rural areas did not always coincide with a growth of opportunities in the urban areas. The view, commonly held today, that changes in one sphere of the economy are offset by changes in other spheres, was, in this case, not justified by the facts. Even when the opportunities in the industrial sector began to expand, those who were considered desirable for the new production processes were not necessarily those who were displaced by the earlier conditions. Thus, the demand for child labor in the growing textile industry did not directly help the displaced adult population find employment.

Piven and Cloward have shown that relief systems in Europe, particularly in England and France, were a response to fluctuations in the economic sphere. As conditions became worse, and the potential threat of violence appeared, relief systems were changed to allow the support of a greater number of those considered to be in need. Using the English Poor Laws as an example, they demonstrate how these were liberalized during periods of mass distress and discontent and acted as a safety-valve for social pressure. When economic conditions improved the laws were changed to make it more difficult, once again, to obtain aid from public funds.[5] Figures are cited to show that at different periods of time during the eighteenth and nineteenth century the proportion of the population dependent upon public relief funds for their subsistence rose to 10 percent.[6]

By the end of the nineteenth century in England, a general feeling of economic well-being permeated the world view of the dominant middle class. However, the survey work of Booth [7] in London and Rowntree [8] in York contradicted this euphoric economic vision. Both of these researchers demonstrated that approximately 30 percent of the population in each of these urban centers lived below the subsistence level as they defined it. It should be noted that these definitions of subsistence were probably more indicative of adequacy or comfort level than survival. What these studies demonstrated, and, what many similar studies of particular societies have recently confirmed, is that general economic prosperity does not, *in and of itself,* result in an elimination of material deprivation. A more essential element is the way the products of economic prosperity, the wealth generated, is distributed among the general population.

Despite the figures which indicate that a high level of material deprivation was characteristic of the British population from the end of the feudal period through the nineteenth century, our general assumption that there has been a decrease in the extent of material deprivation in the world, and particularly in those societies which have become highly industrialized, is not negated. We would contend that there existed an even higher proportion of those who were materially deprived during feudal times, although statistics are not available which would permit us to test the validity of this statement. One of the incontrovertible facts about England's economic growth through both the mercantile and industrial revolutions was the emergence of a large and powerful middle class which had to be recruited from the lower segments of the previously existing social stratification system.

It was the new visibility of the poor and the growing belief that poverty had no positive attributes, that it produced negative anti-social behavior and that it was *not* inevitable that led to a concern with the poor in the nineteenth century. Material deprivation was less significant than in primitive and traditional agrarian society, but it was much more widespread than need be in an open productive system in which no ideological supports for the poor were maintained.

CHANGE IN POPULAR BELIEFS ABOUT CAUSATION

In the previous discussion of traditional agrarian society the point has been emphasized that the concept of the poor as a specific category of the population was lacking and therefore little explanation for the existence of this vague category was needed. There were those who were afflicted by divine intervention (the maimed, widows and orphans) and those who, because of their traditional occupation or lifestyle, were regarded as spiritually defiled (and who were only incidentally poor). However, the great changes which we have briefly summarized led to a new perception of the poor and beliefs about the causes of poverty were modified. One emerging belief was that some of the poor were in that condition because they refused to work. This notion appears quite early in the transitional period; during the reign of Elizabeth when specific laws were formulated to deal with the "sturdy" beggar.[9] The sturdy beggar was obviously a member of the poor category who preferred begging to working as a way of life. In the sixteenth century, a beggar or impoverished non-worker without a license convicted a third time could expect to be put to death.

To refuse to work for lawful wages (according to the Act of 1572) was therefore made a punishable offense, and those who refused the work provided for them by the overseers of the parish were to be whipped and stocked to bring them to a better frame of mind. Begging and vagabondage were doomed, if legal measures could kill. All persons of fourteen years of age or more, if convicted of wandering, begging and the "roguish trade of life," were to be "greviously whipped and burnt through the gristle of the right ear with a hot iron of the compass of an inch about." Their only chance of escape was if some good-hearted parishioner offered them a year's employment, in which case the penalty was abrogated. For a third offense in this kind the penalty was death.[10]

Despite these harsh measures the problem of those who did not work persisted and reinforced some of the popularly held beliefs about the causes of poverty. In traditional society, there was no specifically defined social category known as the poor who were believed to share a negative social value and an immoral lifestyle. Such a group becomes the bottommost element of the new stratification system in a society where material success is considered evidence of goodness and salvation.

With the expansion of the economy in the eighteenth and nineteenth centuries the general belief that a large segment of the poor consisted

of those who refused to work was reinforced. The development of
public assistance legislation such as the Poor Laws, the establishment
of Workhouses and the attempts to eliminate "out-door" relief (support
given to those who were not living within the confines of an institution) can all be seen as policies based upon a basic belief that there were
large numbers of the poor who preferred not to work and desired to live
on the charity of the community or parish. When Mayhew did his classic
work on the London poor in the middle of the nineteenth century he
devoted an entire volume of this four-volume work to "Those That Will
Not Work." [11] Among those described in this volume are prostitutes,
thieves, swindlers and beggars. All are viewed as predators upon the
larger community and unworthy of public support or sympathy.

A different view was that poverty was the result of changing economic
forces which were beyond the control of the individual. While this view
became less important than the previously mentioned view based on
the generalized work ethic, the State for the first time recognized its
responsibility for the poor and implemented the first public welfare
program. Starting with the enclosure movement and continuing through
the industrial revolution people were displaced from their land and
their occupations by man-made rather than natural forces. Even in Elizabethan times it was recognized that employment opportunities were not
sufficient to take care of the entire working population:

In 1575 the justices (respected men who controlled local community
affairs) were required to raise money by taxation and with it to provide a
common stock of wool, hemp, flax, iron, etc., for the employment of the
out-of-work poor. They were to pay for the work done, and any recipients
of this state aid who spoiled their material were to be sent to the house of
correction provided in each county. Thus, when normal employment failed,
the State took upon itself the task of seeing that the able-bodied received
sustenance, but only in return for work done.[12]

According to Jordan, many of the new class of wealthy urban intel-
lectuals and businessmen of Elizabethan England viewed the economic
changes of the time as the major source of material deprivation, before
the Protestant ethic with its strong emphasis upon individual responsibility had fully developed. Some of the writings of this time point to
the social upheaval which the system was experiencing as the major
source of increasing poverty. This was viewed as a social malfunction
the relief of which, was *society's responsibility*. The breakdown of the
traditional relations between master and serf; the depopulation of the
peasant village and the increasing mobility of the population were

emphasized as causative agents. This eventually led to the declaration of public responsibility for the poor as well as massive private action.[13]

As machines replaced human labor large numbers of individuals and those dependent upon them lost their livelihood. We have previously mentioned the plight of the skilled weavers when faced with competition from machines and the following excerpt from a beggar's prepared speech is probably not far from the truth:

> We are poor working-men from _____ which cannot obtain bread by our labour, owing to the new alternations and inventions which the master-manufacturers have introduced, which spares them the cost of employing hands, and does the work by machinery instead. . . . Our masters have turned us off, and without bread and knowing no other trade but that which we was born and bred to, we are compelled to ask your kind assistance. . . . As we have said, masters now employs machinery and steam-engines instead of men, forgetting that steam engines have no families of wives or children, and consequently are not called on to provide for them. . . . Foreign competition has drove our masters to this step, and we working men are the suffers thereby.[14]

Although the previous passage is cited by Halliday to demonstrate the techniques used by beggars who were not, in fact, displaced weavers, the speech itself is based upon public knowledge of the difficulties faced by those who were actually affected and their families. Early in Elizabeth's reign as beliefs about the causes of poverty changed, a feeling of public responsibility for the poor led to the promulgation of the Elizabethan Poor Laws. They were intended primarily to help the "worthy" or deserving poor in a social system which was coming to recognize poverty as a condition which was frequently beyond the control of the individual. Before the Poor Laws, it was left to private charity to care for the needy. However, after Henry VIII closed the monasteries and confiscated church land and wealth, charity was not able to cope with those needing support. In the early edicts relating to poverty and the care of the poor through alms giving, moral exhortation and public ridicule were used as weapons to force the wealthy to contribute to the support of the poor. However, as it became apparent that the charitable instincts of private individuals could not be relied upon, new legislation was introduced. Each parish had to take care of its own indigent population and taxes, called the poor rates, were enacted to support those deemed worthy of maintenance. As the numbers of the poor increased, so were the rates raised.

In addition to public support, Jordan notes that many wealthy businessmen felt that society was responsible for the increase in poverty. He cites the massive private activities developed to "rehabilitate" the vagrant and the debtor. Debtors in prison were let out in the custody of these social worthies who would aid them through loan plans and systems of purchased apprenticeship and job placement.[15]

DEVELOPMENT OF ACADEMIC VIEWS

Another change which occurred during the industrialization of England was the *intellectual and academic* preoccupation with the causes of poverty. In the feudal period and in the Great Traditions which we have previously described, the intellectual and scholarly elite did not devote much of their attention to the description and analysis of the life of the poor. To a certain extent this growing concern can be traced to the growing "visibility" of the poor in urban areas, as well as the need to explain the persistence of the poor in a society which was ex-expanding its economy at a very rapid rate.

Among those who attempted to explain the existence of poverty during the early stages of industrial expansion was Malthus. In his view, poverty was attributable to the propensity of the poor to procreate and their inability to conserve whatever resources were available to them. Taking a view completely opposed to the one which we have suggested, Malthus predicted that the proportion of the population which could be characterized as materially deprived would increase. His suggestion that food resources increased by small amounts (arithmetic progression) while there was a larger rate of population growth (geometric progression), could only lead to the view that material deprivation or poverty would become even more widespread during the course of human history.[16] Actually food resources and the other factors related to subsistence have increased at a greater rate than the total world population. (What is most disturbing however, is that the greatest increments in production have taken place in those nations of the world which have to some degree reduced and controlled the growth rate of their own population. It is in the underdeveloped nations of the world that increases in food and other subsistence items have been limited, while population growth has continued at a high rate; these societies come closest to demonstrating the validity of the Malthusian prediction.) It should be recognized that Malthus placed the blame for poverty squarely upon the poor themselves who are not able to control their animal urge to gratify their sexual needs, an argument which continues to be heard in the contemporary debate on poverty.

Malthus, who had experience with the Industrial Revolution in its early phases, was a proponent of what is usually referred to as classical economics. One of the basic assumptions of this academic tradition was that the economy was in a state of equilibrium. Although this assumption could be challenged by actual events in the economic sphere, these events were viewed as short-term and correctable over time without any outside interference. In effect, the economic system was viewed as self-regulating. To maintain equilibrium of the economy, it was necessary to have a large surplus labor force since classical economists saw wages as a major factor of production which could readily be manipulated by the capitalist. An oversupply of workers led to low wages, which meant that the capitalist could accumulate more capital and invest in the developing industrial and capitalist system. A large surplus of labor also set the stage for free capitalistic competition which would insure a healthy economy. Even if this process led to the depressed living conditions of a large segment of society, it was an essential ingredient of the capitalist system. To help justify a position which disregarded the miserable living conditions of the distressed masses, classical economists endorsed the Malthusian view that any increase in wages would simply lead to a higher birthrate and an increase in population so that the poor would be no better off than they had been before. It was further suggested that low wages as an economic check on population growth besides being of benefit to the poor, were a means of avoiding potential problems for the entire social system.

A view of the social system which emerged in the latter part of the nineteenth century was related to the theories of biological evolution. This view is referred to as Social Darwinism, although many of its basic assumptions were unrelated to Charles Darwin's explanation of the origin and survival of biological species. For the Social Darwinist, poverty was the consequence of the inherited characteristics of the individual. Competition, or, in Herbert Spencer's phrase, "the survival of the fittest," was considered the ruling force in social life. Those members of the human species best equipped to survive would survive. Thus, those in poverty were ill-equipped to meet the demands of social life and should, therefore, be allowed to die out.[17]

Perhaps the most famous spokesman of this theory was Herbert Spencer. The following extract is representative of his thinking:

It seems hard that an unskillfulness which with all his efforts he cannot overcome, should entail hunger upon the artisan. It seems hard that a labourer incapacitated by sickness from competing with his stronger fellows, should have to bear the resulting privations. It seems hard that widows and orphans should be left to struggle for life or death. Nevertheless, when regarded not separately, but in connection with the interests of universal humanity, these harsh fatalities are seen to be full of the highest beneficence—the same beneficence which brings to early graves the children of diseased parents, and singles out the low-spirited, the intemperate, and the debilitated as the victims of an epidemic.[18]

What strikes the reader today most is the failure to distinguish between categories of the poor. As we have seen, in medieval times and in the Great Tradition of agrarian societies, a distinction was made between the deserving and the undeserving poor.

Oviously, Spencer and his colleagues were opposed by others who felt that society should do something to mitigate the horrible conditions faced by those in poverty. Both Sumner in the United States and Spencer in England attacked their critics, Sumner by calling them champions of "the survival of the unfittest" [19] and Spencer in the following terms:

Blind to the fact, that under the natural order of things society is constantly excreting its unhealthy, imbecile, slow, vacillating, faithless members, these unthinking, though well-meaning, men advocate an interference which not only stops the purifying process, but even increases the vitiation—absolutely encourages the multiplication of the reckless and incompetent by offering them an unfailing provision, and *dis*courages the multiplication of the competent and provident by heightening the prospective difficulty of maintaining a family. And thus, in their eagerness to prevent the really salutary sufferings that surround us, these sigh-wise and groan-foolish people bequeath to posterity a continually increasing curse.[20]

A revolutionary doctrine of the nineteenth century which viewed poverty as inherent in the capitalistic system was that proposed by Karl Marx. In many ways, the Marxian view parallels that of the classical economists except that his view of the exploitation of labor is negative rather than positive. Unlike the equilibrium approach of the classical economist Marx viewed the capitalistic system as one which contains the seeds of its own destruction. In the constant efforts of the capitalist to increase profits by exploiting labor, Marx foresaw a growing polarization between the owners and the workers and an increase in poverty. Although Marx recognized the tendency of the poor (a reserve army of surplus labor) to reproduce at a higher rate than the general population, he does not attribute this to immorality or slothfulness, but rather blames it upon the capitalist system which uses up the life of the worker and requires him to be rapidly replaced.[21]

Still another nineteenth-century approach to poverty was that of the descriptive sociologist. Unlike the previous approaches which were based upon speculation, descriptive sociology was empirically derived. It was also unlike the previous "dismal" approaches in that it was optimistic. As such, it was an example of the general Victorian habit of thought which regarded all social problems as capable of solution through the application of knowledge. The early sociologist viewed poverty as a product of the social system, but the system was defined as mutable. Poverty was not the fault of the individual but the responsibility of a faulty economic system. Surveys of the conditions of poverty to pinpoint the locus of the problems would lead to proposed solutions. Housing, employment, nutrition, and disease were investigated to demonstrate the material deprivation of those in poverty. It is worth noting that a great deal of emphasis was placed upon the living conditions of the poor, primarily housing, which has remained a central focus in several views of poverty since that time. Unlike the previous academic approaches, the early sociologist believed that once the objective conditions of poverty were described, these conditions could be changed without reference to the entire social and economic system. Poverty was seen as a social maladjustment which could be cured in a piecemeal fashion. This notion often referred to by its critics as "the Band-Aid approach," is still prevalent today.

A different approach to the explanation of the condition of poverty which has unfortunately been confused with that of the descriptive sociologist is found in the early assumptions of social workers. Those suffering from material deprivation were seen as individuals or family groups who were migrants from an alien culture or those who had been poorly socialized, so that they did not acquire behavior and motivation appropriate to their changed circumstances. In some cases, poor socialization was traced to early loss of parents, disorganized family life, immoral or alcoholic parents, cruelty, child abuse, and so forth. In some respects, this view of poverty anticipates the concept of the culture of poverty and other cultural explanations of poverty prevalent today (such as cultural deprivation).

From the social evaluation of the poor to the social "necessity" of poverty in an expanding industrial economy, our investigation has covered a broad spectrum of views. From some societal perspectives poverty is an inevitable consequence of capitalist development and, in effect, it has been argued that the poor are always with us. Classical economists and Social Darwinists saw poverty and unemployment as inevitable for the economic and social systems. Others saw poverty as a temporary condition and one which would be erased when the dominant class in society committed itself to the solution of this problem or when the productive system expanded rapidly enough to allow a more just distribution of wealth to everyone in society.

Explanations of the causes of poverty, like most other explanations of natural and sociocultural phenomena, can be viewed as a part of the world view or ideology of a particular culture at a specific time. Thus, if a societal world view emphasizes an individual's responsibility for his present condition of life, then it follows that those living in poverty are responsible for their own condition. If, on the other hand, the world view emphasizes the idea that the social system sets up the condition into which individuals must fit, then obviously those in poverty are in that condition because of requirements of the social system.

Many of the dominant ideas about poverty which we have been describing can be summarized in the following way:

Figure 1. Explanations of the Causes of Poverty.

	Innate	*Acquired*
INDIVIDUAL	1	2
SOCIETAL	3	4

Cell 1. Explanations which fit into this cell are characterized by emphasis upon the individual's innate characteristics such as:

    a. inherited or congenital physical disabilities

    b. mental inferiority (lack of intelligence)

    c. inborn immorality or character flaws

The analysis of the poor suggested by Malthus, which emphasizes their propensity to excessive procreation, would be an ideal example of a Cell 1 explanation. In addition, many of the restrictions placed upon the relief of the poor in transitional England would appear to be based upon the notion that the poor are inherently indolent and lazy. If sturdy beggars and vagrants (as opposed to the "impotent" poor) were to be supported by the parish their numbers would increase. The establishment of the workhouse and the curtailment of "outdoor relief" (where the recipient was allowed to live at home) are specific examples of the treatment of the poor which was based upon these underlying beliefs about the causes of poverty. Even though some poor were believed to be capable of learning to appreciate work, many were regarded as having a character flaw. To a certain extent part of the Social Darwinist position could be included within this category of explanation since it was assumed that there were some inherent flaws in the individual which hampered him in the competitive struggle for survival. Finally, explanations such as those offered by charity sources which emphasized the depravity of the poor or their heredity would fit this category.

Cell 2. Explanations which fit into this cell are chiefly those individual characteristics which are acquired after birth through experience such as:

a. physical disabilities resulting from illness or accident
b. ignorance (the lack of acquisition of useful knowledge)
c. failure to conform to social norms

Although many of the explanations of the causes of poverty suggest that it is the poor themselves who are responsible for their present condition, there appears to be a distinction between those which suggest that there is something inborn which leads individuals in this direction and those which suggest that the poor person has not accepted "proper" social attitudes toward work and mobility. Such explanations came to the fore with the emphasis upon the innate goodness of work found in the Protestant Ethic. Those who did not appear to share this particular value emphasis (the unemployed) were obviously people who had been incorrectly educated. Thus, one of the goals of the workhouse movement in England and charity in the United States was to teach people the value of work, if they had not already learned this. The growing insistence that the poor must work at something if they were to receive any support is a further indication of the emerging emphasis upon teaching the poor the value of work. Those explanations which emphasize the laziness, intemperance and improvidence of the poor also fit into this category. The social work notions assumed that people were poor because they were of alien cultures. The ultimate development of this approach occurs in the concepts of the culture of poverty and cultural deprivation: the poor are unsocialized, have been socialized incorrectly or have learned different styles of behavior.

Cell 3. Explanations which fit into this cell are related to the nature of society, for example:

a. the necessity of social hierarchy
b. the need for a large surplus of labor
c. the need for competition

Classical economics would be a prime example of a Cell 3 explanation. In addition, that aspect of Social Darwinism which views competition as inherent in the social system has its place here. It also views the poor as a category of individuals who are not fitted by nature to deal with the demands of a competitive society. The Marxist view of poverty in the *capitalist* system also fits this cell.

Cell 4. Explanations which fit into this cell are not characterized by basic structural attributes, but by events which occur in the life cycle or history of a society such as:

a. epidemics, natural disasters
b. rapid social change which destroys social equilibrium (automation, migration, war, conquest)
c. economic fluctuation such as depressions

Marx's view of poverty would seem to fit the type of explanations subsumed by Cell 4 as well as 3. Poverty is viewed as inherent in capitalist society, but it could be eliminated or kept from appearing in socialist societies. The existence of poverty in primitive societies was also denied because of what Marx considered to be the existence of primitive communism in many of the hunting and gathering groups of the world. He did not view them as poor in the same way that the lumpenproletariat of the growing army of unemployed workers were viewed as poor. The explanations of descriptive sociologists would also fit in this category since, in their view, the most appalling conditions of poverty could be ameliorated without fundamental change in the system. Post-transition welfare views fit into this cell as well.

Thus, in the attitudes to poverty to be found in the transitional period in England there were continual shifts of emphasis between individual-oriented explanations on the one hand, and the arguments of social forces on the other. One minor trend was a movement away from the perception of inherent traits toward a perception of acquired attributes.

Official Policy and Poverty

ENGLISH POLICY

Official policy toward poverty also reflected varying uses of different ideological positions regarding individual or social system weakness. Symbolic of society's disapproving attitude to the poor is the workhouse, an institution which was maintained in Britain from the sixteenth century through the beginning of the twentieth century. The framework within which workhouses operated were the much-amended Poor Laws of Elizabethan times. These subsequent amendments reflected changes in the views of the dominant class. Workhouses were one instrument in the entire program of poor relief. The following description of workhouses in the English Black Country is taken from a longer work by the British historian George Barnsby.

The Black Country is an area of less than one hundred square miles north of Birmingham. It stands on what was the thickest seam of coal in Britain and as soon as some of the technical problems related to the utilization of the coal were solved the area became a center for the developing industrial activities in Britain.

The swiftly changing villages of the Black Country inherited the Poor Relief facilities common to the rest of the country. Workhouses, run with varying degrees of competence and sympathy, provided indoor or outdoor relief as appeared most appropriate to Overseers of the Poor at any given time. [Editors' note: Indoor relief was that provided to full-time residents of the workhouse, while outdoor relief was provided to those who lived outside the confines of the workhouse but came there to work or lived outside and were supported without working.]

What the conditions inside these workhouses were is difficult to judge. "Bastille" was an apt epithet for them since no one was allowed to visit the workhouse, even the Guardians requiring permission from the Workhouse Master before they could enter. Guardians were the locally elected officials responsible for the Poor Relief. They were men of property, tradesmen, small businessmen, craftsmen, etc., who were elected by limited franchise. However, the basic administration of the workhouses was under central governmental direction rather than local authorities, particularly after the passage of the Poor Law Amendment Act of 1834, and thus the local Guardians did not have direct control over most activities in the workhouses. Thus, one of the first general descriptions of a Black Country workhouse appeared in September, 1876, in the *Miners' Examiner* a working-class newspaper:

A Visit to a Black Country Workhouse

We were admitted by a tall janitor. Entrants are stripped, their clothes are put in a hot air stove and they are given a cold bath. In the morning male casuals are put to breaking 3 hundred pounds of stones before being sent on their way rejoicing with a breakfast of dry bread. The building had evidently grown with the poverty of the parish. We were shown through a wilderness of long bedrooms with floors clean and white with rows of small, iron bedsteads, much more healthy than the crowded bedrooms in which a large proportion of the toiling masses sleep. We were next conducted through the day rooms. Here a number of old men sat on benches listlessly waiting on lagging time. They looked curiously at us as we crossed one of the yards which limit the liberty of the paupers. The able–bodied are not allowed to spend their time thus, the delights of oakum picking being reserved for them to while away the time. We were shown old rope ends hard and dirty with oil. These are dried and hammered until they are soft enough to handle, to be separated by fingers and torn to shreds. Few skilled workers were found in the House. The women were generally more cheerful than the men and the children were scampering round the Workhouse yard. One little fellow was called "Tommy Unknown."

In the hospital there were many sick men and women prostrate with disease. We were conducted to the asylum where fifty or sixty women were of all ages and degrees of imbecility. Some moved with restless wildness like wild beasts, others gazed stonily into space. Among the idiots on the men's side were many eccentric characters. One had attacked an old man, himself an imbecile, and bitten off his ear and part of his hand. Others looked quite sensible—these were epileptics. One man had sat in a corner for forty years without speaking, having said he would never speak again and kept his vow. We are convinced that this is one of the best–managed poor law establishments in the country.

The ultimate aim of the Poor Law Amendment Act of 1834 was to abolish outdoor relief entirely and drastically reduce indoor relief by application of the principle of "least eligibility" whereby conditions within the workhouse were made worse than those of the least favourably employed person outside. The Act of 1834 also consolidated smaller units into one large workhouse, which was frequently located at the very edge of heavily populated areas thus making it difficult for people to remain outside the workhouse and "commute." Still another effect of the law was to standardize diet all over the country and eliminate local forms of charity.

Thus, the famous Christmas dinner in the workhouse does not emerge until the latter part of the nineteenth century. In 1837 plum puddings donated by charitable persons for the inmates of Wolverhampton workhouse were returned to the donors.

Despite the goals of the 1834 Act to eliminate out relief and reduce workhouse relief, they were never attained. As late as 1891 in Wolverhampton, out relief was denied. However, the workhouse could not accommodate all those who applied and out relief had to be reinstituted. Working against the attempts to curtail relief payments were the increasing general population (between 1831 and 1861 the population of the Black Country doubled) and the economic fluctuations which led to periods of high unemployment interspersed with periods of high employment. Despite these fluctuations the amount spent for poor relief of all types remained relatively static throughout most of the century.

Within the workhouse several categories of people were lodged. Among these were the aged, the chronically sick, the insane, orphans, women, and a small proportion of able bodied men. For the able bodied men work in the stoneyards was required for which they received payments of 9 pence a day. Throughout all of the various approaches to the poor in the Black Country a distinction between the "deserving" and "undeserving" was maintained.[22]

The thrust of the legislation devoted to conditions in the workhouses would indicate that mid-nineteenth century thinking in England still emphasized the punitive and educational aspects of the workhouse experience. In addition, by making conditions in the workhouse as uninviting as possible the hope was to discourage members of the parish from entering the house or using the yard. It can be assumed that the able-bodied were most actively discouraged from entering this institution. Despite these policies, when economic conditions deteriorated and massive unemployment occurred, the door to the workhouse had to be opened.

Despite the increasing harshness of workhouse policy understanding of the difficulties faced by the poor workingman grew. The recognition that workers lacked control over their own working conditions led to change in public policies. Thus, measures designed to aid the hardworking poor were approved. These measures are generally referred to as the Speenhamland Laws. Polyani notes:

The justices of Berkshire, meeting at the Pelikan Inn, in Speenhamland, near Newbury, on May 6, 1795, in a time of great distress, decided that subsidies in the aid of wages should be granted in accordance with a scale dependent upon the price of bread, so that a minimum income should be assured to the poor *irrespective of their earnings*. The magistrates' famous recommendation ran: When the gallon loaf of bread of definite quality "shall cost 1 shilling, then every poor and industrious person shall have for his support 3 shillings weekly, either procured by his own or his family's labor, *or an allowance from the poor rates,* and for the support of his wife and every other of his family, 1 shilling, 6 pence; when the gallon of bread shall cost 1 shilling, 6 pence, then 4 shillings a week, plus 1 shilling, 10 pence; on every pence which the bread price raises above 1 shilling he shall have 3 pence for himself and 1 pence for the others".[23]

The suggestions adopted at Speenhamland never actually reached the statute book, but they were widely adopted throughout the country. In effect, we have the first instance of a guaranteed annual income for a large industrial nation. Workers could be paid at whatever rate their employers determined, but if those rates fell below the mandated minimum income, they had to be supplemented from the public funds. The assumption that all those residing within a given parish had the right to a minimum income guaranteed by the local community, what Polyani refers to as a "right to live" declaration, can only be based upon public recognition that those in poverty were enmeshed in a situation which was beyond their own ability to control. However, as time went on, popular and official thinking about the indolent poor became less generous, and such attempts at income redistribution fell by the wayside.

In the twentieth century in England, interventionist policies have superseded nineteenth-century laissez-faire. Social welfare programs have been implemented at a surprising rate and at the present time this nation can be viewed as one major example of a welfare state. Provision through a national scheme of assistance guarantees that every citizen has the right to a minimal level of subsistence. Health is provided for by a national health service, unemployment is taken care of by compensation and employment exchanges, low wages are alleviated through supplementary programs of support, and old age is provided for by a system of pensions. In addition, those families with large numbers of dependents are helped by a family allowance program which provides support. In most large cities in England local municipalities provide housing for the major proportion of the indigenous population. All of these programs which form part of the social welfare system are designed to eliminate the most debilitating consequences of material deprivation.

THE HISTORY OF PUBLIC POLICY TOWARD POVERTY IN THE UNITED STATES

In the United States public responsibility for the maintenance of the poor was not recognized until much later than in England. However, there was recognition of the plight of the poor and a number of private charitable agencies were developed to help care for them. The nation's first comprehensive agency to care for the poor was the New York Association for Improving the Condition of the Poor, which was established by a group of philanthropists in 1843.[24] A basic assumption of the Agency was ". . . that volunteer personal service to the poor should be revived in great cities in order to counter the prevailing trend to indiscriminate almsgiving." The visitor was to act as a role model for the poor and teach them religious observance, thrift, hard work and temperance. One of the fears expressed by those who supported the Agency was that those helped would become dependent upon the aid received and remain dependent for life. To counter this possibility aid was kept to a minimum and the poor were encouraged to seek employment.

Many officials responsible for dispensing public and private aid could be seen to have rather mixed, ambivalent views about the origins of poverty in the system. Both the system and the individual were simultaneously blamed. In the United States, the officials of the New York Association for Improving the Condition of the Poor thought the causes of pauperism were: ignorance, idleness, intemperance in drinking, want of economy, imprudent and hasty marriages, lotteries, pawnbrokers and houses of ill repute. As we shall see, these are behavioral *responses* to poverty, not causes. It was noted that the most worthy poor would decline charity under any conditions and prefer to suffer rather than become dependent. Another example of American attitudes toward the poor can be seen in the following list of reasons given for the widespread existence of the tramp by charitable, political and social organizations in response to a survey. The reasons given are many, some general, some specific. Many refer to innate weaknesses in the individual: "drink, laziness, tobacco, discontent, shiftlessness, vice, love of roaming, heredity, inability, dishonesty, depravity, worthlessness, improvidence, force of habit, lack of manhood, imbecility. . . ." Many refer to attributes affecting the socialization of the individual: "lack of home training, ignorance, poor example, dime novels, immigration, jails, defective education, uncomfortable homes and 'the Devil.' " Finally, many refer to the social or economic system: "War, unemployment, indiscriminate almsgiving or false charity, strikes, type of civilization, low wages, fees made by magistrates, socialistic ideas, over-population, hospitality of jails and alms houses, industrial system and specialization of labor." [25] Some observers did note basic economic factors as causes of poverty, such as inadequate wages, fluctuations in the economy, and an inequitable distribution of scarce resources such as property and money. However, the overriding impression one receives is that the poor were blamed for their own state—either because they had innate flaws, poor socialization or alien socialization.

Negative Evaluation of the State of Poverty and the Poor

In eighteenth- and nineteenth-century England, and in the United States during the same period, there seems to have emerged a general view of the poor as immoral and depraved. Unlike previous eras when the poor might be viewed as afflicted through divine intervention or the poor might be viewed as necessary for the salvation of the non-poor through giving charity, the emerging view of the poor did not see any redeeming features in this condition. The religious views which had previously sanctioned poverty were in decline in the growing monetized system and poverty was no longer acceptable. Ironically, society approved those who had risen from the ranks of the poor. However, the credit given to "rags to riches" success was consistent with the condemnation of the immorality and slothfulness of those who did not rise above their level. Since it was commonly supposed that anyone who really wanted to work could find a job, little time was wasted on those who did not work and were poor.

In traditional agrarian society the disreputable were placed in this category because of the nature of the tasks they performed and/or the particular lifestyle associated with the people in this occupation. In transitional England the shift in attitudes toward poverty focused upon the poor as a group of people, for the most part, who were unable to obtain any kind of stable employment. This large and heterogeneous group of materially deprived began to be associated with the defiling, immoral lifestyles of the former underclass. Malthus pointed to the tendency of the poor to procreate excessively as the basic source of their poverty. Spencer saw their depraved modes of behavior as a major cause of poverty. A view of the poor as immoral and intemperate began to pervade many of the treatises on poverty. Among the various attributes of the poor we find such items as drink, laziness, ignorance, lack of home training, vice, poor heredity, dishonesty, depravity, improvidence, and lack of manhood.

When we look at the actual descriptions of behavior, we find that some alleged attributes are more accurate than others. Some behavioral responses are adaptive to conditions of poverty while others are simply not accurate. As we have previously noted some of the behavior of the poor was viewed as innate, while many other aspects were viewed as acquired or learned. Where the negatively valued behavior of the poor was viewed as learned, it became the job of the larger society, either through the workhouse in England or the charitable visitor in the United States, to re-educate them and teach them proper patterns of behavior, particularly as these influenced the work situation.

Victorian Ethnography of the Poor—Mayhew

In the middle of the nineteenth century, Henry Mayhew, a journalist, began a survey of the conditions of the life of the poor in London which stands today as a monument to ethnographic effort. Mayhew spent several years talking with members of the lowest class of the London population and observing their patterns of behavior. Much of the material collected was published in newspapers and eventually brought together in a four volume work which is a description of "Those that *will* work, those that *cannot* work, and those that *will not* work." [26]

One particular group which is described in great detail in Mayhew's first volume is the costermongers. The term "costermonger" is used for a variety of peddlars who purchase their wares at local markets and sell them during the remainder of the day. The similarity of this group to others found in the developing nations of the world is marked. Some sell cooked food and others uncooked food. Other items sold are second-hand clothing, household gadgets, and so on. Some have permanent stations while others constantly move about.

Costermongering is an occupation which draws individuals who have been unsuccessful in other occupational careers. However, the true costermonger seems to scoff at the feeble efforts of displaced industrial workers to earn a living in this way. The following excerpt from an interview with a "born and bred" costermonger illustrates these attitudes.

"From the numbers of mechanics," said one smart costermonger to me, "that I know of in my own district, I should say there's now more than 1,000 costers in London that were once *mechanics or labourers*. They are driven to it as a last resource, when they can't get work at their trade. They don't do well, at least four out of five, or three out of four don't. They're not up to the dodges of the business. They go to market with fear, and don't know how to venture a bargain if one offer. They're inferior salesmen too, and if they have fish left that won't keep, it's a dead loss to them, for they aren't up to the trick of selling it cheap at a distance where the coster ain't known; or of quitting it to another, for candle-light sale, cheap, to the Irish or to the 'lushingtons' that haven't a proper taste for fish. Some of these poor fellows lose every penny. They're mostly middle-aged when they begin costering. They'll generally commence with oranges or herrings. We pity them. We say, 'Poor fellows! they'll find it out by-and-bye.' It's awful to see some poor women, too, trying to pick up a living in the streets by selling nuts or oranges. It's awful to see them for they can't set about it right; besides that, there's too many before they start. They don't find a living, it's only another way of starving." [27]

Costermongering is a highly precarious way of life, even for those who have grown up in the trade. One must learn how to bargain with those in the markets and how to inflate prices and adulterate goods to increase the levels of profit. Few costers seem to be free of debt and these are incurred on a daily basis as well as those times when larger scale capital investments are needed to buy donkeys, carts and barrows. Mayhew notes that the ordinary interest paid by a coster for a loan is 20 percent per week on whatever amount has been borrowed.[28]

One of the intriguing descriptions is that of the relations of costers with the police. Evidently the police are viewed as the enemy and anything which can be done to the police without getting caught is sanctioned. One coster observed:

"Can you wonder at it, sir," said a costermonger to me, "that I hate the police? They drive us about, we must move on, we can't stand here, and we can't pitch there. But if we're cracked up, that is if we're forced to go into the Union (I've known it both at Clerkenwell and the City of London workhouses,) why the parish gives us money to buy a barrow, or a shallow, or to hire them, and leave the house and start for ourselves: and what's the use of that, if the police won't let us sell our goods?—Which is right, the parish or the police?" [29]

One of the notable characteristics of this group is the high proportion of consensual unions rather than church or legal marriages found among them. Once again, we shall see in Chapter 5 that this is a common response to poverty in the contemporary world as well. Mayhew estimated that no more than one out of ten couples had legal sanctions for their union. He lists as possible reasons for the extent of consensual unions the following:

1. paramours cannot afford to pay the marriage fees;
2. paramours do not believe in the sanctity of the ceremony;
3. paramours object to marry them for pecuniary or family reasons; and
4. [paramours] would forfeit their income by marrying as officers' widows in receipt of pensions. . . .[30]

Mayhew describes the marital arrangements of the costers and the legitimacy of their offspring in the following words:

Only one-tenth—at the outside one-tenth—of the couples living together and carrying on the costermongering trade, are married. Of the rights of "legitimate" or "illegitimate" children the costermongers understand nothing, and account it a mere waste of money and time to go through the ceremony of wedlock when a pair can live together, and be quite as well regarded by their fellows, without it. The married women associate with the unmarried mothers of families without the slighest scruple. There is no honour attached to the marriage state, and no shame to concubinage. Neither are the unmarried women less faithful to their "partners" than the married; but I understand that, of the two classes, the unmarried betray the most jealousy.[31]

Perhaps the best view of what the life of a coster was like can be obtained from the following description of the life of a coster boy.

"My father," he told me in a thick unimpassioned voice, "was a waggoner, and worked the country roads. There was two on us at home with mother, and we used to play along with the boys of our court, in Golding-lane, at buttons and marbles. I recollects nothing more than this—only the big boys used to cheat like bricks and thump us if we grumbled—that's all I recollects of my infancy, as you calls it. Father I've heard tell died when I was three and brother only a year old. It was worse luck for us!— Mother was so easy with us. I once went to school for a couple of weeks, but the cove used to fetch me a wipe over the knuckles with his stick, and as I wasn't going to stand that there, why you see I aint no great schollard. We did as we liked with mother, she was so precious easy, and I never learned anything but playing buttons and making leaden 'bonces,' that's all," (here the youth laughed slightly.) "Mother used to be up and out very early washing in families—anything for a living. She was a good mother to us. We was left at home with the key of the room and some bread and butter for dinner. Afore she got into work—and it was a goodish long time—we was shocking hard up, and she pawned nigh everything. Sometimes, when we had'nt no grub at all, the other lads, perhaps, would give us some of their bread and butter, but often our stomachs used to ache with the hunger, and we would cry when we was werry far gone. She used to be at work from six in the morning till ten o'clock at night, which was a long time for a child's belly to hold out again, and when it was dark we would go and lie down on the bed and try and sleep until she came home with the food. I was eight year old then.

"A man as know'd mother, said to her, 'Your boy's got nothing to do, let him come along with me and yarn a few ha'pence,' and so I became a coster. He gave me 4d. a morning and my breakfast. I worked with him about three year, until I learnt the markets, and then I and brother got baskets of our own, and used to keep mother. One day with another, the two on us together could make 2s.6d. by selling greens of a morning, and going round to the publics with nuts of a evening, till about ten o'clock at night. Mother used to have a bit of fried meat or a stew ready for us when we got home, and by using up the stock as we couldn't sell, we used to manage pretty tidy. When I was fourteen I took up with a girl. She lived in the same house as we did, and I used to walk out of a night with her and give her half-pints of beer at the publics. She were about thirteen, and used to dress werry nice, though she weren't above middling pretty. Now I'm working for another man as gives me a shilling a week, victuals, washing, and lodging, just as if I was one of the family.

"On a Sunday I goes out selling, and all I yarns I keeps. As for going to church, why, I can't afford it,—besides, to tell the truth, I don't like it well enough." [32]

The prevalent use of second-hand clothing and household furnishings is described by Mayhew and an interesting informal money-raising mechanism exists in the form of a raffle. In time of illness, one small possession is raffled to raise money for the sick individual.

The second and third volumes of Mayhew's work deal with two other categories of the street-folk. These are scavengers and casual laborers. We find a rather startling similarity between the marginal occupations of the London poor and the poor of the developing nations of the world (a finding which is borne out in Chapter 5). Of these various categories of street occupations, scavenging or finding, is one of the most debilitating and materially unrewarding ones. Mayhew describes the living conditions of "bone-grubbers" in the following words:

The houses are of the poorest description, and seem as if they tumbled into their places at random. Foul channels, huge dust-heaps, and a variety of other unsightly objects, occupy every open space, and dabbling among these are crowds of ragged dirty children who grub and wallow, as if in their native element. None reside in these places but the poorest and most wretched of the population, and, as might almost be expected, this, the cheapest and filthiest locality of London, is the head-quarters of the *bone-grubbers* and other *street-finders*.[33]

Another form of scavenging, referred to as "mud-larking," consisted of walking along the banks and in the shallow waters of the Thames and picking up whatever one could find. This form of scavenging was primarily restricted to younger boys and girls and one described his life in the following way:

He stated that his father was a sailor who had been hurt on board ship, and been unable to go to sea for the last two years. He had two brothers and a sister, one of them older than himself; and his elder brother was a mud-lark like himself. The two had been mud-larking more than a year; they went because they saw other boys go, and knew that they got money for the things they found. They were often hungry, and glad to do anything to get something to eat. Their father was not able to earn anything, and their mother could get but little to do. They gave all the money they earned to their mother. They didn't gamble, and play at pitch and toss when they had got some money, but some of the big boys did on the Sunday, when they didn't go a mud-larking. He couldn't tell why they did nothing on a Sunday, "only they didn't"; though sometimes they looked about to see where the best place would be on the next day. He didn't go to the ragged school; he should like to know how to read a book, though he couldn't tell what good it would do him. He didn't like mud-larking, would be glad of something else, but didn't know anything else that he could do.[34]

Among the street laborers described by Mayhew are those involved in construction. He notes the instability of this form of employment because of weather conditions and speculative enterprises based upon the money market. When weather conditions are bad construction work is halted; when money is available there is a demand for such labor but when the money market becomes tight jobs in this industry are hard to find.[35]

Another category of workers which is influenced by numerous conditions beyond their control are the dockworkers. The London docks were a source of employment for large numbers of men. The work was hard, required intensive human energy inputs, and was cyclical rather than steady. Mayhew distinguished the casual laborers from those more

regularly employed at particular docks, but notes the precariousness of
even the latter group's employment and income. He also notes the
diversity of previous occupations followed by those who worked on the
docks while he was doing this study.

Those who are unable to live by the occupation to which they have been
educated can obtain a living there without any previous training. Hence
we find men of every calling labouring at the docks. There are decayed
and bankrupt master-butchers, master-bakers, publicans, grocers, old sol-
diers, old sailors, Polish refugees, broken-down gentlemen, discharged
lawyers' clerks, suspended government clerks, almsmen, pensioners, servants, thieves—indeed, every one who wants a loaf, and is willing to work
for it. The London Dock is one of the few places in the metropolis where
men can get employment without either character or recommendation, so
that the labourers employed there are naturally a most incongruous as-
sembly.[36]

Volume Four of this series, which includes work by several authors,
concentrates upon those who will not work and includes prostitutes,
thieves, swindlers and beggars. The basically corporate structure of
populations of thieves and prostitutes are noted, but it is suggested that
this structure is breaking down under the impact of amateurs who are
being recruited into these fields because of hard times. Halliday de-
lineates the relationship between certain categories of prostitutes and
beggars in the following description:

The relations which subsist between prostitutes and the beggars reveal
some curious traits. Beggars will enter a public house because they see some
women at the bar who will assist their suit. They offer their little wares
to some gentlemen at the bar, and the women will say, "Give the poor
devil something" or "buy bouquets for us," or if the commodity should be
laces or buttons, they say, "Don't take the poor old woman's things; give
her the money." And the gentlemen, just to show off, and appear liberal,
do as they are told. Possibly, but for the pleading of their gay companions,
they would have answered the appeal with a curse and gruff command to
be gone. I once saw an old woman kiss a bedizened prostitute's hand, in real
gratitude for a service of this kind. I don't know that I ever witnessed anything more touching in my life. The woman, who a few minutes before
had been flaunting about the bar in the reckless manner peculiar to her
class, was quite moved by the old beggar's act, and I saw a tear mount in
her eye and slowly trickle down her painted cheek, making a white channel
through the rouge as it fell. But in a moment she dashed it away, and the
next was flaunting and singing as before.[37]

Begging is a residual means of obtaining a livelihood in most areas of the world. Halliday describes many of the beggars who pose as sellers of goods, such as match boxes.[38] The following description of the career pattern followed by one individual who was well known to Mayhew indicates certain parallels to patterns in developing societies.

I have traced one boy, by the identifying mark of a most villanous squint, through a career of ten years. When I first saw him he was a mere child of about four years of age. His mother sent him with a ragged little girl (his sister) into publichouse bars to beg. Their diminutive size attracted attention and excited charity. By–and–by, possibly in consequence of the interference of the police, they carried pennyworths of flowers with them, at other times matches, and at others halfpenny sheets of songs. After this the boy and the girl appeared dressed in sailor's costume (both as boys), and sung duets. I remember that one of the duets, which had a spoken part, was not very decent; the poor children evidently did not understand what they said; but the thoughtless people at the bar laughed and gave them money. By–and–by the boy became too big for this kind of work, and I next met him selling fuzees. After the lapse of about a year he started in the shoe-black line. His station was at the end of Endell Street, near the baths; but as he did not belong to one of the regularly organized brigades, he was hunted about by the police, and could not make a living. On the death of the crossing-sweeper at the corner he succeeded to that functionary's broom, and in his new capacity was regarded by the police as a useful member of society. The last time I saw him he was in possession of a costermonger's barrow selling mackerel.[39]

Thus Mayhew attempted to describe the slum-dwellers of London. Mayhew's poor were engaged in the same occupations which are characteristic of the poor in contemporary developing societies. He is especially concerned with the street vendor whom he describes in great variety specializing in fish, vegetables, eatables and drinkables, razors, pocket knives, key rings, cigars, toys, second-hand goods and a wide variety of other small consumer items. In addition, he lists scavengers, nine types of street cleansers, and the casual heavy laborer.[40] Mayhew indicates that these occupations are filled by unempolyed industrial workers when times are bad, thus confirming that they serve as a floating supply of unskilled labor.

Mayhew's surprisingly objective first-hand observations of the behavior of the poor may strike the modern reader of contemporary descriptions of the behavior of the poor as remarkably alike. As we shall see in Chapters 5 and 6, many of the behavioral responses of the un-

stable laboring class in nineteenth-century London described by Mayhew
are precise analogues to the coping responses of those with low and unstable income in the United States and Third World nations today.

Notes

1. William McNeill, *History of Western Civilization* (Chicago: University
   of Chicago Press, 1969), p. 377.
2. McNeill, *ibid.*, pp. 376–380.
3. McNeill, *ibid.*, pp. 372–390.
4. Henry Mayhew, *London Labour and the London Poor*, vols. 1–4
   (First published 1861–62; reissued London: Frank Cass and Co., Ltd.,
   1967).
5. F. F. Piven and R. A. Cloward, "The Relief of Welfare," *Transaction*,
   vol. 8, no. 7, May 1971, pp. 1–39, 52–53.
6. *Ibid.*, p. 36.
7. Charles Booth et al., *Life and Labour of the People in London* (New
   York: Macmillan, 1902).
8. B. S. Rowntree, *Poverty: A Study of Town Life* (London: Macmillan
   and Co., Ltd., 1902).
9. Mayhew, *op. cit.*
10. M. S. Byrne, *Elizabethan Life in Town and Country* (London: Uni-
    versity Paperbacks, 1961), p. 171.
11. Mayhew, *op. cit.*, vol. 4.
12. Byrne, *op. cit.*, p. 167.
13. W. K. Jordan, *Philanthropy in England 1480–1660* (New York: Rus-
    sell Sage Foundation, 1959).
14. Andrew Halliday, "Beggars," in Mayhew, *op. cit.*, vol. 4, pp. 447–448.
15. Jordan, *op. cit.*
16. T. Malthus, *An Essay on the Principle of Population* (First published
    1798) (New York: E. P. Dutton & Co., Inc., 1914).
17. Herbert Spencer, "Poverty Purifies Society," Will and Vatter (eds.),
    Poverty in Affluence (New York: Harcourt, Brace & World, Inc.,
    1965), p. 58; William Sumner, "Survival of the Unfittest," Will and
    Vatter, *ibid.*, p. 60.
18. Spencer, *op. cit.*, p. 58.
19. Sumner, *op. cit.*, pp. 60–61.
20. Spencer, *op. cit.*, p. 59.
21. Karl Marx, *Capital: A Critique of Political Economy* (Chicago: C. H.
    Kerr and Co., 1906–1909).
22. George Barnsby, "Attitudes to the Poor Law in Britain in the Nine-

teenth Century as Exemplified in the Black Country." Paper prepared by Professor Barnsby in September 1970 for this volume. Unfortunately, the limitation of space has forced us to abstract from this contribution, but not reproduce it in full as we should have liked.

23. Karl Polyani, *The Great Transformation* (Boston: Beacon Press, 1944), p. 78.

24. Dorothy Becker, "The Visitor to the New York City Poor, 1843–1920," *Social Service Review,* vol. 35, December 1961, pp. 382–396.

25. Frank Leonard, "Helping the Unemployed in the 19th Century: The Case of the American Tramp," *Social Service Review,* vol. 40, 1966, pp. 429–434.

26. *London Labour and the London Poor,* vols. 1–4.

27. *Ibid.,* vol. 1, p. 7.

28. *Ibid.,* p. 29.

29. *Ibid.,* p. 20.

30. *Ibid.,* pp. 20–21.

31. *Ibid.,* p. 20.

32. *Ibid.,* p. 39

33. *Ibid.,* vols. 2, 3.

34. *Ibid.,* p. 156.

35. *Ibid.,* p. 324.

36. *Ibid.,* vol. 3, p. 301.

37. Halliday, *op. cit.,* p. 439.

38. *Ibid.,* pp. 438–440.

39. Mayhew, *op. cit.,* vol. 1, p. 439.

40. *Ibid.,* vols. 1–4.

Chapter 4

Material Deprivation: A Cross-Cultural View in Contemporary Developing Societies

IT is clear that economic and technological change in Western society produced a new kind of socio-economic order. In the new system, not only was the incidence of material deprivation affected, but, as a consequence, its social meaning changed as well. Poverty was no longer rationalized and justified. Instead, the poor were identified with the most despised social strata and poverty came to be viewed explicitly as a problem not only requiring, but also susceptible of solution.

To what extent are these changed views on the character of poverty and the nature of the poor common to all urban industrial systems? Are there striking similarities in the attitudes toward poverty in urban industrial societies as there were in traditional agrarian systems? Are Western attitudes toward poverty and the poor uniquely Western, or can we expect to see them duplicated in the rest of the world as the industrial transition takes place? In this chapter we shall discuss the implications of the technological-economic revolution in the non-industrial capitalist world.

The question of the existence of material deprivation in contemporary socialist countries, although it arises, is not treated here. The major reason for this omission is that data which the authors consider to be impartial and valid are extremely difficult to obtain. The re-emergence or persistence of petty capitalism and state capitalism in Soviet Russia either challenges the Marxist's assumption that the basic evils of a capitalistic system will be eliminated in a socialist economy, or indicates that a truly Marxist economic system has not yet emerged. From all accounts of the Soviet brand of socialism, class distinctions have not been eradicated. Furthermore, ethnographic descriptions of everyday life activities of the urban masses are not available. Much the same can be said of the Cuban situation where, in addition, the time elapsed since the Revolution is quite short. In the case of China, controlled release of information and limited studies by foreign observers make it impossible to assess the degree to which material deprivation has been eliminated.

The Transition in Contemporary Developing Societies

The process which took place in England during a period of more than three hundred years might be labeled "the modernization process." Similar processes are now occurring in varied forms in many other nations of the world. Differences are related to the fact that the process has a different starting point and occurs in a contracted time span.

As conscious policy, all of these nations want to raise the standard of living of the population as well as to enhance their political position in the world arena and, to that end, are going through a transitional phase. In all of them, the development of agriculture, commerce and industry is crucial. As the productive capacity increases, there is a growing belief in the ability of man to control his environment. Just as in the West, the nature of material deprivation and attitudes toward material deprivation have changed, so, we can anticipate a similar change in the developing nations.

In discussing the variety of changes which took place in England between the sixteenth and the nineteenth centuries, we must recognize that the growth of colonialism played an important part. If we shift our focus from development in England and Western Europe to the dependent colonies, we see that a complementary and in some cases parallel process had been set in motion. Before the nineteenth century, colonies existed as places from which wealth could be directly drawn in the form of precious minerals, spices and handicrafts. As the harnassing of new energy sources stimulated industrialization, the role of the colonies changed to that of markets for manufactured goods from the mother country. One consequence of this process was the expansion of internal markets within the colonies and the broadened significance of money as a general medium of exchange and standard of value. In economies where basic goods and services had been produced by the consumer himself or exchanged through traditions of reciprocal kinship or occupational roles, money exchanges replaced traditional exchange. Traditional currencies such as cows or scarce shells had had very narrow utility being used only in a limited range of transactions. Money, on the other hand, became an all-purpose medium. Land and other goods which were formerly the inherited property of a family, kinship group or community were now bought and sold in the open market for cash. As money became a generalized medium of exchange, the need for it grew. Lerner refers to this as the development of a "cash nexus between the desires and satisfactions." [1]

A basic response today to the growing need for cash in rural areas is either a conversion from subsistence agriculture to cash crops or the sale of labor for wages. Since opportunities for the sale of labor in rural areas are limited, many rural dwellers shift to urban areas where they can more readily sell their labor.

Many recent anthropological studies of communities in developing societies have focused upon the increasing impact of higher levels of the social system upon the village, especially through the impact of cash crops and wage labor. Emphasizing the market as a major factor related to vast social changes among a variety of African peoples, the contributors to the volume *Markets in Africa* consistently emphasize the growing importance of money among such diverse people as the Fulani, the Kipsigis and the Arusha. As a particular example, we might note the substitution of money for the traditional currency of cattle in the establishment of bride-wealth.[2] Oscar Lewis, in his study of an Indian village, mentions the attempt by landowning *jatis* (castes) to substitute cash payments for payments in kind in exchange for the services of hereditary servants.[3] Hammel [4] and Lewis [5] note for their respective Peruvian and Mexican villages that cash payments are increasingly used as a substitute for communal work. In both areas a citizen's traditional obligation was to provide communal labor in return for use of land. Erasmus also notes the decline of traditional reciprocal labor groups in the face of cash labor.[6] Thus, cash seems to replace traditional currency and reciprocal exchange in a wide variety of transitional societies.

Sources of Cash in Rural Areas

CASH CROPS

As cash becomes the general medium of exchange, the need for it becomes more pervasive. Those in rural areas generally have the two alternatives mentioned above, to shift to cash-cropping or to sell their labor where there is a market for it, in rural, urban, or foreign areas.

There are numerous examples from a variety of world areas which illustrate the shift from subsistence to cash agriculture. A classic description of the impact of colonialism on cash-cropping in Mexico and Guatemala can be found in the work of Wolf who implies similar developments took place in Dutch Java.[7] In India, Rao's comparative study of two villages illustrates the basic differences between the communities as a result of both a shift to cash-cropping and nearby urban industrial employment.[8] In comparing a Taiwanese and Sumatran farmer, Halpern indicates that a very large segment of agricultural production from even their small-scale farms enters the cash-oriented market.[9] Much attention has been given recently to the cocoa farmers in West Africa [10] and we have seen television commercials about the cash-cropping coffee growers of Latin America (for example, Juan Valdez and those mythical cash-croppers who negotiate with *El Exigente*). A more scholarly description of independent coffee cash-croppers can be found in Wolf.[11] An early study of the shift from subsistence to cash-oriented agriculture is the case study of the Tanalese in Madagascar done by Linton in the 1930s. Although this study antedated recent anthropological interest in the economic development process, Linton's work showed the tremendous impact of this shift. As a result of market-oriented rice production, many aspects of social organization and ideology underwent rapid and marked change.[12] The same process has occurred in the rest of the world as cash has become important. All of these examples illustrate the pervasive emphasis upon money and the needs for cash which are characteristic of the developing world.

RURAL LABOR

Although we have suggested that opportunities for selling labor in the rural areas are limited, some do in fact exist. As the basic reciprocity which characterizes much of peasant life breaks down, certain services become converted into wage labor, for example, domestic work and local construction work. In addition, displaced craftsmen, sharecroppers, tenants and small landholders can become agricultural laborers working locally for cash.

For those in the village displaced by the intrusion of the cash economy, an alternative to remaining in the village is to leave and move to plantations. Some crops which have commercial value like sugar cannot be grown profitably in the small-scale cash-crop agriculture described above. These crops are grown primarily on large-scale commercial estates which use wage laborers who have been described in many monographs and sometimes referred to as the "rural proletariat." [13] These large-scale commercial agricultural enterprises may be located within national boundaries or they may involve emigration as illustrated by Lopreato in his discussion of an Italian village and its transition.[14] It should be noted also that the migration process involves differences in time as well as space. In many instances, such as the *bracero* migration (Mexican peasants entering the United States for agricultural wage labor), the movement is almost always short-term and temporary. In other cases, movement in search of wage labor initially viewed as temporary may become permanent. Many studies have described this process of migration for all areas of the world.[15] In general, the movement to large-scale commercial agricultural enterprises is likely to be seasonal and of less permanent duration than movement to cities. Since rural-urban migration is very closely related to the development of urban poverty we shall enlarge upon this aspect in a later section.

CHANGES IN CONSUMPTION

Change to a cash-oriented economic system has great implications for the kind of work one does. To survive, one must either produce goods which have cash value or sell one's labor for cash. A complex system of relations exists between work, production, cash and consumption. New goods and services enter the market system and increase the need for cash to purchase them as they become part of the desired consumption pattern. Many of these items which were not part of the traditional pattern are given high prestige value. Foster notes this near universal trend to using purchased items such as clothing and jewelry as prestige items for conspicuous consumption.[16] Newly available items take on prestige value and become symbols of a particular position in a new stratification system based more directly on cash and consumption. In direct contrast to this growing emphasis on cash and status, the more traditional peasant community avoided conspicuous consumption because of the finite nature of available resources. This view is changed as productive capacity increases through improved technology. Thus, appliances and other capital goods become important in allotting prestige and status in a Colombian town,[17] the bicycle and mechanical grass-cutter confer high status in the Indian village; [18] and automobiles, watches, telephones, and radios are ubiquitous symbols of social status in the non-Western as well as the Western world.

In Chapter 2, we discussed the negative attitude toward the accumulation and manipulation of money which existed in traditional societies. Since prestige and power were not directly dependent upon the possession of money and the merchant classes were not allowed to convert money into power and prestige, the accumulation of money was not considered important. The shift to a value orientation in which money can be converted into prestige and power does not take place without resistance from the traditional value system. In most of the cases we have been discussing above, it is apparent that the emphasis upon money has won out. However, this is not always the case, nor is the process a simple one.

Sometimes, the desire for new prestige items, for which money is necessary, does not outweigh the desire to avoid a breakdown in traditional social structure. Often the means to acquire cash contradicts the traditional value system. A recent case study which illustrates the point centers upon a Samoan village where the villagers desired Western goods. Several attempts were made to develop a cash reserve to purchase the desired goods. These included wage labor, an attempt to grow a cash crop (copra), and the establishment of a community store. In each case some aspect of the traditional system such as notions about land tenure and kinship obligations were violated by the new activity, and the villagers gave up the venture.[19]

In other instances there are no objections to the means employed for acquiring cash, but cash is used to achieve *traditional* prestige goals rather than for the consumption of *new* prestige items. Thus, the otherworldly orientation of the fiesta cycle in Zinacantan, Mexico, continues to drain the cash reserves of the successful community members.[20] Salz provides a similar example for Bolivian Indians.[21] In India, a villager who migrated to the city to become the driver of a *tonga* (horse-drawn vehicle) says he wishes to earn money only to buy a farm for his sisters. After that his one great wish is to follow the traditional route to blessedness. He wants to live in a lonely place and be a "holy man." [22]

In a similar vein, Lerner describes the persistence of an ambivalent attitude to money in the Middle East and the difficulty of developing a "sense of cash." [23] He says of a Turkish village, "to talk much of money is an impropriety. To reveal excessive *desire* for money is . . . Allah defend us! . . . an impiety." [24]

Industrialization

Industrial development, using new sources of energy and new organization of production, has been given impetus in many former colonial dependencies by the growth of independence and nationalism. As industrial production increases, new opportunities for the sale of labor emerge and there is a shift in the occupational structure of the system. There is also an increased participation in the commercial market by a large segment of the population.[25] Both of these results intensify the processes we have previously discussed. Furthermore, industrial production leads to an increasing concern with the rational and efficient use of human resources. Thus, according to Moore, more open access to education, intergenerational mobility and a more open social system are among the first consequences of the process.[26] The ideology of an open system is one of the major forces producing a changing view of urban industrial poverty.

Another set of changes which results from an increasing emphasis on industrial production relates to the concept of work. Work is now something that happens away from the home. Hours of work are regular and scheduled. It is also easier to make a distinction between employment and unemployment. Previously, the notion of unemployment was not developed. Agricultural work varies seasonally. Thus, plowing, planting, weeding and harvesting, require large work inputs while other phases in the growing cycle require little effort. During the slack season, people are not concerned with putting all their time to other good use, but this does not mean that they are unemployed. Artisans, merchants, menials who belong to organized guilds are not viewed as unemployed even when they are not engaged in daily work. In addition, farmers and artisans may take pride in doing their craft well for it is part of their birthright. However, they do not generalize this concern to other forms of work. As Lopreato points out, work in a traditional peasant community is considered necessary but not necessarily moral, that is, work in itself does not have any intrinsic value.[27] In modern Western society, work of all kinds is valued for its own sake. Conversely, non-productive leisure-time activity is devalued. Where time is a factor of production, it is considered immoral to "waste" time.

As Weber and others have pointed out, the development of these attitudes toward work was a necessary condition for the development of capitalism and industrialization.[28] In the newly developing areas, Moore points out that nationalism serves as a functional equivalent to the generalized work ethic as an impetus to development.[29] Production for the good of the nation-state (emperor, king, and so on), is often an incentive to work. The consequences of the work ethic for the evaluation of the poor have been previously mentioned, and we shall discuss them at length in the remaining chapters.

RURAL–URBAN MIGRATION

A basic response to both the expanding reliance on cash and growing industrialization is the movement of population from the country to the city. Most demographic studies of urban populations indicate that the spectacular growth of the urban segment is largely attributed to migration from rural areas. Such movement is usually analyzed in terms of push–pull factors. The push factors are those characteristic of the rural area which drive the individual out of his community. The pull factors are those characteristic of the urban situation which draw individuals to the city. As we have previously noted, governmental policies may have a direct impact upon this process. This was the case in the English enclosure movement. It was also the case in the British colonial policy in Africa which introduced taxes that could only be paid in cash, thus forcing Africans to move to urban areas where their labor was required.[30] Other political events which induce extremely rapid influx to the cities are war (as can be seen in contemporary Saigon), and political partition such as that which forced movement of Indians and Pakistanis in 1947. The Palestinian refugee is another case of political migration resulting from both war and partition. The forced migrant who cannot return to his place of origin is usually referred to as a refugee rather than a migrant.

In contrast to direct political intervention, migration in most developing areas of the world is a response to deteriorating economic conditions in the rural areas resulting from population growth, increasing indebtedness, declining land productivity and displacement of traditional service and craft occupations through technological innovation and competing manufactured goods. A classic example of the last process is the case of water carriers, in Gujerat, India, who were displaced by mechanically excavated household wells and were thus pushed to urban centers to seek work.[31]

Movement of people from rural to urban areas is one of the most significant demographic changes occurring at the present time. For most Americans, the significance of this process outside the United States is not very apparent. However, it is very real in every developing society in the world and parallels a similar process in England and the United States. Urban centers such as Lima, Peru; Tokyo, Japan; Bombay and Calcutta, India; Hong Kong; Singapore, Malaysia; Manila, Philippines; Cairo, Egypt; Kampala, Uganda; and Lagos, Nigeria; have doubled and tripled their size in short periods of time and contain high proportions of people who were born in rural areas. For most of the cities mentioned above, population growth as a result of migration has been greater than the increase in job opportunities. Thus, a large segment of the migrants, particularly those without requisite skills, form a pool of intermittently employed or totally unemployed laborers. In contrast to the village where survival is not so affected by cash employment, to survive in the city one must have cash. As one of the pedicab drivers in Bangkok stated in an interview, "In the Northeast (Thailand) if you don't have money you can still get by, in Bangkok if you don't have money you die." [32]

The discrepancy between stable employment opportunities and urban growth has been frequently noted. [33] Even if a small segment of the total national population lives in cities, that small proportion may have a very low level of stable jobs. Thus, India with less than 20 percent of its population in urban areas contains fewer job opportunities for urban residents than the United States where 80 percent live in cities. This discrepancy between the great increase in the size of urban population and the smaller increase in employment opportunities becomes a major condition for the emergence of poverty in contemporary developing societies.

FOCUSING ON URBAN AREAS

Because the urban area is the one in which the urban industrial transition is most advanced and since rural areas conversely retain many of the economic, social and ideological attributes of traditional agrarian societies, we will concentrate on the urban sector in our ensuing discussion. Although we have suggested that the basic conditions for the emergence of the new kind of poverty (based on a cash economy), are found in rural areas as nations develop, the greatest impact of modernization is felt in the urban areas. Traditional behavioral and ideological characteristics can be more easily maintained in a peasant village, even one moving into a cash economy. The isolation of such rural communities, the possibility of maintaining some subsistence activity and traditional exchange, in lieu of a cash need and the draining off of individuals most receptive to change through the migration process, all allow the maintenance of traditional attitudes towards material deprivation in rural areas.

Urban Poverty

THE EXTENT OF POVERTY

Despite the recent impact of technology upon production in the non-Western world, the benefits up to now have been fairly well confined to the nations of Europe and North America. To a degree, the continued impoverishment of most of the people in the world can be seen as a result of the improvement of living conditions for the small Western minority. For most of the urban industrialized nations of the world the process of development was based upon colonial expansion. Thus, dependent areas were kept out of the full developmental process by being utilized as major producers of raw materials and large-scale markets for manufactured goods from the mother country.

At the present time, most of the former colonies have become independent nation-states with a basic "urge for industrialization." Many of these newly created countries have established planning bodies whose major goal is to stimulate the economic growth of the nation, primarily through the expansion of industrial production. However, many barriers to the expansion of the economy exist at the present time. As Myrdal and others have noted, the developed nations of the world have been increasing their affluence at a much higher rate than the underdeveloped nations.[34] Thus, the rich nations are becoming richer while the poor nations are becoming poorer. In spite of this, some increments in economic growth have taken place in many of the developing nations. One further factor related to the failure to develop at a faster rate has been the "population explosion." In contrast, there has been relative population stability in the more economically advanced nations.

In discussing changes in the attitudes to poverty and the poor, the extent of poverty throughout the developing world should be considered as a vital factor. There is no simple measure, however, which can be used as an objective and accurate index of this phenomenon. A recent assessment of world poverty used several indices. These were per capita annual income, availability of medical services, infant mortality, and caloric deficiencies. Despite all of the flaws of using per capita national income as a comparative index for the assessment of the extent of poverty, it is the best available measure and has been most extensively used.

Simpson has used a per capita national income figure of $300 as the dividing line between those nations which are poor and those which are not. A listing of those nations which fall below this figure, together with their per capita national income, and population appears in Table 1.

Table 1. Nations with Less than $300 Per Capita National Income, Total Population, and Actual Per Capita Annual National Income

Nation	Population (Millions)	Income Per Capita (Dollars)
Afgahanistan	15.7	47
Albania	1.9	239
Algeria	11.9	195
Angola	5.2	56
Bolivia	3.7	144
Brazil	82.2	217
Burma	24.7	56
Burundi	3.2	38
Cambodia	6.1	112
Cameroon	5.2	104
Central African Republic	1.4	123
Ceylon	11.2	130
Chad	3.3	60
China	700.0	147
Colombia	18.1	237
Congo (Kinshasa)	15.6	66
Dahomey	2.4	55
Dominican Republic	3.6	212
Ecuador	5.2	183
El Salvador	2.9	236
Ethiopia	22.6	42
Ghana	7.7	245
Guatemala	4.4	281
Guinea	3.5	83
Haiti	4.4	80
Honduras	2.3	194
Hong Kong	3.7	291
India	486.8	86
Indonesia	104.5	85
Iran	24.8	211
Iraq	8.2	193
Ivory Coast	3.8	188
Jordan	2.0	179

Source: Based on D. Simpson, "The Dimensions of World Poverty," *Scientific American*, vol. 219, 1968, pp. 6 and 7.

Nation	Population (Millions)	Income Per Capita (Dollars)
Kenya	9.3	77
Korea, North	12.1	88
Korea, South	28.4	88
Laos	2.6	59
Lebanon	2.4	204
Liberia	1.0	148
Madagascar	6.4	83
Malawi	3.9	38
Malaya	8.0	257
Mali	4.6	57
Mauritania	1.1	106
Mongolia	1.1	250
Morocco	13.3	174
Mozambique	7.0	40
Nepal	10.1	66
Nicaragua	1.7	298
Niger	3.3	78
Nigeria	57.5	63
Pakistan	102.9	89
Paraguay	2.0	186
Peru	11.7	218
Philippines	32.3	219
Rhodesia	4.3	206
Rwanda	3.1	38
Saudi Arabia	6.8	125
Senegal	3.5	149
Sierra Leone	2.4	123
Somalia	2.5	48
Sudan	13.5	90
Syria	5.3	156
Taiwan	12.4	185
Tanzania	10.8	64
Thailand	30.6	105
Togo	1.6	82
Tunisia	4.4	179
Turkey	31.2	244
Uganda	7.6	77
United Arab Republic	29.6	96
Upper Volta	4.9	35
Vietnam, North	19.0	113
Vietnam, South	16.1	113
Yemen	5.0	36
Yemen, South	1.1	246
Zambia	3.7	174

Although per capita national income may be the best measure for the existence of poverty in the total system, the actual figures do not reflect the extent of individual poverty. Thus, Simpson, quoting Kuznets, has suggested that the *upper income* groups in those countries with an average per capita annual income of $300 or less *have an even greater share* of the total national income than do those same groups in the richer nations. From this statement it is quite apparent that a major factor in assessing the incidence of material deprivation among individuals and family units is the actual distribution of the available national income. It is quite possible that a nation with a relatively low per capita annual income in the aggregate may have fewer poor individuals than a nation with a higher average, if different patterns of distribution of the existing wealth have been developed. Unfortunately, as Simpson has indicated the distribution figures are simply not available.[35]

Setting aside some of the problems related to the use of per capita annual income, some general observations can be made. Most of those nations which appear in Table 1 are located in Asia, Africa and Latin America. As Simpson has indicated:

About 2.1 billion people, or 64 percent of the world's population live in countries whose average income is less than $300, and almost 1.9 billion of these people live in countries whose average income falls below $200. About 67 percent of the people in this group live in only four countries: China, India, Indonesia and Pakistan.[36]

We cannot directly compare the extent of material deprivation today with the extent in agrarian societies of the past because comparable statistics do not exist for the latter. However, it seems safe to assume that per capita productivity was lower in agrarian societies due to technological simplicity.

Another area of comparison about which it is difficult to make definitive statements is distribution. If we assume that the modes of distribution were as inequitable as those which exist in contemporary advanced capitalist societies, and we believe they were more inequitable, then the incidence of materially deprived individuals must have been greater in such societies because the total productivity was lower. Put in its simplest terms, when the size of the pie increases and distribution does not become more inequitable, then the leftovers are increased. This statement should not be interpreted as a vindication of the present system, but rather as an attempt to compare the present with traditional systems. It might be argued that as the size of the pie increases, there is less justification for a distribution system which actively denies fair shares to a section of the population.

Some comparisons can be made between the extent of poverty in the Western transition and the contemporary transition. It is obvious that early medical innovations resulting in lower mortality, particularly child mortality rates, and the striking growth in population, which precedes productivity increases, have greatly enlarged the population of the materially deprived in the contemporary transitional world. In addition, the unbalanced relationship in the world market resulting from colonialism and international inequality, economic and political, is another basic difference in the process today. On the other hand, there are also major parallels in the nature of change. Examples of these are the impact of cash on the economic marketplace as well as on the prestige system, changes in occupational structure and rural–urban migration. In this way those socio-economic variables which have the greatest impact on social attitudes toward poverty and the poor are parallel to those which occurred in the historical Western case.

SOCIETAL PERCEPTION OF MATERIAL DEPRIVATION

In the following section, it should be noted that the data were collected from a wide variety of disparate sources which do not directly deal with the concept of poverty per se. It is therefore not possible to pull together precisely comparable material dealing with all aspects of poverty.[37]

Modernization in the contemporary world has produced changes in attitudes similar to those in the West. There is a movement away from the traditional justifications and rationalizations for the existence of poverty. Material deprivation is now viewed as bereft of virtuous, spiritual implications. It is not a blessed state producing greater harmony with the supernatural and bringing its own rewards in the afterlife. Also, poverty is no longer regarded as inevitable, but as an avoidable problem which the system can solve.

As one example of this emerging view we have the United Nations Declaration of Human Rights which includes freedom from want as a basic right. The early Western capitalist perspective certainly did not consider the right to a decent standard of living a basic human right. This belief is to be found in the developing world at an earlier point in the transition than it was in the West. This is partly a result of direct diffusion of welfare notions from the West. Diffusion is made easier because the kind of labor-intensive, wage-minimizing system required early in Western capitalism is not *essential* for the larger manufacturing enterprises in the developing world. Other alternatives exist for major industry.

As Gutkind has pointed out in relation to Africa:

> Although it is true that one hundred years ago in Europe and North America, an upward birthrate was considered vital to radical economic transformation based on labor intensive methods, today the evolution of technology has put an end to such a strategy.
> . . . The African economies are now more than ever part and parcel of a world network of trade dominated by the economically powerful who expect to exchange their own products under highly competitive conditions. This presents the African nations with a clear challenge to produce their own products in the most competitive manner possible, that is, through the utilization of the most competitive technology. . . . Labor intensive methods are not generally geared to the reduction of the cost of the units produced. For example, the Minister of Works, Communications, and Power of the government of Kenya told the House that his Ministry was not considering building more roads with hand labor because the cost was more than double that of using machines.[38]

Capital can be brought from outside the system and capital intensive automated techniques can be borrowed. Labor is also more expensive in larger firms for several reasons. The early introduction of protective labor legislation makes labor more costly and tax policies to encourage development make mechanization through capital relatively advantageous. The introduction of post-Keynesian economic thinking also emphasizes the relationship of consumption to development rather than wage minimization as in classical early economic theory. All of these factors mitigate against the necessity of an extreme work ethic. It was the work ethic which prevented the early development of the notion of freedom from want as a basic right in the West. Japan is a non-Western nation which industrialized relatively early in time and most extensively. Japan also went through a labor-intensive period of development and experienced a change in its views on poverty and the poor similar to the ideological transition in the West. Thus, in Japan, there developed a work ethic which reflected the notion that poverty was produced by individual indolence. This served to prevent the acceptance of welfare as a basic right until recently.[39] In contrast, new nations, such as India and Burma, whose independent constitutions postdate World War II, have from the start made freedom from want a fundamental social right and a major national goal.

Once it is accepted that poverty is avoidable, social policies to reduce or remove deprivation are framed. The notions of charity characteristic of traditional agrarian societies stemmed from the belief in the inevitability of poverty. Charity was practiced in the belief that almsgiving yielded spiritual returns. In the modern system, while the eradication of poverty is seen to benefit not only the poor, but also society as a whole, there are no longer spiritual rewards. Since poverty is now seen as a social threat (the association of poverty with antisocial behavior) and an economic threat (unproductive waste of manpower), eradication is necessary to increase productivity and social stability. Charity in the traditional sense is outmoded and systematic social legislation prevails. Unfortunately, most of the developing societies are not in an economic position to implement these goals.

Social welfare legislation and the development of social work services in the developing nations can be seen to have derived directly from the Western world through the instruments of international aid and the overseas training of most social work professionals. Thus the ideas precede the productive capacity to implement them. Furthermore, because the goal of social welfare has to compete for limited resources with the primary social goal of economic development itself, the implementation is less extensive than intended.

If we make a distinction between official acceptance of social welfare goals and popular acceptance, we can again contrast the experience of the West with the contemporary developing world. In the West, both official and popular acceptance of the goal of social welfare was slow to develop. Official reluctance was due largely to the labor-intensive wage-minimizing aspects of early capital formation. Popular reluctance was due to the moralistic judgment of the behavior of the poor. The pronounced work ethic and the tendency to blame individuals for their own condition were consequences of this phase. The Japanese parallels to this are also described by Taira.[40] In both the West and Japan, the last few decades have seen the growth of official acceptance of welfare as an individual right and recognition of poverty as a condition which negatively affects production. However, popular beliefs still lag behind and are reflected in political reluctance in the welfare field. In sum, while ideology was a major impediment to the development of welfare in the West, technological limitations as well as ideology are the major impediments in the contemporary developing areas.

A further word of caution is necessary in evaluating the prospects for the elimination of poverty in many of the developing nations. Although the avoidance of an overemphasis upon the work ethic and an increase in productivity may appear to be sufficient for the effective elimination of material deprivation through social welfare, it must be recognized that in many of these nations, despite the acceptance of national "right to live" legislation and constitutions, traditional elites remain quite powerful and usually opposed to such national goals. It is extremely doubtful that such elites will passively allow a re-allocation of resources which would be necessary to eliminate poverty even if it were official policy and technological capacity made the goal feasible.

As an example, let us consider the attempt to redistribute land in India. Many state governments have legislated to limit the amount of land a single individual can own. It was hoped that the excess land could then be turned over to landless agricultural laborers or tenant farmers. However, the larger landowners quickly developed a technique for recording land ownership in the names of sons and daughters which had the effect of curbing the impact of official legislation. Another example of traditional responses can be seen in the effects of the "green revolution" in Pakistan and other parts of South Asia. The green revolution refers primarily to recent innovations in staple grain crops which allow a tremendous increase in productivity. As a result, large landowners are dispossessing their tenants and driving out the small cultivators in order to maximize their own returns. We have already seen how the effects of sheep herding and enclosures created such a movement in England.

Furthermore, although official recognition of welfare as a right is common, we have little direct evidence of popular acceptance in developing societies. It seems likely that, whatever the official policy may be, popular attitudes are still largely determined by traditional agrarian beliefs.

MOBILITY, ACHIEVEMENT AND INDIVIDUALISM

Economic development would appear to be strongly associated with an emphasis upon the individual's own responsibility for his own actions and their consequences. However, the degree of emphasis may vary and in many cases the extremity of the Western emphasis will be avoided. Real social mobility is achieved by the more rational use of manpower resources. Such rationality results from man's new belief in his ability to increase production infinitely. This leads to severance of the individual from his corporate group and the "self-made" man emerges as a real and ideal phenomenon. The truly self-made man is one who can exercise control over his own life chances in the same way that the technological system can control nature. As Peacock and Kirsch state,

In any event, it is still a fact that with modernization both the idealized rate of mobility and the actual rate tend to rise. . . . One reason for increased mobility is that modernization weakens the bond between the individual and the group into which he was born; it becomes easier for him to move away from that group and up (or down) into a new group.[41]

That the stratification system is no longer believed to be divinely ordained can be seen in the fact that Indian castes no longer try to raise their prestige primarily by the creation of myths which invoke divine support (Sanskritization), but now consolidate their position through the development of economic and political power. The development of the Christian Democratic movement in Western Europe and parts of Latin America which urges social justice and social reform in this world also demonstrates the movement away from a fatalistic belief in the divine ordination of social hierarchy. No longer is happiness achieved by fleeing this world, but by reforming it. Moreover, money is now not a defiling element, but a generalized medium for the evaluation of an individual's social worth.

The transition from closed stratification systems to open ones is reflected in the trend toward the replacement of traditional elites by new self-made middle classes in much of the developing world. Parallels to the Horatio Alger stories can be found (albeit much less frequently than believed) everywhere, even among former members of scheduled castes in India.[42] The nouveaux riches in Latin America have also been frequently described.[43]

One mechanism through which the new ideology of open mobility is supported is that of mass education. Halpern sees the school as the major purveyor of change in the rural area.[44] Much has been written about the plight of the "school-leaver" in Africa who has received a good primary education and has developed a desire for upward mobility. The problem is caused by this group's preference for white-collar jobs which are extremely scarce and their frequent refusal of the available work which is marginal and menial in nature and provides no opportunity for advancement. Thus many are believed to be voluntarily unemployed rather than working at a low paid, menial, dead-end job.[45] In urban areas where education is more generally available, the transmission of a value system closely related to the new ideology is an important function of the school. To a degree, what one learns is an exaggerated belief that one's effort can produce success and that failure is one's own responsibility.

Even without formal education the belief in open mobility is transmitted. Patch describes this as a strongly held belief among lower-class Peruvians:

The residents of the Terminal (the market in Lima) believe that success is achieved by individual initiative. The person himself has control over his destiny; it is not fate which determines whether he will succeed or fail. . . . On the other hand the urban poor . . . clearly see the lower rungs of the ladder of upward mobility and accomplishment. The rungs are marked with signs of material success and demands for conformity to mores appropriate to a particular group. They see success as achieved, not as ascribed from birth by a transcendent God.[46]

According to Gutkind there is a strong belief in an open system and the possibilities of success in Africa where the role models of bush migrants who are part of the new elite are frequent.[47] However, fatalistic determinism has given way to belief in individual control and responsibility only in an uneven fashion, and, in the developing world, the belief is by no means always as strong as it was in the Western transition.

The expected movement of the individual in the system precludes the existence of stable corporate groups into which an individual is born and to which he is committed for life. To use Peacock and Kirsch's attributes of modernism, the modern individual may use a voluntary organization as a context in pursuing his own *individual* goals, but this instrumental use of a group for individual gain is different from the ascribed agrarian groups in which the member internalized *group* goals as his own. In the developing world, as in the West, we also find evidence that the economically successful tend to sever their ties with their ascribed groups since such ties would drain their resources.[48]

While transition to an open system and to an emphasis on mobility is occurring in all modernizing societies, one can still claim that the excessive individualism which interfered with the social welfare goal in the Western transition is not developing elsewhere. In the West, as we have seen, there was a change of attitude, and, whereas poverty was once considered part of God's plan, it came to be believed that individual immorality and laziness were to blame. Only recently has the view that the social and economic systems are significant causes of poverty gained some degree of acceptance. In the contemporary non-Western world, it is quite possible for attitudes to undergo a different development, from belief in divinely ordained causation directly to belief in causation by a man-made, mutable economic system. Thus the emphasis on individualism in the developing world may be slower in developing, less intense and less significant than in the West. This alternative transition can be seen in its most extreme form in socialist nations and to a lesser extent in the welfare states.

WELFARE POLICIES

It is not feasible here to provide a lengthy description of welfare legislation in a cross-cultural perspective, but some observations can be made. First, many of the programs developed in response to the new antipoverty commitment in developing nations are directly borrowed from Western models. This is true of the voluntary, private social service agencies as well. Not only are the personnel trained in the West, but the specific socially defined categories protected by social legislation are also borrowed from the West in spite of differences in social and demographic situations. Thus, the formerly employed elderly and the female or minor survivors of male heads of household who were gainfully employed (those defined as deserving in the first Western social security programs) are frequently the categories provided for in spite of the fact that traditional beliefs held other groups to be deserving of support. In Africa, particularly, the suggestion has frequently been made that instead of importing Western institutions, indigenous aid institutions be expanded. However, the tribal heterogeneity in most African nations makes nationwide *indigenous* programs difficult and instead European models continue to be borrowed.

Furthermore, because of limited resources, such diffused programs have often been adopted piecemeal. Rohrlich states that outside of Euro-American societies, the only truly comprehensive programs protecting all categories of social risks are found in Japan and Israel.[49] Programs for the unemployed involving income maintenance, training and rehabilitation are not at all widespread. Africa, areas of Asia and Latin America lag behind the West in unemployment compensation. However, Mexico and Uruguay have adopted advanced unemployment programs in the last decade. Health programs have not been very effective because of the lack of facilities and personnel.

It is a mistake to assume that the nature of the political or economic system of a nation-state will directly determine welfare policy. While many new states in Africa are socialist in ideology and economy, their actual social welfare programs may be sparse and provide little for the unemployed, the technologically displaced or even the "handicapped." In such states it is assumed that material deprivation will be eradicated automatically by socialism so that specific welfare programs are not necessary. The Soviet Union, in fact, is not generous in the benefits it provides for such categories as the disabled, the invalid and elderly.

It is also a mistake, as we indicated above, to equate the existence of official legislated programs with their actual implementation. Many of the quite elaborate programs developed by social planners in Latin America and Asia are implemented merely as small pilot projects because of the lack of funds and trained personnel. Thus, commitment and recognition of the legitimacy of welfare are commonly found while operating programs are not.

Finally, looking at actual working programs can be deceiving in terms of the commitment of a nation. While appropriations and legislative programs have been expanded in Great Britain and Japan since World War II, the poor in these nations today have a smaller share of the national prosperity than they did in the past. Their proportional share in the expanding National Income has declined relative to their proportion in the population.[50] A truly cross-cultural examination of welfare programs would have to measure not only official and popular commitment, legislation and implementation, but also the proportional share of the poor in national wealth in relation to their proportion in the population.

Who Are the Poor?

In developing societies, we again see a convergence of the materially deprived with those traditionally located at the bottom of the prestige system. Thus a socially defined attribute, "poorness," which had come into existence in agrarian societies in a limited and unspecified sense, becomes a concrete attribute of a specific social category. A new cluster of occupations requiring no skills, which produce low and sporadic cash income become alternative sources of cash for the unstable laboring class. While we shall use the term marginal occupation or marginal employment in this volume, other terms frequently used for this type of employment are: peripheral, casual, precarious, unstable, redundant, and so on. The well-known term underemployment and the concept of an "odd-jobs" occupation or "jack-of-all-trades" also refer to this phenomenon.

Much of the recruitment to these occupations is from rural migration, but much also results from second and third generation urban residents who enter the urban labor market at the lowest level. The presence of ethnic, religious or racial minority groups which face discriminatory employment practices also reduces the access to permanent, stable and well-paying jobs.

For the segments of the population enmeshed in marginal occupations, the work situation involves intermittent employment and unemployment; low wages when employed and high inputs of time and/or energy on the job in relation to income. Such circumstances produce the objective conditions of material deprivation and socially defined poverty in the urban industrial setting. In any discussion of poverty, it is important to understand that the insecurity of income is perhaps even more significant than the low-level of income. Income insecurity has recently been discovered to correlate very significantly with the lack of economic success of urban migrants.[51]

Because of the technological and organizational similarities of societies in the transition from agrarian to urban industrial systems, there are great similarities in those segments of the system which are materially deprived. These are individuals whose unstable jobs and fluctuating non-vertical careers produce insecure and low income, as well as periods of no income. The pool of jobs which is part of the transitional occupational structure in both the historic English and contemporary non-Western cases is remarkably similar in both cases. The jobs result from three basic shifts. First, there are new pre-mechanized and pre-organized jobs which involve heavy labor and time inputs. Second, there are transformed underclass activities which change in organization. Finally, there is the proliferation of redundant petty commercial activities.

STABLE LOW-STATUS JOBS

In order to clarify the definition of the set of marginal occupations, one can contrast these activities with several types of occupations which share some attributes but differ in the crucial constellation of income level and income insecurity. Analogous to the jobs requiring heavy inputs of pre-mechanized labor are those traditionally found in the no-

tion of blue-collar work in the United States. Since considerable confusion has existed between the unstable laboring class and the stable
blue-collar class in American social science, it is not surprising that the
distinction is frequently overlooked in developing nations where the
two segments have not even crystallized as yet. Stable blue-collar jobs
are relatively rare in developing societies, but they consist for the most
part of skilled or semi-skilled factory jobs. These jobs are desirable in
that they provide some security and regularity of income which is
protected to some degree by labor legislation. Frequently, such jobs
provide fringe benefits in the form of bonuses and severance payments
which are often used as capital for small-scale investments. The jobs
also provide higher income than their marginal analogues, sometimes
yielding three to five times the monthly income of the latter.[52] Careers
are vertical, usually involving movement to activities which are hierarchically ranked in a bureaucratic structure and provide higher income
than previous jobs. In contrast, marginal careers do not involve higher
ranked, related jobs nor successively higher income. Peattie notes the
beginning divergence of the stable working class from the unstable
laboring class in the Venezuelan community she studied. The two
groups differ in world view and lifestyle.[53] It should be mentioned that
many unskilled jobs in large factories in contrast to skilled and semi-
skilled positions are unstable. Gutkind points out the high turnover of
labor in West and East Africa.[54] The work gang is an institutionalized
form of heavy labor which partially mitigates against low and insecure
income in times of reasonable opportunity. A group of laborers organized under a leader can secure relatively stable, quasi-contractual
work commanding much higher salaries than the individual dayworker.

Another distinction must be made between the petty trader and the
small businessman. The *suq* shop in the Middle Eastern city, the stall in
a Latin American urban central market, and the small stall operator
anywhere may have less overhead than the large-scale modern entrepreneur in a modern specialty or department store. However, he should
not be confused with the marginal street-seller, for even the market stall
requires considerable overhead in rental or municipal tax and an inventory of a much larger scale than that of a street vendor. In turn, the net
returns are greater. Peddlers have almost no capital invested and
purchase inventory daily on credit. Thus, if they exist at all, their net
profits are minimal.

Analogous to the distinction between street vendors and shopkeepers,
is the distinction between marginal illicit activities available to the

amateur and the activities of professionals in vice trades. The professional as a member of a semi-organized group which restricts competition and protects the practitioner from the law is at quite a different economic level from the sporadic amateur practitioner whose income is marginal. The amateur counterpart loses by virtue of his lack of professional socialization and his non-participation in the rationalized allocation of personnel in the professional sphere. The schools for thieves described by Dickens for London and their counterparts described by Patch for Lima produce professional thieves who enter long-term careers characterized by increased skill, income and prestige among peers.

It is imperative to keep the above distinctions clear. Leeds has suggested that in many areas, there is a clear distinction between the formal labor market (stable jobs covered by government labor, taxation and welfare regulations) and the informal labor market in their processes of labor recruitment, turnover, and so forth. He also points out that the native population itself recognizes the distinction in the two types of labor markets and differentiates between them linguistically. Thus in Peru, informal labor is sometimes called *cachuelo* while in Brazil the word *biscate* is often used. This casual employment market includes not only odd jobs and marginal occupations, but "a series of contractual forms . . . (comprising) a *system* for getting around the severe constraints of the formal labor market. . . ." [55]

The analogous groups of activities, marginal and non-marginal, are frequently confused in the literature. Part of the confusion is due to conceptual fuzziness, but most of it is due to the blurring of the two kinds of workers in empirical reality. As we shall see, many careers lead from truly marginal occupations to stable blue-collar jobs, larger-scale commercial enterprises or professional level illicit occupations. Also, occupants of all these non-middle-class statuses tend to be residents of the same communities and frequently members of the same families. The incipient new occupational structure is just beginning the process of sorting people out. The clearcut division between the stable and unstable laboring class is not as precise as it is in the advanced industrial nations.

SOURCES OF CASH THROUGH WORK

The sources of cash used by the new unstable laboring groups are varied and can basically be divided into those for which work is performed and those which involve no work. The definition of "work" itself can vary so that in some areas a beggar is defined as providing a service while in others he is considered as not working.

From the point of view of the individual recruit, marginal sources of cash require no skills and are thus most accessible. From the point of view of the larger system and its economic development goals these jobs are wasteful of energy and time. The labor force is redundant, that is, if many individuals left the marginal activity, total productivity would be the same. In some cases, as in the scavenging activities (or resource recycling) the work may provide some function for development, but in òther cases such work retards development.

Two major characteristics of these sources of cash is that they are unstable, noncontinuous or sporadic and they are often interchangeable. When one kind of job is not available, individuals will frequently switch their activity to an alternative which is available among the same cluster of unskilled occupations. Thus, Geertz notes that the ranks of petty tradesmen are swelled when the demand for other unskilled labor is low.[56] In Hong Kong, when construction workers are unable to find work in their line, they will meet at a particular locale where information will be exchanged about which factories or government agencies will be hiring labor for that day.[57] According to Frank in his summary of urban poverty in Latin America, "Many people shift frequently between irregular unskilled employment and often only partial self-employment and they must always look forward to having any particular source of income only for a short time." [58] Studies of beggars in India indicate that very few able-bodied men are full-time beggars. They only resort to begging as an economic activity when they are unable to get jobs as laborers, and during major religious events when the population is more willing to give alms.[59]

One can divide the jobs under consideration into two groups. There are those which involve the sale of labor and those which involve the sale of goods. Of the jobs involving the sale of labor, there are some which are wasteful of energy such as portage, dock work and heavy construction (earth moving and manual brickmaking) those which are wasteful of time (messengers, watchmen) and combinations of the two such as domestic activity and driving human-propelled transportation devices (see Table 2). In selling goods, there is petty commerce as in the case of the door-to-door peddler, street hawker or the ambulatory seller of petty services (barber, shoeshine boy, and so on). The amateur streetwalker, bootlegger and illegal lottery salesman would fall in the category of illicit practitioner.

Table 2. Classification of Poverty Level Occupations

Occupation	High Energy Input	High Time Input[1]	Structural Instability[2]	Personnel Instability[3]
Beggars		X		
Carriers of goods	X	X	X	
Construction Workers (pre-mechanized and unorganized)	X		X	
"Coolies"	X	X	X	
Domestics		X		X
Drivers (pre-mechanized vehicles)		X		
Prostitutes (Amateur)		X		X
Scavengers		X	X	
Sweatshop workers		X	X	X
Thieves (Amateur)		X		X
Streetsellers		X		X

[1] By high time input we mean those occupations which require the physical presence of the individual for long periods of time. Frequently he is not performing his specific occupational functions for most of that period of time.

[2] By structural instability we mean those occupations for which there is variable demand depending upon macro-economic conditions which are not controlled by the worker.

[3] By personnel instability we mean those occupations in which there is a high labor turnover primarily as a result of the decision by the worker to give up his job.

SELLERS OF LABOR

High energy occupations referred to as "coolie" work in parts of Asia or "peon" work elsewhere are often related to construction and dockwork. They frequently involve the departure of a casual laborer from his home each day to a central place where he is hired for day work. Although construction workers in the United States possess skills because of the high degree of mechanization in earth moving and related activities, and are organized into trade unions and command high salaries, in many other areas of the world construction laborers do not have these attributes. It is rare for the construction worker in non-Western areas who can look forward to full employment or, when he is employed, an income high enough to carry him through the year. Thus, he must look for alternative sources of cash to meet his needs. As Vidyarthi has shown, construction workers brought in to help build a steel plant in Bihar, India, reported that they had been unemployed for extensive periods of time before obtaining their present job.[60] Construction workers in Hong Kong face the same situation as we noted above and must be willing to take alternative jobs.

The literature indicates that periods of planned and massive construction activity which are related to international public works aid and planned cities always seem to attract a much larger number of workers than are required. These projects are very visible and subject to a more efficient recruitment communication system than other types of work. Milone refers to the magnet-like attraction to migrant labor of the building activities (hotels, roads, monuments, and others) which centered around the 1962 Asian Games in Djakarta.[61] Vidyarthi notes that even when the construction workers in Bihar were no longer needed, and there was no work for them, they remained on the site because they had housing there and no better prospects for a job elsewhere.[62] The same phenomenon has been noted for the planned cities of Brasilia in Brazil and Cuidad Guayana in Venezuela.[63]

The instability of construction work in Hong Kong is illustrated by the fact that a construction worker could rarely count on more than twenty days of work per month. Although by American standards this might appear to be adequate, the wage for construction workers in Hong Kong is such that employment for twenty days means a marginal level of subsistence.[64] Frank characterizes construction work in Latin America as "notoriously occasional and unstable," and yet it is one which many people resort to as a prime source of income.[65]

For most port cities, a vital part of the economic activities consists of shipping and therefore low-skilled laborers who load and unload ships are needed. Zachariah indicates the tremendous demand for dockworkers in Bombay.[66] Again, work is not continuous and wages are very low. This is especially true in lesser ports such as Tripoli, Lebanon, where, unlike Beirut, the shipping volume is very variable and unpredictable so that labor needs are not continuous.[67] This kind of work also requires a tremendous effort for a short period of time. When a ship comes in, it must be unloaded immediately, especially if the cargo is perishable, if other means of transport are waiting for the transfer of goods, if the harbor berth is needed, or if the ship has other ports of call. This work requires higher, more intense inputs of energy and lasts for a shorter time even than construction work. In a study of migrants to Calcutta, it was found that dockwork was so unattractive that only members of scheduled castes (untouchables) would take such jobs. Work conditions made the situation so undesirable that many migrants after short-term residence in Calcutta would return to their village.[68]

Another large group of occupational activities which are not necessarily unstable nor energy-intensive, are those of domestic servants. What makes these jobs unattractive is the social stigma attached to them and the lack of individual autonomy. Unlike the other occupations which have been described, the domestic servant provides personal services to a single client family. To a certain extent, the use of domestic servants is the most intimate of face-to-face exploitation. In most traditional peasant societies, domestic servants are attached to particular household units through ties of loyalty and paternalistic obligations often passed down in family lines. This relationship is transformed under the impact of monetization where cash payments become the basis of the relationship. In transitional societies where household tasks require higher energy and time investment than in modern society and where food preparation is not industrialized, domestic servants are in high demand. More explicitly, the lack of vacuum cleaners, washing machines and good food preservation techniques require human manpower substitutes. Many of the tasks of the domestic servant, however, are viewed negatively. Moreover, domestic servants are required to spend most of their time working in the household and most are required to sleep in and have little time off. Because of the difficult personal relationship in this type of work and the difficulties this work presents for a mother with children, there is a high turnover in domestic work.[69]

In less industrialized areas, like Tripoli, Libya, and Kingston, Jamaica, the best opportunities for recent migrants are in domestic work.[70] While men perform domestic jobs in parts of Africa and Asia, it is usually the most important source of cash for women when they are employed. Several domestic chores which women can perform for others within their own homes are laundering and sewing.

In contrast to household services primarily supplied by females, there are some which are supplied more frequently by men. Where the concept of a municipal police department is not fully developed and where burglar alarm systems do not exist, most homes and businesses require the services of private employees who protect property. These watchmen may spend several weeks in the home of a vacationing family, patrol a residential neighborhood or a business establishment. The instability of watchman jobs in Kano and the extremely low wages offered are indications that this occupation falls squarely in the poverty classification.[71] In the major market in Lima, Peru, porters (*carga-*

dores) who work in the marketplace during the day, live in the market and are paid for watching the stalls during the night.[72] When watchman jobs are part of a complex of multiple jobs rather than the only source of income, material deprivation may not be characteristic. These jobs are time-wasting, rather than energy-consuming. With the growth in urbanism and industrialization, however, there is a tendency to organize these activities on a larger-scale basis. Firms of security guards like the Pinkertons allocate manpower on a more rational basis. Municipal police services expand and mechanical surveillance devices also help to displace this occupation. Although there is a high cost factor for these services, they are subscribed to in advanced societies.

Another set of major occupations characterized by higher energy input than domestic work as well as lower social status are those of waste removers such as street sweepers, garbage collectors, chimney sweeps, and janitors. These services are essential in any large urban center and are increasingly being organized by municipal authorities, although they are still organized privately in many developing nations. In Hong Kong, privately employed garbage collectors must provide their own equipment consisting of either a carrying pole or a primitive wagon and some baskets. In addition to the income derived from the collection service itself, collectors are also able to sell such items as used tin and aluminum which relates this occupation to scavenging.[73] Those who follow these occupations face less job instability than those in the occupations thus far discussed, but this positive attribute is offset by the social stigma still attached to dirt- and refuse-related activities. A study of street sweepers in Jubbalpore, India, has indicated the extremely low status of street sweepers there.[74]

In many cities of the developing areas of the world, jobs related to pre-mechanized transportation and communication fit into the category of occupations which are low in income, unstable, intermittent, of low skill level, and require intensive energy or time investment. As we might expect, the transition to technologically advanced transportation and communication facilities allows the maintenance of some traditional activities in these areas and may even stimulate the expansion of traditional forms in the earliest stages. As the city expands, as workplace and residence become separated and transportation systems do not grow correspondingly, the need for human-energy transportation vehicles increases. Thus, at the early stages of growth, traditional facilities such as bicycle rickshaws, pedicabs, wheelbarrows, carrying poles and other crude wheeled vehicles used to transport goods and/or people become increasingly important. Whiteford describes such human transport as follows:

In spite of the great increase in the number of trucks in Mexico a considerable amount of freight was still moved on human backs. When a bed and mattress were sold a *cargador* was called. He took the coil of rope, which was the badge of his occupation, from his shoulder and tied them together into a load which he could lift onto his back. Trunks, racks of pottery, sacks of grain, pieces of machinery, furniture, crates of chickens, and almost anything else which could be lifted could be seen at one time or another strapped to the back of a *cargador* and bound for delivery.[75]

Depending on the extent of competition from other more expensive forms of transportation (animal and engine powered), particular occupations may have continuous clientele and provide "decent" cash incomes. However, this is only true during the earliest stages of urban growth for as transportation becomes mechanized, these occupations become marginal and the income derived from them becomes lower and insecure. The change in the position of this occupation can be illustrated by a recent report in the *New York Times* of the decline in the number of Hong Kong rickshaw drivers due to lessening demand.[76] In Djakarta, there is less demand for pedicab (*betchak*) drivers and government efforts to convert them to automobile taxi drivers have been unsuccessful because the skills required for the two occupations are quite different. The automobile drivers require some mechanical skills and a degree of literacy.[77] In the transportation of goods, we see trucks replace the human backs, carrying poles, baskets and primitive wheeled vehicles which were used to carry packs of any size, especially around the commercial areas of the city.

Similarly, there are changes in communication activities. Where telephones are scarce and the mails are unreliable, most personal and business communications are carried by hand from one location to another. Advertising done through sandwich boards and handbills also require manpower. Unlike transportation, this activity is not high-energy consuming. However, like the jobs of drivers and porters, messengers spend a good deal of work time merely waiting for the need to arise for their services, and then waiting for answers. While the time demands for these activities are greater than those of high-energy jobs, these activities are potentially more continuous than the others. However, there is an increasing rate of turnover in this activity and there is always a large pool of available messengers loitering around the office area of the central city, thus creating a superfluous, redundant supply of labor. Whiteford describes the errand boys in Popayán, Colombia, who sit "in the doorway of a lawyer's office to tell his clients where to find him." [78]

Another insecure, marginal occupation, perhaps most closely analogous to the blue-collar factory worker, comprises jobs in marginal manufacturing enterprises. The sweatshop employee epitomizes this group of workers. This individual is an unskilled worker who is employed in a very small-scale enterprise; the smallness of scale is indicated by low capitalization, few employees and short-term production planning. The positions are usually unstable and lowly paid. The few workers employed are exploited; they receive low wages, they are paid on a piecemeal basis, and work long hours. Since most workers in the establishment have an expectation of employer-employee relationships approximating the old personalistic artisan-apprentice model, they are disillusioned by the real relationship. The employer, a marginal entrepreneur speculating on changing demand and very vulnerable, because of his low level of investment cannot behave as a patron to his employees if he is to achieve profit. Thus the turnover in these jobs is high, often because of mutual choice. In the *Children of Sanchez,* Manuel Sanchez's career consists of little more than a series of such jobs, and his sisters are similarly employed.[79] Such employment also pervades the occupational structure of Hong Kong slums and those in Singapore, among others.

SELLERS OF GOODS

Vending. We have previously noted that in a cash economy, an individual in search of money can either sell his services or sell goods. We are obviously not concerned in this volume with highly capitalized merchants, storeowners, or wholesalers. Our primary focus is on the small-scale seller of goods who is probably ambulatory and sells low cost goods in small quantities. This cluster of occupations may be pursued by either males or females and in many cities, by both. Unless credit is extended by a wholesaler, one obvious requirement of this occupation is a small cash outlay. Peddlers, hawkers and street-vendors are terms variously used for people in these occupations. The goods are diverse although most vendors specialize in one category.

A basic characteristic which distinguishes the kind of selling activities with which we are concerned at the moment from what might be termed true capitalist activities is the scale of the enterprise. Most petty tradesmen have very limited inventories of goods for sale usually acquired on a day-to-day basis. They sell small quantities for little profit because of the competition among themselves and with the more developed retail structure. Another distinctive characteristic of this set of activities is the small or nonexistent capital expenditure for overhead. Frank points out that these are not true capitalistic ventures.[80] Unlike the true entrepreneur, the petty tradesman does not require a store, a warehouse or even a market stall (which is usually a costly item rented from or taxed by the municipality), and he does not require the utilities (fuel, electricity) required by these facilities. Although the old, tiny shops on crowded, narrow streets described by Gulick in Tripoli, Lebanon, do not sound like establishments with high overhead costs or large-scale business, they *are* costly to maintain as well as characterized by a steady clientele and fairly high income.[81] Marris makes a clearcut distinction between the Lagos trader with a shop or stall and a regular clientele on the one hand, and the "less well-established women traders (who) hawk their goods about the streets, and work hardest for least profit." [82] The latter often have a stock limited to "a few odd remnants of cloth." [83] Another overhead expenditure avoided by the petty tradesman is that of record keeping. In fact, as Peattie points out, the petty tradesman in a slum in Venezuela is rarely in a position to estimate his real income or rate of profit.[84] Capital expenditures for equipment for street vendors can involve anything from a single basket or a portable stand to wheeled push carts, charcoal burners and the elaborate tin decanters and porcelain cups of the coffee vendor in Lebanon.[85]

Some petty tradesmen are located in a fixed geographic sector while others are primarily ambulatory. Fixed positions are usually found in those areas of the city which are heavily trafficked such as street corners in the central business district, railway stations, sports stadiums and tourist attractions, as well as on the fringe of the central market. Ambulatory petty tradesmen sell primarily to household units going from door to door and their area of activity is extensive. Petty commerce is also found in the slum itself where an individual may store a small inventory of items to be sold. These items are needed on a daily basis for cooking, sewing, and so forth. Roberts found that forty out of the 400 households in a low-income community in Guatemala City were performing some selling service.[86] Mangin found that sections of one third of the homes in one squatter settlement were used as shops where women sold goods to supplement the household income. He describes commerce in such goods as water, kerosene and other fuel in tiny quantities and in such services as entertainment (as in renting chairs in a home to watch the household television set).[87]

A fundamental question is why do people buy what they do from petty tradesmen. One answer is that the petty tradesman by either coming to the door or being in the path that one usually takes is offering a convenience. In the burgeoning city of the developing nation, one reason why convenience is so important is that good transportation facilities are lacking, food storage techniques are not highly developed and shops and markets are dispersed. Thus, convenience becomes an important reason for the maintenance of these marginal economic activities. In addition, the vendor is frequently looked upon as an individual who needs help in his obvious struggle to avoid outright begging. While slum enterprises provide convenience too, they are also organized to enable the slum dweller to buy miniscule amounts of goods such as several tablespoons of margarine,[88] which are unavailable in regular establishments. They also extend credit to their customers.

Household vendors and slum entrepreneurs tend to specialize in the sale of food and household utensils for cooking, laundry and sewing. Those located at major thoroughfares tend to sell cooked or prepared food, drinks and trinkets to take home.

From the perspective of the professional economist, these petty tradesmen provide no real economic increment to the larger system. It would be difficult to give them any weight at all in such economic measurements as the Gross National Product or Gross National Income. If they did not exist, productivity would be the same. Hawkers do not earn enough to be true investors in the economic system. Once again, their efforts are time-consuming and yield low monetary rewards. They are redundant in the labor force and their condition is sometimes referred to as "hidden unemployment." [89] However, from a social point of view, these individuals provide the service of convenience at a given stage in development; they may perform a vital distribution function. They do not perceive themselves as unemployed. These activities are also very versatile in that they may be pursued by anyone without reference to sex, age or condition (within the limits or cultural proscription) and provide a good alternative source of cash at any stage in one's career. Thus, Caldarola says that such small businesses develop and disappear "like weeds." [90] And as indicated above, Geertz mentions that the number of petty tradesmen in Java increases greatly when economic conditions are poor and job opportunities scarce.[91] It is interesting to note that Mayhew noticed this tendency in London in the mid-nineteenth century.[92] While skilled laborers might flock to petty vending as a last resort when jobs are unavailable, these sources of cash are sometimes regarded as desirable by unskilled workers. Abu-Lughod writes that while casual labor jobs in Cairo are much more taxing than rural labor, petty vending is not.[93] In addition, petty tradesmen are sometimes viewed as "better-off" than casual laborers because they are self-employed and have greater control over their conditions of work. Thus, Peattie notices a preference for self-employed commerce in Venezuela [94] and Caldarola notes the same tendency in Japan.[95] Another advantage of street hawking is the possibility it offers for success and expansion. However, in most cases the street vendor is materially deprived.

Although the capital outlay for many vending activities may seem very low from our point of view, they are frequently beyond the economic reach of the vendor without some sort of credit. Data obtained in Hong Kong suggests that credit may vary from twenty to thirty Hong Kong dollars to several hundred Hong Kong dollars (one Hong Kong dollar equals fifteen cents in United States currency) and the period of time for which credit is extended may be as short as the working day or as long as several months. As a stable relationship develops between a hawker and his supplier, the amount of credit and time allotted tends to increase. Sellers of home-processed cooked foods or sweetmeats seem to require no credit. They buy supplies for the next day's sales with this day's profits. On the other hand, sellers of fruits, vegetables and hard goods seem generally to require loans for inventory.[96]

Artisanal Vending. In the previous discussion, we have distinguished between those occupations which involve the sale of labor and those which involve the sale of goods as sources of cash. However, certain occupations still exist which are carryovers from an earlier artisan tradition in which one individual combined both functions of production and sale within the same role. One finds many examples of those who make and/or mend items either at home or on the street where they are sold. Thus, they resemble vendors in the scale of enterprise even though they are sometimes selling their labor to a greater degree than they are selling a product. Some examples of these craftsmen, are the ambulatory rattan furniture makers (in Asia), potters, bicycle repairmen, shoemakers, carpenters, seamstresses, tailors, and knife menders. Some of these occupations used to yield a steady and relatively high income. Now, however, competition with mass-produced consumer goods or services has affected the demand for the product so that purchases become very sporadic. Geertz illustrates how the traditional carpenter in Java has become economically marginal now that other sources of wooden goods and woodworking labor are available.[97] Other services, such as bicycle repairing, develop as a response to changing conditions.

Scavenging. A very widespread and frequently overlooked source of cash in underdeveloped societies is scavenging. This general occupation is highly correlated to the nature of the economy in developing nations. Most of these nations are limited in resources because such resources are either not present, having been exploited by colonial powers, or are not easily extracted with the given technology. Thus, whatever resources enter the production cycle must be conserved to as great an extent as possible. Such items as paper, rags, glass, and scrap metal are vital in the production process and are therefore regenerated or recycled through the collection of discarded items. It is interesting to note that in the United States, recycling is now being stressed as a conservation movement after decades of wasteful destruction of resources.

Unlike petty trade, these occupations are important to the larger economic system, as well as to the individual. The major sources of scavenging activities are the refuse of large industry and offices. However, these tasks are usually handled by large-scale contractors who purchase and resell the waste products of industry and firms. Household refuse and street litter provide another source of goods and often petty scavengers take care of these jobs by picking litter from the street and picking through household and business refuse. These petty scavengers sell their collected items to dealers. Frequently a dealer will have a number of scavengers supplying him and may develop a rather personal relationship with them.

The diary of a São Paulo scavenger indicates that a personal relationship can exist between the scavenger and the dealer. Maria de Jesus has two different dealers, one to whom she sells junk and one to whom she sells paper. Maria relates the occasion upon which one of her dealers gave her enough money to buy a pair of shoes for her daughter although the amount of goods she had turned in did not warrant that large a payment.[98] Yet, de Jesus's scavenging activities usually brought in less than enough income to feed herself and her children. Income varied from day to day and on a good day she would obtain enough to buy some food delicacy. The uncertainty of cash income is reflected in her writing and emphasized in the constant complaint that she is unable to satisfy the needs of her children.

In Japan, ragpicking has a long history. According to Taira rag dealers employ rag pickers whom they exploit. The dealer buys unspecialized waste by the pound from the picker, often cheating on the weight and then subdivides the waste into categories and sells it to specialized wholesalers. The rag dealer often further exploits his pickers by providing them with shanty dwellings for which they pay rent so that he may oversee their activity. Since ragpicking is defined as extremely demeaning, it is difficult to use this occupation as a basis for upward mobility.[99]

CARRYOVERS OF ILLICIT OCCUPATIONS

There are a number of other poverty occupations which are usually viewed as illicit or immoral. Among these lowly-valued occupational roles are prostitutes, pimps, thieves, sellers of stolen goods, beggars, bootleggers and gamblers (or hustlers). All these occupations were once part of the traditional agrarian social structure and in the past they had a high degree of internal organization as did most corporate occupational groups. They controlled the recruitment and behavior of their members. However, as large numbers of rural migrants enter the city and are unable to find employment in other areas, some move into these occupations in an amateur fashion. They are not fully committed to the activity as a "profession," but are amateurs who view the activity as an alternative source of cash, part-time and/or casual. In his study of prostitutes in Lebanon, Khalaf distinguishes between those who live in the organized brothel area and the increased number of "free-lance hustlers." [100]

Prostitution. Prostitution is an occupation which is generally viewed as degrading. Part of the difficulty in discussing prostitutes in relation to poverty is that the occupation varies so much in terms of income, pattern of solicitation, and so on. Traditionally, prostitutes were confined to special quarters which facilitated organization and social control, but today there is a marked increase in casual prostitution, not only in Lebanon, but also in many other areas.[101] Many nations have now made it their policy to eliminate prostitution and clean up the red-light district. This has had the effect of breaking down professionalism. The decentralization of prostitution in Lahore, Pakistan and the increased use of bus stalls and street-walking to solicit have made it possible for a non-professional to use occasional prostitution as a source of cash. The demand for prostitution has also increased as a result of the large-scale migration to the city of males without their families. Khalaf's survey of prostitutes in Lebanon demonstrated that they themselves had occupied other poverty occupations, especially domestic servant work, before beginning prostitution and that their fathers, and if they were married, their husbands, were predominantly unskilled laborers or, if they lived in the towns, petty merchants.[102]

Begging. Change in the thinking that lay behind the Great Traditions in many of the developing nations has led to a reassessment of the position of the beggar. At the present time, the existence of large numbers of beggars is viewed as a basic social problem and national programs have been launched to rehabilitate them.

There is no clearcut distinction between the beggar who simply solicits alms and one who performs some slight service such as singing, wiping a car windshield, saying a prayer or selling some slight trinket not even desired by the purchaser. It is even possible that the ubiquitous shoeshiner, of Latin America and the Middle East, belongs in this category although he expends quite a bit of energy and is thought by some to be a petty capitalist having more in common with the itinerant peddler or artisan.[103] Since rates of urban underemployment and unemployment are extremely high in developing areas,[104] the question is, why more people, with no basic source of income do not beg. There are two answers: one is the basic negative evaluation of begging and the second is the inability of certain categories of people (that is, able-bodied men) to induce enough sympathy to obtain alms. An Indian observer says:

If we still find that there are people who would rather suffer the uncertainties of a casual construction labourer, a street-side coolie, a petty hawker, etc., than stretch out an arm and ask for alms from passers-by, it is because of the psychological barriers that every society creates and maintains more or less successfully between "honest work" and begging.[105]

In one of the few ethnographic descriptions of beggars and begging (in a Southern Mexican city), the psychic and social costs of this activity are described. Beggars are excluded from normal social interaction with others and are treated as non-persons.[106]

Women with children and children alone, as well as maimed adults, constitute the bulk of the beggar population. Gulick describes a young peasant woman with a small child on her hip leaning against a wall. The child sucks his thumb or plays in the gutter or nurses throughout the day while the mother sits with her hand outstretched.[107] This is a familiar sight throughout the developing areas of the world. A study in Ahmedabad, India, indicates that there are very few mature able-bodied men among the beggars.[108] In fact, for able-bodied men, begging is often an alternative source of cash only during religious ceremonies.

The Mexican study found that beggars were mostly male, probably because of the traditional protection of women. However, most of the males were elderly or had visible physical disabilities which were prominently displayed. Those with no visible problem would use an aggressive verbal technique to describe non-apparent chronic illnesses in order to solicit alms. Many of the Mexican beggars were found to be using begging as a seasonal alternative to their regular work when it was not available. They would leave their home region and come to this city where they were not known so that they would not become permanently stigmatized.[109]

Just as there are ambulatory and stationary peddlers, so too, there are beggars who go from door to door and those with a fixed locale. Those in fixed locations have some degree of organization in order to allocate space and avoid disruptive competition. In Colombia, children go from door to door in middle-class areas begging for *sobres* ("leftovers"). One indication of the modernization of begging is the recent "union-like" demand of Pakistani beggars that they be given a minimum amount of alms with increments based on the amount of deference shown to the donor.[110] Beggars in India argue that begging is as much work as many other activities. They talk of work hours and leisure hours.[111]

Thieves. Petty thievery is another source of income which may occupy an individual either on a full-time or part-time basis. As in prostitution, there is a big difference between the professional thief who is skilled and the member of a partially organized community of thieves, and the amateur thief who steals occasionally to acquire cash, goods for consumption, or goods for sale. The thieves' market is to be found in most developing areas. This activity is closely related to scavenging. In many cases the scavenger may help himself to "rags" on a clothesline, and so on. Once again, the social stigma, and in this case, the risk attached to these illegal acts prevent a large proportion of the population from participating in them.

Patch, whose descriptions of the thieves in Lima is one of the most thorough in the ethnographic literature, indicates that in many ways petty thievery is considered just another business in and around the marketplace. Such activities are perhaps more risky, in terms of the threat of punishment, but they are also more lucrative. Police harassment of the peddler without a license and the deliberate oversight of some criminal activity by the police make the community attitude toward crime somewhat ambivalent, since the law seems to work capriciously.[112]

Patch discusses the complex specialization among professional thieves and describes the training sessions for youthful apprentices often run by aging ex-convicts. All this reminds one of the London of Mayhew and Dickens. A young boy who is an amateur "fruit bird" (casual market shoplifter) acquires the more professionalized skills of a *carterista* (purse snatcher) or *lancerista* (pickpocket). Later he will become a *ratero* (unarmed house burglar) or *hampon* (skilled in weaponry, a true thug). Another alternative is to become a *cuentista* (conman who works his games on gullible recently arrived rural migrants). It is obvious that the professional career involves considerable skill, training, and participation in an organized community. On the other hand, one can remain an amateur "fruit bird," and continue casual, sporadic, illicit acts. Such types are described by de Jesus when she mentions an incident in which a group of boys rolled a drunk who had collapsed in the *favela*.[113]

Gambling. Gambling, as an occupation or an alternative source of income, is a rather complex phenomenon. As in our previous descriptions, we are not here concerned with the professional gambler or gambling activities which require large outlays of money or the acquisition of highly developed skills. Throughout much of the literature on slum communities, some individuals are mentioned who derive all or almost all of their marginal income from gambling activities. In one Japanese community, 3 percent of the population are classified as vagrants who try to make money out of various forms of gambling.[114] Patch indicates the importance of gambling in a slum area in Lima.[115] However, in most cases, gambling is an additional source of income rather than a full-time occupation. Many gamble but few earn their livelihood in this manner. Lotteries as a form of gambling are commonly found and vary from national enterprises (in Latin America and the Middle East) to small associations organized for this purpose. Lottery selling is often structurally analogous to petty trade. For the Japanese flophouse dweller, pinball machines provide a potential source of income although the player usually loses. In the analysis of the budget of one flophouse dweller, it was indicated that slightly less than one-tenth of his total meager income was spent on pinball machines.[116]

Bootlegging. In Africa, in particular, the illicit manufacture of bootlegged liquor provides a very important means of livelihood for many unskilled laborers. In many slum studies, the proportion of the population engaged in this activity is significant. One must again make the distinction between a bootlegger whose scale of capital investment and profits are large and his casual counterpart.[117]

CHANGES IN OCCUPATIONAL STRUCTURE

All of the marginal occupations which characterize the low-income groups in modernizing nations are products of changes which have disrupted the traditional occupational structure. Some involve entirely new kinds of work activity. Others are extensions of traditional sources of livelihood which have been changed by the development process.

Construction as a primary means of gaining a livelihood was not very widespread in peasant societies. Large-scale construction labor was recruited on the basis of an individual's obligation to the state or to a noble patron. In other cases, slaves and prisoners were used for public works. Homes for most of the population were built by individuals and their friends or kin. As a result of the growing population in urban centers and the general impact of development, construction has become a major new occupation. In this instance, both the demand for such labor and the supply of laborers has increased with development. However, the demand is sporadic and dependent on the business cycle (the boom and bust cycle).

Among the more traditional occupations which have undergone rapid change are prostitution, theft and begging. Traditionally, these occupations were organized and leaders controlled the recruitment, socialization and the behavior of their members. However, as a large number of rural migrants enter the city and are unable to find employment, they flood the labor force in these activities and a large number of casual practitioners not committed to a career begin to perform the same activities.

The opportunity structure in these activities has also expanded as male migration patterns increase the demand for prostitutes, and the increase in wealth and consumption increase the opportunities in theft.

Petty commerce has expanded in part as the result of the proliferation of goods and services and the dispersal of population prior to efficient transportation facilities and large-scale retail distribution. However, the demand for such activities has been surpassed by the redundant oversupply of labor.

UNEMPLOYMENT–UNDEREMPLOYMENT

The terms underemployment and unemployment are often associated with discussions of the livelihood of the materially deprived. Poverty occupations lead to underemployment because the demand for labor is low relative to the supply. Thus such activities often produce incomes at or slightly above the subsistence level. Moreover, the irregular demand for labor, the oversupply of labor and the lack of long-term contractual agreements which would provide a measure of income security produce frequent periods of unemployment. Unemployment periods are significant in the life histories of those involved in marginal occupations. Similarly, unemployment is a statistical fact in the slum communities studied all over the world. However, it is rare to find unemployment statistics in community census data. Given the unstable nature of most of these activities, it is hard to tell the difference between temporary unemployment, underemployment and permanent unemployment, but long-term unemployment does seem to be characteristic of a fairly large proportion of the population in some areas. One study indicated that between 18 and 25 percent of the squatter population around Caracas were unemployed,[118] and Peattie found that one-third of the men in the Venezuelan community she studied (aged nineteen to sixty) reported themselves as unemployed.[119] Gutkind studied a large group of long-term unemployed in Lagos and Nairobi. He predicted phenomenally high rates of long-term unemployment in the future.[120] Gutkind's work indicates the problem of the definition of unemployment. His subjects are defined as unemployed from the point of view of stable salaried jobs. In actuality, many of those in his sample were sporadically engaged in marginal activities. He describes the younger group as having "occasional jobs as washing cars, carrying loads, watching market stalls, looking after young children, hawking combs, pencils, cigarettes or cloth and generally picking up whatever casual work they could find."[121]

Those self-employed in such marginal activities and others such as scavenging and begging are usually not officially recognized as employed although they do eke out a marginal livelihood.

CROSS-CULTURAL COMPARISONS

Differences. Since poverty occupations seem to be less career specialties than a pool of alternative sources of cash, they are fairly open in recruitment. However, there are some limits in recruitment related to sex and age generally or to the specific definition of sex and age roles in a particular culture. Thus, prostitution is obviously related to both sex and age limitations. Other occupations such as begging and running errands seem to be primarily occupations for the very young and very old.

The effect of a particular culture's definition of the division of labor is illustrated by the fact that earthmovers in construction work in India are frequently women, and porters in the Himalayan region are predominantly women. Domestics in parts of Africa and Asia are as likely to be male as female. Sometimes a sexual division of labor exists within the category of domestic work so that some tasks such as laundering are performed by males while women take on other work. While the Islamic practices concerning the seclusion of women (*purdah*) prohibit women from hawking activities in most Islamic countries, in Lagos, Nigeria, women are predominant in trading activities and Marris states that there seem to be no differences in the nature of male and female trading activities.[122]

Within the category of occupations which are characterized by low income, low skill level, high time and energy input, non-continuity and low evaluation, there are significant differences in their relative evaluation in different societies. We have already indicated that the low opinion of occupations such as begging, prostitution and petty thievery keeps the vast majority of the unemployed from participating in them. However, persistent beliefs, particularly those relating to anti-materialism, as in India and Islam even today, make begging less defiling than the other occupations. *Purdah,* the seclusion and protection of women, on the other hand, leads to a more negative evaluation of prostitution in the Islamic countries.

As another example of differential cultural evaluations we find that dockworkers in India are almost exclusively recruited from scheduled castes while hawkers usually come from clean castes. In parts of Latin America dockwork is not considered as bad. Taira implies that within the low income occupations in Tokyo, ragpicking which requires "stooping in the street" is only to be undertaken as a last resort, other forms of scavenging being preferred.[123] In South Africa, messengers are considered almost middle-class while in Latin America they have lower status.[124]

It should be pointed out that the "native's" way of classifying activities and differentiating between them does not coincide with the criteria we have imposed for our analysis. For instance, the classification of different types of hawkers varies from culture to culture. In Lima's major market, many distinctions are made. First there is the distinction between the sellers of new goods and the *cachinero* or seller of stolen goods or goods whose owner recently died. Furthermore, specialization in wares varies. Certain kinds of household utensils which are grouped together for one type of vendor in Lima are distributed among several types of specialists in Mayhew's London. Finally, distinctions are made according to the degrees of mobility of the seller or the scale of his enterprise (the two often go together). In one case, an indigenous distinction is made between those who "shout their wares," and those who use no aggressive sales pitch.

Unfortunately, except for some historical writing on elites, very little work had been done on indigenous classifications of occupations. The variety of ways in which poverty level occupations are classified or grouped, the social evaluation of the different occupations, and a more realistic view of the internal ranking system for a wide variety of societies cannot be determined at this time. Future studies, more specifically geared to delineating the indigenous views of poverty-level occupations will help us determine the cross-cultural differences in these areas.

Similarities. In spite of some of the obvious differences in the culturally specific division of labor and the evaluation of these occupations, there is a striking similarity in their distribution cross-culturally. Most studies which concentrate on the slum community or migrants as a category indicate similar occupational structures in all world areas. Marginal occupations predominate while the more stable analogues are lightly sprinkled among the population. It should be remembered that there is heterogeneity in terms of level of occupation in most slum communities.

Thus in a Japanese flophouse community, Caldarola states that 50 percent of the population are casual, unskilled laborers in transportation and construction who are called "standing poles" because of the way they wait for daily labor contracts. Thirteen percent are day-workers who seek employment through the government, 9 percent are self-employed itinerant artisans and peddlers. Twenty-five percent are steadily employed blue-collar workers.[125]

De Vos and Wagatsuma indicate that 40 percent of those living in one Japanese slum community earned their income through relief work (a government administered day-work program). Another 20 percent were privately employed day-laborers. The rest were, in order of frequency, rag and junk men, street sweepers and shoeshiners.[126]

Street sleepers (those who sleep on mats outdoors in the center of the city) in Calcutta are characterized as doing ". . . casual work as porters, pedal–bike rickshaw drivers and construction helpers." [127] In a study of Delhi slums, it appeared that 13 percent of the population were unskilled laborers, 10.5 percent petty shopkeepers and 7.8 percent hawkers, while smaller percentages were made up of such skilled crafts as masons, plumbers and tailors and such unskilled occupations as sweepers and washermen.[128] Zachariah says of Bombay, "It thus appears that one out of every four migrant workers in Bombay is a casual laborer or *peon,* a cook, a waiter, a hawker or petty trader." [129]

A survey of slum dwellers in Hong Kong finds the occupants to be owners of small businesses, hawkers of vegetables and cooked food, laborers on a daily rate (some skilled, such as plumbers and carpenters, some unskilled, "coolies") and salaried government workers with job security.[130] Kaye lists specific unskilled occupations for the residents of Upper Nankin Street in Singapore. Some of the more frequently mentioned were earthmovers, laborers, packers, odd-job workers, itinerant hawkers, street vendors, cleaners, drain sweepers, porters, unloaders, office cleaners and rickshaw drivers. There were also at least as many skilled and semi-skilled workers in this community.[131] McGee lists the poorest members of a squatter settlement in Djakarta as *betcha* (bicycle rickshaw) drivers, dockworkers, construction laborers and the unemployed. He also indicates the presence of some skilled and even professional workers.[132]

Abu-Lughod suggests that most of the migrants in Cairo whom she studied are casual laborers or engage in less energy-consuming activities such as itinerant peddling, shoe-shining, tea-making and domestic service.[133] Harrison lists the occupations for a squatter colony in Tripoli, Libya, as laborers, nightwatchmen, cleaners, launderers, houseboys, domestic servants, prostitutes and child beggars.[134]

The pattern is the same in Latin America. For the general region,

Frank stresses the importance of heavy labor as well as ". . . self-employed 'entrepreneurs' such as in street vending, odd jobs and of course domestic employment." [135] Whiteford differentiates between skilled manual labor (upper-lower class) and lower-lower class in two Latin American cities. He includes in lower-lower occupations those activities characterized by carrying, lifting, scrubbing, sweeping, digging and watching.[136] In all areas, while skilled and unskilled workers are both present, the marginal occupations dominate and are striking in their similarity from place to place.

NON-WORK SOURCES OF CASH

Public welfare programs and private charity provide sources of cash and often goods without involving work. Both these sources are non-traditional in nature, for organized charity which is large-scale and systematic did not exist in traditional agrarian societies. Instead charity was characterized by sporadic almsgiving often on a personal basis. Public welfare is an even more recent phenomenon. When these sources are available, they may be used to supplement a meager income or to entirely support the household unit. In a study of two Hong Kong communities, for those in the lowest income categories, charities were a significant source of income. In the poorest family, private charity accounted for 40 percent of its income.[137] De Jesus describes the monthly distribution of food by one of the local mission groups [138] and Whiteford describes the soup kitchens and other donations of goods and services by the Ladies of Charity, a lay-church group in Popayán, Colombia.[139] Second-hand clothing redistributed through private charity is widespread. Because of the newness and limited implementation of welfare programs in the developing world, *public* assistance does not play a significant role in household income, although this varies between particular nation states.

Another widespread source of income not involving work activities among the poor is rents. Although this sounds unusual to middle-class individuals used to other patterns of real estate, in areas where housing is scarce due to rapid urban growth, it is not unusual for an extremely crowded household unit to rent bedspace or even a whole room (often half their living space) since the cash is more useful than space. This pattern is described as prevalent in Port Said slums, among the Nubian migrants to Cairo [140] and is widespread in South Africa [141] and Lagos,[142] for example.

Movement Away from Marginal Occupations

There are several different career patterns or occupational sequences which are typical of those who start off in the urban industrial setting in marginal occupations. The paths away from the material deprivation characteristic of marginal sources of income depend to a large extent on external factors outside the control of the individual, but sometimes conscious behavioral choice plays a part.

CIRCULAR MIGRATION

One common pattern is to continually move between the urban industrial system and the traditional agrarian system still existing in rural areas. The term frequently applied to this process is "circular migration." This involves the use of urban jobs which produce cash incomes merely to support a traditional rural way of life. Often male migrants will live austerely in the city for a few years avoiding an urban standard of living. They can then return home with a cash reserve and only return to the city periodically thereafter to replenish their cash resources. This pattern characterizes a large proportion of rural–urban migration in India. The urban centers are filled with males who live in male boardinghouses and send their cash home to their families. They also return to the village frequently to visit and take care of kinship and ritual obligations.

Circular migration is also a marked characteristic of African urbanization although many commentators feel that there is an increasing commitment to urban life.[143] The nightwatchmen of Kano provide a colorful example of circular migrants. They are actually members of a nomadic tribe from north of this Nigerian city. They enter the city to earn cash as nightwatchmen, and they save most of their income since they sleep and eat at their jobs. They then return to their traditional way of life.[144] Textor describes the pattern of pedicab drivers from the Northeast portion of Thailand who come to Bangkok and reside for several years only to return with their savings to the Northeast to live more comfortably in their agricultural settings.[145] The Caribbean is also characterized by this phenomenon. People migrate to towns, to other islands and even to other countries, such as England and the United States, to earn, save and return to their homeland. Latin American rural–urban migration involves circularity to a lesser extent.

The circular migrant is not committed to the urban industrial system and is using marginal occupations to avoid material deprivation in the traditional agrarian setting. However, it is questionable whether the return to rural lifeways will long remain a viable alternative for the urban migrant.

ENCLAVES

Another alternative is to remain in the city, but remain as part of an enclaved community insulated from the pressures of an urban lifestyle, including an urban standard of comfort. Thus, populations can remain located in the city but perpetuate a traditional way of life. Such communities are not fully dependent on cash for their goods and services. They manage to produce some of their own food and retain traditional patterns for the exchange of goods and services. They also avoid a cash evaluation of individual social worth and are satisfied to live at a lower standard of material comfort. Residents may be socially defined as poor by outsiders, but do not perceive of themselves in this way. Thus the circumstances typical of the urban industrial poor are avoided. Truly enclaved populations which have all of the aforementioned attributes are hard to find in the literature, but there are many communities which approximate this type.

In the Middle East, the residents of the Cities of the Dead on the outskirts of Cairo seem to come close to this description.[146] Gulick describes a similar persistence of tradition among the Alawites and Maronites in Tripoli, Lebanon. In describing certain squatting communities in Bagdad, he also mentions the maintenance of traditional patterns of *shaykh* rule, tribal law codes, guest houses and the use of women in paying indemnities.[147] Suzuki presents an example of migrants from an Anatolian village who reconstructed traditional patterns of community co-residence, endogamy and mutual aid funds in the city of Ankara.[148]

The Xhosa Reds described by Mayer in East London are noted for their traditional institutions and behavior.[149] McGee describes the occasional occurrence of traditional enclaves in the Southeast Asian city,[150] and a further classic example of this type are the former outcast communities of Japan which remain integrated and insulated from modern Japanese life.[151] In all of these instances, marginal occupations and material deprivation do not have the same meaning as they do for individuals whose aspirations are keyed to an urban industrial way of life.

This type of enclaved population is not very common in Latin America where commentators frequently point out the speed with which the migrant becomes enmeshed in the cash economy and relates to material symbols of status. However, the Mixtec migrants in Mexico City described by Butterworth do seem to approximate an enclave.[152]

UPWARD MOBILITY

Another career pattern which can be followed is that of moving away from the marginal occupational cycle by increasing the amount and security of income. Obviously this involves a career characterized by upward mobility in which the marginal job is merely a temporary phase. There are several common paths which enable one to move upward from marginal occupations and a parallel set of facilitating external variables which make the move more or less possible.

The external variables are those largely out of the realm of individual choice. They are beyond an individual's control for the most part. One variable is the opportunity structure extant at the time when the individual enters the urban industrial job market (either as a migrant or an emerging urban-born young adult). This factor depends on the phase in the business cycle at the time of entrance as well as such things as the proliferation of foreign aid projects. To arrive at a time when a major industry is beginning to recruit is quite different from arriving just after the completion of a major construction project has released a large number of the recently employed onto the market. Changes in government policy can also affect the employment scene especially in controlled economies. If communication of opportunity were more sophisticated and efficient, the clever individual could plan fortuitous moves to take advantage of these changing circumstances. However, the plans of the policy-makers often go awry and even economists have difficulty in predicting the boom–bust fluctuations in the economy. Comparative data on the length of time it takes for a migrant to find a job varies from city to city,[153] thus indicating a measurable difference in opportunity structure.

Another important factor beyond the individual's control is his health. Medical expenses in the urban setting can destroy any chance of success. Group data [154] indicates that old people and women of childbearing age are especially prone to medical misfortune as can be seen in the case of Don Valentín who migrated to Lima and whose life chances were effectively destroyed by the illness and frequent childbearing of his wife.[155] The observer who has group data at his disposal could predict that it is probably less risky to enter the urban labor force before marriage and the beginning of the reproductive cycle or later in the domestic cycle but before age becomes a health handicap. However, it is almost impossible for a migrant to perceive such differences in probability. Individuals differ in their basic health condition and their potential for fertility. It is these differences, beyond the control of the individual, which have a tremendous effect on his life chances.

One final external variable which significantly affects the nature of one's occupational career is the degree of occupational discrimination imposed on a particular ethnic–racial group. In this instance, we are not talking about an ethnic cultural *preference* for certain occupations (related to the skills and values of the culture of origin), but of forces generated by the host culture which impose limits on opportunity structure. Obviously, this variable is very important in the development of the United States. Analogous discriminatory patterns can also be found in the rest of the world. In Lima, Peru, the *serrano* (highland migrant) faces severe discrimination in the *criollo* (coastal) society.[156] The scheduled caste member (untouchable) in India also finds the job market severely constricted in relation to other groups.[157]

One obvious means for upward mobility for those who sell labor is to acquire marketable technical skills. Very often this is done as the result of on-the-job training. It is not always rational to market these skills, however, as Dietz points out in one instance.[158] One of his subjects patiently learned to operate a brickmaking machine only to find later that it was economically more advantageous for him to remain in his unskilled construction gang even though he had no permanent contract and had to spend time and money commuting to work. He felt he could fall back on brickmaking, however, if times became bad in construction.

Peattie provides us with a classic example of upward mobility through the acquisition of technical skills in Venezuela.[159] Jorge was the son of an agricultural worker who himself began his career as a farm worker. He drifted into petty commerce until he arrived in La Laja (a squatter settlement in industrial Ciudad Guayana). His arrival was fortuitously timed as the major industry, the Iron Mines Company was just beginning to recruit ordinary laborers. His foreman became interested in him and he was given the opportunity to acquire electrician skills on the job. After seven years he was laid off by the company, a risk frequently present in blue-collar work but cushioned by severance pay. He found a job as an electrical repairman, but always dreamed of investing in his own business. Thus, he left this new job voluntarily to open a grocery store. When this business failed he fell back on his skills and became an electrician at the steel plant where he rose steadily within the company to become a foreman. His many raises have enabled him to realize all his aspirations and he continues to work while also investing in a bar run by his kinsmen.

Another major path to moving upward is through the acquisition of lump sum capital for investment. There are several patterns through which this is accomplished. One common pattern is to use a cooperative organization often patterned after a traditional corporate group. These cooperatives are to be distinguished from groups used to save for emergencies or ordinary consumption. We are talking about investment groups from which capital is obtained and used to change one's way of life and launch new ventures. The African literature contains many references to these groupings. Raum describes the *mgalelo* (savings group) in which three members hand over the bulk of their weekly wages in rotation to each individual. Such a lump sum can facilitate an investment.[160] The Latin American housing cooperatives described by Dietz are often used by the individual to move upward and change his luck.[161] The judicious use of bonuses and severance pay as lump sums for investment are also frequently mentioned. Bonuses at holidays in Hong Kong and Japan can amount to as much as twice the monthly salary.[162] Protective labor legislation in parts of Latin America provide lump sum capital at the termination of employment which can be used for investment.[163] It must also be added that having a lump sum for investment by no means assures success. In the case of Don Valentín, a cattle dealer who moved his family to Lima where they met failure, a substantial initial investment in a market stall with a large inventory ended in producing almost no return on the investment.[164]

At first glance, certain types of poverty occupations are more conducive to capital expansion than others. It is obvious that petty commerce can conceivably lead to large-scale commerce, but this depends on many variables like the unit price of items, their perishability, portability and the control of competition. Selling cooked food which requires little overhead is not an easily expandable enterprise because of perishability and the impossibility of developing a large inventory without overhead (storage facilities). On the other hand, other items require a creditor relationship with one's supplier which reduces autonomy and potential for expansion. Even if some upward mobility is achieved, it is just as easy to slide back down the ladder. Eraclio, described by Patch, is a

youth who achieved upward mobility through petty commerce.[165] After
working as a truck unloader and basket porter at the market, he began
selling household utensils as an *ambulante* (mobile seller located on the
fringe of the legitimate market). After some days of failure, the en-
terprising boy began to see the necessity of developing a salespitch to
attract customers. His sales increased and in a short period his profit
doubled. (Another way of increasing the volume of sales is to use a
shill to help you bargain with customers.) After clearing between sixty
and eighty *soles* per day in profit, a rate which seems typical of *ambulantes* in Lima's market, the boy reached a net profit rate of 150 to 200
soles per day or twice the average rate. At the time of the study he was
planning to purchase a permanent stall at a better class market.[166] On
the other hand, two other migrants who began as *ambulantes* clearing the
average rate and who were pooling their profits and sharing costs in
the hopes of becoming wholesalers met disaster when one of them was
conscripted off the street for the Peruvian army and his portable stand
and inventory were confiscated by the municipality. His friend, who
could no longer manage his room rent or operating costs, returned to
the village of his origin.[167] The Hong Kong literature also provides
insight into the possibilities and probabilities of a hawker's expansion.[168]

Illicit occupations are very conducive to upward mobility if one breaks
into the professional network. These activities offer tremendous opportunity because of the increasing opportunity structure. However, it is not
only the normative antipathy to a way of life defined as immoral and
defiling which keeps the labor force supply low. The control of the
labor supply by the organized profession is also a factor. In his study
of prostitutes in Lebanon, Khalaf provides an example of a former
amateur hustler who moves into brothel life, but she is unique.[169]
Patch's descriptions of Lima's market provide glimpses of the difficulties of breaking into the thug way of life.[170]

Some marginal occupations are structured in such a way as to allow the
individual to obtain cash from more than one work activity at the same
time. We have previously noted that nightwatchmen in market areas in
Lima also work as market porters during the day. Nightwatching in
general provides time for the performance of many odd jobs during
the day. It would also appear to be possible for errand boys to pick up
other odd jobs during intervals between errands. It would not be incorrect to suggest that street vendors and pedicab drivers are frequently in
a position to engage in illicit activities related to gambling or prostitution. We have also noted the coexistence of scavenging activities with

petty theft. Any activity involving self-employment and autonomy like scavenging and street vending can be combined easily with other jobs. It is thus possible through a combination of simultaneous work activities to acquire capital to live above a materially deprived level or even to invest for upward mobility.

Another route to upward mobility is the judicious utilization of income from multiple wage-earners in the household. Part of the success of this alternative depends upon the life cycle phase of the household, the presence of unmarried, non-dependent individuals who contribute income is an advantage to the household. It is possible to time the use of a wife's services in child care and her entrance into the job market so as to maximize income. With multiple wage-earners, some of the risky but high-yield alternatives like starting new business ventures can be explored since there are other sources of income to fall back on.[171]

In Hong Kong there are a number of alternative patterns of multiple household earners usually yielding higher and more secure sources of income than for comparable households with one earner. Among hawkers it is not unusual for a husband and a wife to work as a team. Men who are employed as tailors frequently use their wives as assistants. Sometimes husband and wife may work in the same factory. Typical of the employment of wives in Hong Kong is that they prefer to work within the house rather than in factories outside. A number of women make plastic flowers while others take in ironing and washing. Where wives are employed as subsidiary earners their income is usually much lower than that of the main earner. However, there are a number of cases in which the women do earn more than their husbands and a result seems to be that the women become the major decision-makers in the household unit. Sometimes children are also employed. Traditionally, the Chinese have been unwilling to allow their daughters to work outside of the household unit. However, in Hong Kong some of these traditional prohibitions are breaking down and they are allowed to work in factories outside the home.[172]

It should not be assumed, however, that multiple wage-earning is always a stepping stone to mobility. It is often a necessity and frequently provides no movement out of the cycle of marginal occupations. The wife of Jesus Sanchez always worked. Two of her major jobs were the sale of cake crumbs she obtained in a bakery, and the sale of second-hand goods. Her income made a difference, but not a major difference.[173] In the household of Don Valentín everyone worked. While he ran his unsuccessful stall with the help of his daughter, his wife prepared and sold meals in the market from a moving cart with a primus stove. The little boys sold newspapers and shined shoes. The income of the household was still insecure and low in spite of all this activity.[174] Households headed by females often contain working children but these households too are living in extremely marginal circumstances.

A final means of moving up from the cycle of marginal jobs is through a conversion or revitalization experience. Peattie discusses this process in general when she says that some of the individuals in the community she studied seem to undergo a conversion of their self-images and world views and begin to believe that through discipline and self-control they can control their own destiny.[175] This occurs without any organized revitalization movement. However, it is to be assumed that the experience of the individuals in question has been more rewarding than those who do not change their world view. Without facilitating external factors, such beliefs will not arise nor will they be sustained. Sometimes organized movements lead to such conversions. This is true in some of the evangelical movements in Latin America and some of the sects in Africa. One such movement led to massive behavioral and ideological changes in a small group of ragpickers in Japan. In Ant's Villa, a whole community of marginal economic participants (ragpickers) moved up in the social system through a religious revitalization movement. Here, several formerly elite and middle-class individuals who had been downwardly mobile (turned to nightwatchman and ragpicking jobs) helped to organize and rationalize the ragpicking activities of the community making them profitable. This, in addition to conversion to active Christianity by many members of the community, had many repercussions on behavior and life.[176] The crucial element here was probably the commercial skills and know-how of some of the participants. The successful enterprise provided a secure economic milieu for the changes in world view and behavior which followed.

All of the career routes thus far discussed have led *away* from the cycle of marginal occupations either through geographic mobility, through insulation within an enclave, or through upward mobility resulting from a combination of fortuitous circumstances and behavioral choice. One of the more common patterns of occupational sequence, however, is to continue relying on various marginal sources of cash, and to develop a career of these alternatives. Thus one never achieves or sustains high levels of income; neither does one achieve income stability. This is the life of the urban poor, a more or less permanently deprived group, whose children, in all probability, will find it more difficult to rise.[177]

Although the literature of poverty abounds in statements about the succession of low-skilled jobs, there are few life history accounts available which allow us to see the pattern of use of alternative, unrelated sources of cash. One such case which does make possible a picture of the sequence can be derived from the autobiography of Maria de Jesus in São Paulo, Brazil. Basically, de Jesus is a scavenger. She distinguishes between the paper and the tin which she collects since these commodities are sold to two different dealers. In addition, de Jesus admits to a history of casual, intermittent prostitution although she claims she is finished with that "way of life." Begging is an activity whiich she abhors and she accuses many of her neighbors of begging. However, based upon statements about gifts which she and her children receive, one can only assume that some form of begging is taking place. De Jesus also suggests that when her scavenging yield is poor, she will iron clothes. She has also been a domestic at points in her life.[178]

The careers of Don Valentín Punarejo and Manuel Sanchez are similar. Don Valentín has been mentioned frequently. He ran an unsuccessful stall in the marketplace in Lima and later took a step down to try his hand as an *ambulante* (mobile, small-scale peddler). He also worked as an occasional *peon* (heavy laborer) and finally became a watchman in an enclosure which served as a dwelling for him and a storage place for crates. It was his job to repair as well as to watch them.[179] Manual Sanchez worked as a shoemaker's assistant, a beltmaker in a sweatshop, a street vendor of lottery tickets, a mason's assistant, a nightwatchman, a shill for a friend's stall, a second-hand vendor, a gambler for profit and his longest term employment was in a small glass-making shop.[180]

In spite of the possible alternatives to marginal careers, Mangin and Gutkind, two anthropologists who have made detailed studies of the poor in Latin America and Africa respectively, predict that unemployment rates will increase and that marginal alternatives will become even less rewarding. They also foresee that while first generation migrants, the bulk of the urban population today, will remain relatively satisfied with their lot, the aspirations of the second and third generations will be greater and increasingly non-achievable.[181]

While marginal occupations account for most of the urban poor in transitional societies, they recede in importance in the advanced industrial West. In Chapter 6, a discussion of the poor in the United States, we shall see the differences and the similarities in the relationship between the occupational structure and poverty in the two types of social systems.

Notes

1. Daniel Lerner, *The Passing of Traditional Society: Modernizing the Middle East* (New York: The Free Press, 1958).
2. P. Bohannon and G. Dalton (eds.), *Markets in Africa* (Garden City: Doubleday & Company, 1965).
3. Oscar Lewis, *Village Life in Northern India* (Urbana: University of Illinois Press, 1958).
4. E. A. Hammel, *Power in Ica* (Boston: Little, Brown and Company, 1969), p. 111.
5. O. Lewis, *Life in a Mexican Village* (Urbana: University of Illinois Press, 1955), p. 109.
6. Charles Erasmus, "The Occurrence and Disappearance of Reciprocal Farm Labor in Latin America," in D. B. Heath and R. N. Adams (eds.), *Contemporary Cultures and Societies of Latin America* (New York: Random House, Inc., 1965), pp. 189–193.
7. See Eric R. Wolf, "Types of Latin American Peasantry," *American Anthropologist,* vol. 57, 1955, pp. 452–471, and "The Closed Corporate Community in Mesoamerica and Central Java," *Southwestern Journal of Anthropology,* vol. 13, 1957.
8. B. L. Rao, *Community and Development: A Study of Two Indian Villages* (Minneapolis: University of Minnesota Press, 1966).
9. Joel Halpern, *The Changing Village Community* (Englewood Cliffs, N.J.: Prentice-Hall, Inc., 1967).
10. Polly Hill, *The Migrant Cocoa Farmers of South Ghana: A Study of Rural Capitalism* (Cambridge, England: Cambridge University Press, 1963); and *The Gold Coast Cocoa Farmer* (London: Oxford University Press, 1956).
11. E. R. Wolf, "San Jose: Subcultures of a Traditional Coffee Municipality," in J. H. Steward (ed.), *The People of Puerto Rico* (Urbana: University of Illinois Press, 1956), pp 171–264.
12. Ralph Linton, *The Study of Man* (New York: Appleton-Century-Crofts, 1936).
13. S. W. Mintz, "Cañelmar: The Subculture of a Rural Sugar Plantation Proletariat," in Steward, *op. cit.,* pp. 314–417.
14. Joseph Lopreato, *Peasants No More* (San Francisco: Chandler Publishing Co., 1967).
15. See, for example, Donald Bogue and K. C. Zachariah, "Urbanization

and Migration in India," in R. Turner (ed.), *India's Urban Future* (Berkeley: University of California Press, 1962); Edwin Eames and W. Schwab, "Urban Migration in India and Africa," *Human Organization,* vol. 23, 1964, and William Mangin, *Peasants in the City* (Boston: Houghton Mifflin Company, 1970).

16. George Foster, *Traditional Cultures and the Impact of Technological Change* (New York: Harper & Row, Publishers, 1962), pp. 147–150.

17. Miles Richardson, *San Pedro, Colombia: Small Town in a Developing Society* (New York: Holt, Rinehart & Winston, Inc., 1970), pp. 36–50.

18. Eames, "Population and Economic Structure of an Indian Rural Community," *Eastern Anthropologist,* vol. 8, 1954, pp. 173–181.

19. Vaiao and Fay Ala' i Lima, "Samoan Values and Economic Development," *East-West Center Review,* vol. 1, 1965, pp. 3–18.

20. For discussions of the maintenance of the traditional fiesta cycle and its effects on community wealth, see Francis Cancian, *Economics and Prestige in a Maya Community* (Stanford: Stanford University Press, 1965), and Evon T. Vogt, *Zinacantan* (Cambridge: Harvard University Press, 1970).

21. B. Salz, *The Human Element in Industrialization,* American Anthropological Association Memoir 85, 1955, pp. 196–197.

22. *Ibid.,* p. 195.

23. Lerner, *op. cit.,* pp. 128–129, 132, 174.

24. *Ibid.,* p. 25.

25. For a general discussion of the effects of industrialization, see Wilbert Moore, *The Impact of Industry* (Englewood Cliffs, N.J.: Prentice-Hall, Inc., 1965).

26. *Ibid.,* pp. 41–43, 61–67.

27. Lopreato, *op. cit.,* p. 96.

28. Max Weber, *Protestant Ethic and the Spirit of Capitalism* (London: Allen and Unwin, 1930).

29. Moore, *op. cit.,* pp. 36–37.

30. Bohannon and Dalton, *op. cit.*

31. L. N. Chapekar, "Community Development Blocks in Badlapur," *Sociological Bulletin,* vol. 7, 1958, pp. 111–122.

32. Robert Textor, *From Peasant to Pedicab Driver,* Southeast Asia Studies Cultural Report Series no. 9, p. 27 (New Haven: Yale University Press, 1961).

33. Kingsley Davis and H. Golden, "Urbanization and the Development of Preindustrial Areas," *Economic Development and Cultural Change,* vol. 3, 1954, pp. 6–26; Davis, "The Urbanization of the Human Population," *Scientific American,* 1965, pp. 41–53; N. V. Sovani, "The Analysis of Overurbanization," *Economic Development and Cultural Change,* vol. 12, 1964, pp. 113–122.

34. Gunnar Myrdal, *The Challenge of World Poverty: A World Anti-Poverty Program in Outline* (New York: Pantheon Books, Inc., 1970); *Challenge to Affluence* (New York: Pantheon Books, Inc., 1963); and *Rich Lands and Poor: The Road to World Prosperity* (New York: Harper & Row, Publishers, 1957).

35. David Simpson, "The Dimensions of World Poverty," *Scientific American*, vol. 219, 1968, pp. 27–35.

36. *Ibid.*, p. 35.

37. The data in the ensuing discussion have been obtained from a variety of sources which include United Nations documents, monographs by indigenous as well as foreign social scientists and journal articles. For each of the major world areas we have endeavored, where possible, to select studies of urban life, slum communities, marginal occupations, and urban migrants. For our purposes, in-depth case material, biographies, and descriptive narrative accounts were preferable to large-scale statistical survey material.

    In a "salvage" research operation such as the one undertaken here, there are a number of disappointments which must be faced. One major disappointment is the unavailability of foreign documents in most American libraries. Another is the result of a basic discrepancy between the title of a work and its contents; frequently an article appeared in the literature which seemed to be directly relevant to our purposes but which when finally obtained, produced very little hard data. Finally, because few studies have focused directly on poverty, whatever data were available had to be extrapolated from the text.

38. P. C. W. Gutkind, "The Poor in Urban Africa: A Prologue to Modernization, Conflict and the Unfinished Revolution," in W. Bloomberg Jr. and H. J. Schmandt (eds.), *Power, Poverty and Urban Policy,* Urban Affairs Annual Reviews, vol. 2, 1970.

39. Koji Taira, "Public Assistance in Japan: Developments and Trends," *Journal of Asian Studies,* vol. 27, 1967, pp. 95–109.

40. *Ibid.*

41. J. Peacock and T. Kirsch, *The Human Direction* (New York: Appleton-Century-Crofts, 1970), p. 61.

42. Owen Lynch, *The Politics of Untouchability* (New York: Columbia University Press, 1969).

43. For discussions of this phenomenon in Latin America, see Thomas Crevenna (ed.), *Materiales para el estudio de la clase media en la America Latina* (Washington: Panamerican Union, 1950); John J. Johnson, *Political Change in Latin America: The Emergence of the Middle Sectors* (Stanford: Stanford University Press, 1958); and Andrew Whiteford, *Two Cities in Latin America* (Garden City: Doubleday & Company, Inc., 1964).

44. Halpern, *op. cit.*

45. Gutkind, *op. cit.*

46. Richard Patch, "La Parada: Lima's Market," *American Universities*

Field Staff Report, West Coast of South America, vol. 14, 1967, Part III, p. 11.

47. Gutkind, *op. cit.*

48. Marris tells us that the only advantage residents in new housing estates perceived in their new situation was that they were located far from their needy relatives. Peter Marris, *Family and Social Change in an African City* (London: Routledge and Kegan Paul, 1961), p. 73.

49. G. F. Rohrlich, "Social Security in World-Wide Perspective," *Social Service Review,* vol. 38, 1964, pp. 43–54.

50. For Great Britain, see the data comparing the share of the national wealth allocated to the poor prior to World War II with the present in R. M. Titmuss, "The Welfare State: Images and Realities," *Social Service Review,* vol. 37, 1963, pp. 1–11. For the Japanese data, see Taira, *op. cit.*

51. Robert C. Hanson and O. G. Simmons, "Differential Experience Paths of Rural Migrants to the City," *American Behavioral Scientist,* vol. 13, 1969, pp. 14–35.

52. For data on income differentials, see Whiteford, *op. cit.,* and Helen I. Safa, "The Social Isolation of the Urban Poor," in Isaac Deutscher and E. Thompson (eds.), *Among the People: Encounters with the Poor* (New York: Basic Books, Inc., Publishers, 1968).

53. L. R. Peattie, *The View from the Barrio* (Ann Arbor: University of Michigan Press, 1968). For discussion see chapter entitled, "Different Paths to Becoming."

54. Gutkind, *op. cit.*

55. A. Leeds, "The Significant Variables Determining the Characteristics of Squatter Settlements," *America Latina,* vol. 12, 1970, p. 56.

56. C. Geertz, *Peddlers and Princes* (Chicago: University of Chicago Press, 1963), p. 44.

57. "Report on Making Ends Meet," *Journal of the Hong Kong Institute of Social Research,* vol. 1, 1965, 126 pp.

58. Andrew Frank, "Urban Poverty in Latin America," *Studies in Comparative International Development,* vol. 2, 1966, pp. 75–84.

59. A. Petal, "Some Reflections on the Beggar Problem in Ahmedabad," *Sociological Bulletin,* vol. 8, 1959, pp. 5–15.

60. L. P. Vidyarthi, *Sociocultural Implications of Industrialization in India: A Case Study of Tribal Bihar* (Delhi: N. S. Saxena, 1970).

61. Pauline Milone, *Urban Areas in Indonesia,* University of California Institute of International Studies, Research Series, no. 10, 1966, pp. 86–87.

62. Vidyarthi, *op. cit.*

63. Peattie, *op. cit.,* discusses the influx of labor to Ciudad Guayana Venezuela surpassing the planner's estimations. In addition, the temporary construction workers' settlement outside Brazilia which was

supposed to be removed is still standing and fully inhabited by excess migrants.

64. *Journal of the Hong Kong Institute of Social Research, op. cit.*

65. Frank, *op. cit.*

66. Zachariah, "Bombay Migration Study: A Pilot Analysis of Migration to an Asian Metropolis," in G. Breese (ed.), *The City in Newly Developing Countries: Readings on Urbanism and Urbanization* (Englewood Cliffs, N.J.: Prentice-Hall, Inc., 1969), pp. 36–75.

67. John Gulick, *Tripoli: A Modern Arab City* (Cambridge: Harvard University Press, 1967), pp. 92–93.

68. E. Eames, "Some Aspects of Rural Migration from a North Indian Village," *Eastern Anthropologist*, vol. 7, 1953, pp. 13–26.

69. Lee Taylor, *Occupational Sociology* (New York: Oxford University Press, 1968), pp. 567–572.

70. Fernando Henriques, "West Indian Family Organization," *Caribbean Quarterly*, vol. 2, 1951, pp. 16–24.

71. R. Armstrong, "The Nightwatchman of Kano," *Middle Eastern Studies*, vol. 3, 1967, p. 272.

72. Patch, *op. cit.*, Part II.

73. *Journal of the Hong Kong Institute of Social Research, op. cit.*

74. S. Jayaker, *Rural Sweepers in the City* (Mysore City: Wesley Press and Publishing Co., 1952).

75. Whiteford, *op. cit.*, p. 159.

76. *The New York Times,* December 22, 1970.

77. Milone, *op. cit.*, p. 86, note 216.

78. Whiteford, *op. cit.*, p. 195.

79. Lewis, *Children of Sanchez* (New York: Random House, Inc., 1961).

80. Frank, *op. cit.*

81. Gulick, *op. cit.*, pp. 100–103.

82. Marris, *op. cit.*, p. 73.

83. *Ibid.*, p. 77.

84. Peattie, *op. cit.*, p. 36.

85. Gulick, *op. cit.*, p. 1.

86. Bryan Roberts, "The Social Organization of Low Income Families," in R. N. Adams (ed.), *Crucifixion by Power* (Austin: University of Texas Press, 1970), pp. 479–515.

87. Mangin, "Poverty and Politics in Cities of Latin America," in Bloomberg and Schmandt, *op. cit.*

88. Carolina Maria de Jesus, *Child of the Dark: The Diary of Carolina Maria de Jesus* (New York: The New American Library, Inc., 1962).

89. For a definition of "hidden unemployment," see P. Labini, "Precarious Employment in Sicily," *International Labor Review*, vol. 89, 1968, p. 269.

90. Carlo Caldarola, "The Doya-Gai: A Japanese Version of Skid Row," *Pacific Affairs*, vol. 41, 1968–9, pp. 511–525.
91. Geertz, *op. cit.*, pp. 9 and 11.
92. Mayhew, *London Labour and the London Poor*, vol. 1, p. 7.
93. Janet Abu-Lughod, "Migrant Adaptation to City Life," in Breese (ed.), *op. cit.*, pp. 376–388.
94. Peattie, *op. cit.*, pp. 35–37.
95. Caldarola, *op. cit.*
96. For a discussion of the relationships to suppliers of several hawkers, see *Journal of the Hong Kong Institute of Social Research*, *op. cit.*
97. Geertz, *op. cit.*, pp. 60–61.
98. De Jesus, *op. cit.*
99. Taira, "Ragpickers and Community Development: Ant's Villa in Tokyo," *Industrial and Labor Relations Review*, vol. 22, 1968, pp. 3–19.
100. S. Khalaf, *Prostitution in a Changing Society* (Beirut: Khayats, 1965), p. 2.
101. For example, see N. A. Razvi, 'Extent and Avenues of Prostitution," *Pakistani Review*, vol. 13, 1965, pp. 6–7; and H. Lathbridge, "Girls in Danger: On Prostitution," *Far Eastern Economic Review*, vol. 53, 1966, pp. 583–587.
102. Khalaf, *op. cit.*, pp. 18–20.
103. For a discussion of the possibilities for shoeshine entrepreneurs to move upward socially, see "Shoeshine Boys in North Africa: Horatio Alger Revisited," *Viewpoints*, 1967.
104. M. S. Gore, "Society and the Beggar," *Sociological Bulletin*, vol. 7, 1958, pp. 23–48; Patch, *op. cit.*, Part I; de Jesus, *op. cit.*
105. Gore, *op. cit.*
106. Horacio Fabrega, Jr., "Begging in a Southeastern Mexican City," *Human Organization*, vol. 30, Fall 1971, p. 280.
107. Gulick, *op. cit.*, p. 28.
108. Petal, *op. cit.*
109. Fabrega, *op. cit.*, pp. 277–287.
110. In 1969, the beggars' organization in Pakistan called such a strike. (*The New York Times*, April 17, 1969, p. 3).
111. Gore, *op. cit.*
112. Patch, *op. cit.*, Part I.
113. De Jesus, *op. cit.*
114. Caldarola, *op. cit.*
115. Patch, *op. cit.*, Part I.
116. Caldarola, *op. cit.*
117. For discussions of bootlegging and family income, see B. A. Pauw, *The Second Generation* (Capetown: Oxford University Press, 1963);

and Joan Verster, "Social Survey of Western Township, 1964," *African Studies*, vol. 26, 1967, pp. 175–246.

118. Charles Abrams, *Housing in the Modern World* (London: Faber and Faber, 1964), p. 18.

119. Peattie, *op. cit.*, p. 35.

120. Gutkind, "African Responses to Urban Wage Employment," *International Labour Review*, 97, 1968, pp. 135–167.

121. Gutkind, "The Energy of Despair: Social Organization of the Unemployed in Two African Cities: Lagos and Nairobi," *Civilizations*, vol. 17, 1967, pp. 186–211.

122. Marris, *op. cit.*, pp. 67–69.

123. Taira, "Ragpickers and Community Development: Ant's Villa in Tokyo," *op. cit.*, p. 5.

124. Verster, *op. cit.*

125. Caldarola, *op. cit.*

126. G. De Vos and H. Wagatsuma, "The Ecology of Special Buraku," in G. De Vos and H. Wagatsuma (eds.), *Japan's Invisible Race* (Berkeley and Los Angeles: University of California Press, 1966), p. 124.

127. Joseph Lelyveld, "Kishan Babu," in Mangin (ed.), *Peasants in Cities* (Boston: Houghton Mifflin Company, 1970), pp. 135–137.

128. Samaj Bharat Sevak, *Slums of Old Delhi* (New Delhi: Atma Ram & Sons, 1958), p. 92.

129. Zachariah, *op. cit.*

130. *Journal of the Hong Kong Institute of Social Research, op. cit.*

131. Barrington Kaye, *Upper Nankin Street: Singapore* (Singapore: University of Malaya Press, 1966), pp. 196–200.

132. T. G. McGee, *The Southeast Asian City* (New York: Praeger Publishers, Inc., 1967), pp. 159–160.

133. Abu-Lughod, *op. cit.*

134. R. S. Harrison, "Migrants in the City of Tripoli, Libya," *Geographical Review*, vol. 57, 1967, pp. 397–423.

135. Frank, *op. cit.*

136. Whiteford, *op. cit.*, p. 159.

137. *Journal of the Hong Kong Institute of Social Research, op. cit.*

138. De Jesus, *op. cit.*

139. Whiteford, *op. cit.*, p. 206.

140. Gulick, "Village and City: Cultural Continuities in Twentieth Century Middle Eastern Cultures," in Ira Lapidus (ed.), *Middle Eastern Cities* (Berkeley: University of California Press, 1969), pp. 155–156.

141. Such income appears frequently in the households studied by Pauw, *op. cit.*

142. Marris, *op. cit.*

143. Gutkind, "African Responses to Urban Wage Employment," *op. cit.*

144. Armstrong, *op. cit.*

145. Textor, *op. cit.*

146. Abu-Lughod, "Varieties of Urban Experience," in Lapidus (ed.), *op. cit.*, pp. 159–187.

147. Gulick, "Village and City: Cultural Continuities in Twentieth Century Middle Eastern Cultures," *op. cit.*

148. P. Suzuki, "Encounters with Istanbul: Urban Peasants and Village Peasants," *International Journal of Comparative Sociology*, vol. 8, 1967, pp. 208–215.

149. Phillip Mayer, *Townsmen or Tribesmen: Conservatism and the Process of Urabanization in a South African City* (Capetown: Oxford University Press, 1961).

150. McGee, *op. cit.*

151. De Vos and Wagatsuma, *op. cit.*

152. Donald S. Butterworth, "A Study of the Urbanization Process among Mixtec Migrants from Tilantango in Mexico City," in Mangin, *Peasants in Cities* (Boston: Houghton Mifflin Company, 1970), pp. 98–113.

153. Gulick, "Village and City: Cultural Continuities in Twentieth Century Middle Eastern Cultures," pp. 146–148, cites inter-city differences in cases of employment in industry in the Middle East. Joan Nelson, "Urban Poor Disruption or Political Integration in Third World Cities," *World Politics*, vol. 22, 1970, pp. 393–414; page 398 also cites inter-city differences in opportunity. Differences in opportunity in industry between Osaka and Tokyo are cited in Toshio Kuroda, "Occupational Mobility," *Journal of Social and Political Ideas in Japan*, vol. 3, 1965, pp. 36–44.

154. Hanson and Simmons, *op. cit.*

155. Patch, *op. cit.*, Part II.

156. *Ibid.*

157. H. Isaacs, "India's Ex-Untouchables," in Sylvia Fava (ed.), *Urbanism in World Perspective* (New York: Thomas Y. Crowell Company, 1968), pp. 350–352.

158. Henry Dietz, "Urban Squatter Settlements in Peru," *Journal of Inter-American Studies*, vol. 11, 1969, pp. 353–370.

159. Peattie, *op. cit.*, pp. 125–126.

160. O. F. Raum, "Self-Help Associations," *African Studies*, vol. 28, 1969, pp. 119–141.

161. For an example of the latter kind of capital accumulating cooperative see Dietz's description of a housing capital cooperative in Dietz, *op. cit.*

162. See both *Journal of the Hong Kong Institute of Social Research*, *op.*

cit., and Takashi Oka, "Tokyo Housing Shortage Persists Amid Affluence," *The New York Times*, January 5, 1971, p. 8.

163. Peattie, *op. cit.*, p. 37.

164. Patch, *op. cit.*, Part II.

165. *Ibid.*, Part III.

166. *Ibid.*, Part III, pp. 7–8.

167. Patch, *op. cit.*, Part III.

168. One hawker in Hong Kong describes the expansion of his business, in *Journal of the Hong Kong Institute of Social Research, op. cit.*

169. Khalaf, *op. cit.*, p. 19.

170. Patch, *op. cit.*, Part I.

171. J. D. Mooney, "Urban Poverty and Labor Force Participation," *American Economic Review*, vol. 57, 1967, pp. 104–119.

172. *Journal of the Hong Kong Institute of Social Research, op. cit.*

173. Lewis, *Children of Sanchez.*

174. Patch, *op. cit.*, Part II.

175. Peattie, *op. cit.*

176. Taira, *op. cit.*

177. S. M. Miller, "The American Lower Class: A Typological Approach," *Social Research*, vol. 31, 1964, pp. 1–22.

178. De Jesus, *op. cit.*

179. Patch, *op. cit.*, Part II.

180. Lewis, *Children of Sanchez.*

181. Gutkind, "The Poor in Urban Africa," and Mangin, "Poverty and Politics in the Latin American City."

Chapter 5

Coping Responses
of the Urban Poor

IN the nineteenth century, Mayhew and other British commentators noted certain commonalities in the behavioral responses of the urban poor to their resource-poor environment. Very similar patterns of behavior can be seen in the transforming areas of the contemporary non-Western world as well. Unfortunately, the coping behaviors are usually described in specific terms which cannot be generalized to other systems. However, if the basic features are described broadly enough, many similarities can be found.

Oscar Lewis was one of the first to point out the similarities in behavioral responses to material deprivation in capitalist urban industrial society, but due to several important defects in his presentation, his work aroused considerable hostility. His pejorative tone, and his use of the term culture in the notion of the "culture of poverty," were particularly unpopular. As he used it, the term culture implied that the responses, once learned by an individual, become engrained in his personality and the group for life. The assumption is made that internalization occurs early and is intensive. Actually, while these behaviors may become lifetime patterns for some, they are by no means unchangeable. While they tend to coexist with each other, this is because they are each adaptive to material deprivation and not because they form a coherent systematically related cultural system. Unfortunately, the hostility to Lewis's approach has served to mask the striking similarities in behavioral responses to poverty which exist cross-culturally.

Any inquiry into similarities in the behavior of the poor is related to the ecological approach in anthropology. We have already seen, in Chapter 2, that useful generalizations can be made about the ideological formulations of many traditional agrarian societies. Such general features result from the fact that these systems face similar resource sets with similar technologies and organization. In traditional agrarian societies, furthermore, each social stratum is a category with a socially created set of resources to which individuals must adapt. Thus similar classes cross-culturally demonstrate similar responses. This kind of class differentiation can be carried over into the study of capitalist urban industrial society. Classes must adapt to the man-made constraints of their class ecosystem.

Since the social and organizational environments in urban industrial societies share many commonalities, cross-cultural similarities in the adaptations of the most materially deprived segments would be expected since the same resource-poor environment is involved in both material and social terms. In one sense, the cross-cultural similarities are more difficult to describe than in tribal societies or stable agrarian systems in which corporate groups serve to perpetuate the subculture of their members. Because of the degree of mobility in developing social class systems, there are so many divergent experience paths for an individual to follow in his career that it is impossible to describe the system from the individual's point of view. This does not negate the possibility of the development of similar behaviors among peoples located in the same social position in different societies. It just makes the job of describing these behaviors more difficult.

In spite of the expectation that such behavior would be similar, one finds statements like the following:

The British poor described by Booth (1902) were more like the British middle and upper classes than they were like the poor of Istanbul or Naples. . . . The poor of Mexico and Puerto Rico (San Juan and New York varieties) described by Lewis have more in common culturally with the general population of Mexicans and Puerto Ricans than they do with the poor of France or Pakistan.[1]

This statement obviously discounts the importance of cross-cultural similarities among the poor. Mangin does not say that these similarities do not exist, he merely states that they do not matter. His statement reflects hostility to Lewis's formulation and a bias in the direction of the humanistic trend in anthropology which emphasizes the uniqueness of different cultures and the belief that differences are more important than similarities.

The two positions, those of the generalist and the relativist, should be reconcilable since they are both long-term legitimate aims of anthropology. One way to reconcile them is to point out that some areas of cultural behavior seem more closely tied to ecological factors than others. These areas of behavior will be more similar if resources and their uses are similar while the rest of behavior will still vary. The very traits which Mangin singles out in reference to the statement quoted above, that is "cultural views of the world, ideal family and kinship patterns, aspirations, values and even body movements and language habits . . . ," [2] are those which have always been associated with traditional style or what is referred to in the American social science literature as ethnicity. Those which we will describe as adaptive to poverty are commonly associated with the ecosystem or the class position which forms the ecosystem in modern society. Such things as subsistence techniques and certain aspects of social structure are what Steward, a pioneering cultural ecologist, refers to as the cultural core.[3] We are not denying that the poor in different national systems differ from one another in language, style and expressive behavior, but it is being presumptuous to attempt to state which kind of behavior, the similar or the different, is more significant to social science. Certainly both perspectives are necessary and worthwhile.

The discussion of responses requires some clarification. We are trying to show that certain behavioral responses to poverty become widespread because they are adaptive to capitalist urban industrial poverty conditions (low and sporadic income and the negative evaluation of the poor). However, several disclaimers must be made. First, a correlation between the incidence of material deprivation and a particular behavioral trait by no means indicates that poverty is the significant independent variable related to the trait. This is true in several instances where the same behavioral response can be shown to be related logically and empirically to other social variables. For instance, some of the social patterns characteristic of the poor are logically adaptive to and empirically correlated with the unbalanced sex ratio in urban migrant communities when these occur. They can also be related to circular migration patterns as well as to material deprivation. Although these patterns are by no means confined to the poor, nevertheless, they are important factors. In fact, it is probable that when other variables are controlled, these behavior patterns will be more frequent or intense among the urban poor.

Moreover, some traits included here are not only correlated with specific processes of migration, but they may be associated with the whole complex of modernization trends affecting all segments of the population: rural and urban, middle class as well as lower class. However, once again we would expect to find these patterns occurring more frequently, more intensely or emerging earlier among the materially deprived. Thus we are not implying that material deprivation alone produces these patterns but that a non-random relationship exists between poverty and the patterns of behavior.

Another point which needs clarification relates to the "adaptive" or "functional" nature of the behavior patterns. We are discussing these behaviors from the point of view of the materially deprived individual. Thus, from the short-term perspective of the individual, such behavior can be seen as coping, rational, and maximizing. However, from the longer term perspective of the "poor" as a group or of the social system in its entirety, such behavior may be called dysfunctional. In other words it could be argued that some behavior patterns may be negatively affecting the economic and political goals of the total system. However, such areas of dysfunction are only obvious to the specialized observer, the economist, political scientist, and so on. It is essential to point out that much of the behavior of the entrepreneurs, traditional elites and the new middle classes are equally dysfunctional for the goals of the system and much more harmful in the aggregate! The public, however, seems to lie in wait for a chance to denounce the behavior of the poor and the damage it does to stability and development. It is very important to realize that the behaviors which the public views judgmentally are those areas of behavior which probably have few consequences for the total system. It is important to see the difference between what is dysfunctional from the economic-political point of view and what is perceived as dysfunctional by the layman whose perception is colored by rigid notions about goodness and morality. It is also necessary to bear in mind that the degree of dysfunction in the behavior which appears adaptive to material deprivation is probably less significant to the total system than the dysfunctional behavior of the more powerful segments.

In the following discussion of responses to material deprivation, the behavioral traits are divided into several groups. The first group deals with economic responses to cash-poor living in terms of maximizing cash resources, finding substitutes for money and handling emergencies. These responses are probably the most unique to the poor but can be found among individuals following all the types of careers emanating from marginal occupations. They are the behaviors which are most obviously adaptive and rational and least likely to be viewed negatively by the dominant classes. However, there is, unfortunately, some tendency in popular belief to view some of this behavior as evidence that the poor indulge their impulses and cannot defer gratification.

The Means to Maximize Cash

In order to supplement meager sources of cash and especially to obtain emergency funds in times of illness or other personal crises, those with marginal incomes tend to form small-scale mutual aid associations which are sometimes modifications of traditional forms. As an example of one such grouping, there is the *ooi* found in a low income area in Hong Kong. This is a formally organized group with a leader, regular monthly meetings, fixed membership and a fixed monthly contribution which is extremely small. For an indication of cost, see Table 1. Any member of the *ooi* may borrow in a time of crisis. Individuals compete for loans by bidding at a given rate of interest. The one who offers the most interest is the one who gets the loan. Commitment to repay the loan is recognized and rarely does an *ooi* face a defaulting borrower.[4]

In Kampala, Uganda, Gutkind notes that members of minority tribes tend to belong to small credit societies. Contributions to the fund are made on a monthly basis. Each member of the association in turn receives the total monthly fund. If an individual absconds with the funds, he is subject, if and when he is found, to a severe beating.[5] Lewis notes the development of informal credit associations called *tandas* based on the pooling of resources and the drawing of lots in his original fieldwork in Mexico City.[6] Leeds mentions that groups of workmates in Brazil frequently develop informal credit pools called *vaquinas* and *caixinhas* (little cows and little boxes, similar to the English word "kitty"). These pools are used both for emergencies or low-level "penny capitalism."[7] It should be noted that credit associations designed to produce crisis aid or lump sums for major but necessssary purchases can be different from the more capital-forming credit pools discussed earlier which are designed to amass capital for homes and businesses. The latter are not to be viewed as coping responses but as means of achieving upward mobility.[8] Mayhew as we have seen has referred to similar coping mechanisms such as the informal raffle for the sick in nineteenth century England.

Raum discusses a wide range of small groups among urban dwellers in Zwelitsha, South Africa, which are designed to "maximize small monetary resources" [9] strictly through the manipulation of money. The market set consists of market women who cooperate in hiring a taxi to convey goods from the wholesale market. They also are obligated to bid for each other at the wholesale market if one is sick. Raum also includes the "common mess" or joint shopping, cooking and eating pattern of single males as a maximizing technique. Through the bulk purchase and preparation of food, money is used more efficiently. The rotating gift club found among women is also a device to enforce some savings, rotate small pools of money to be used for large but necessary purchases and to provide inexpensive recreation through bulk food preparation and free entertainment.

The principles of distribution used in such quasi-formal cash maximization groups vary according to cultural style. Rotation is the basic principle used in Africa, chance is used in Latin America and the auction in Hong Kong. However the basic features of these cooperative aid ventures remain the same.

In addition to these more structured credit associations, informal borrowing of money, goods and food is also characteristic of those in marginal circumstances. Although informal borrowing is found among all segments of the population, it does not appear to be so frequent, pervasive or normatively accepted. Throughout her diary, de Jesus refers to borrowing such items as a little pork or rice, and so forth, and to lending money to a neighbor to help a sick child.[10]

Pawning is a source of cash usually based on previous savings and investment in the purchase of capital goods. To be useful for this purpose, items must be relatively portable and marketable. We may note the patterned use of pawning among Hong Kong laborers who purchase items such as woolen clothing, small radios, wristwatches, toasters, irons and other small appliances which are easily converted into cash when needed.[11] Kishan Babu, a Calcutta street sleeper tries to retain possession of his wife's single gold earring because this is the one item of value which he can give to his creditor when additional merchandise is needed.[12] Lewis also found pawnbroking to be a major way to raise cash for those in poverty in Mexico City. He notes that beds were owned for only short periods of time because emergency conditions led to the necessity for pawning or selling beds and other furniture. In addition, radios were mentioned as being pawned in a "clandestine" pawnship charging 20 percent interest on the loan.[13] These usurious rates of interest can be found in other loansharking ventures which provide access to cash when other sources are unavailable. Raum provides an example of the loan group or *noncedo* where up to four relatively well-to-do men pool their resources to lend money to people in need. Loans are usually on a short-term basis often requiring up to 100 percent interest.[14]

National lotteries like those found in Latin America and the Middle East as well as local numbers games like the Chinese game of *fahfee* found in South Africa can also be used to provide small windfalls. Since only partial tickets can be afforded by the deprived, the winnings are unspectacular. However, they can be used for occasional large purchases. Marta Sanchez tells how her father used two minor lottery winnings to purchase a large metal bed and a radio. Incidentally, both were typically pawnable items.[15]

The utilization of second-hand goods is another means of conserving income. The two major items of concern here are clothing and furniture. One can both *sell* his possessions to acquire quick cash or he may *purchase* used goods to maximize limited cash resources. In Japan, hawkers of second-hand clothes are prominent.[16] It should be noted that Mayhew also wrote about hawkers of second-hand household utensils and linen as well as clothes.[17] One observer of street sleepers in Calcutta states that several families supported themselves by acquiring stainless steel pots on credit and then carrying them from door to door to exchange for old clothes. The clothes, in turn, were used by the families directly or sold to a wholesaler. The cash acquired barely paid for the family food and repayment to the supplier.[18] The second-hand market in Mexico City, where the wife of Jesus Sanchez was a vendor, is described by Lewis in the *Children of Sanchez*.

Frequently, used goods are acquired directly, without the need for cash. A favela dweller in São Paulo, Brazil, notes that most scavengers in the São Paulo favela acquire shoes for their families directly through scavenging. Second-hand clothing is also frequently distributed by charitable institutions.[19] One family in Hong Kong stated that they paid no money at all for clothes since they received altered clothes given by a charitable organization.[20] Another source of used clothing is the largess of a mistress to a domestic servant. According to an eighteenth century English social commentator, one obligation of an employer to a domestic is to produce ". . . from time to time some part of your wardrobe or cast-off clothing." [21] This seems to be common in many traditions. Pauw also indicates the frequent payment in goods made to domestic servants in South Africa.[22]

Related to the sale of second-hand goods is the sale of stolen goods. Patch describes a marketplace for stolen goods in Lima with its division of labor and its own normative patterns.[23] This market also serves to redistribute the belongings of the recently deceased which according to the belief system should not be used, but which are sold for cash by the materially deprived and purchased cheaply by others of the same group. The thieves' market in Mexico City is mentioned in Lewis's work and such institutions seem to be found all over the world.[24]

The dominant classes become moralistic about some of the techniques for maximizing cash particularly those which rely on elements of chance and de-emphasize individual control. They are also judgmental about the frequent small purchases which are seen as inefficient budgeting practices. The high frequency of snacking and street eating instead of regular domestic meals is seen as harmful socially, nutritionally and financially. The housing conditions of the poor which provide little facility for cooking or storage, the nature of the time-consuming occupations of vending, messenger carrying and scavenging engaged in by various members of the household and the unreliable sources of income on a daily basis make these practices rational and necessary. This hand-to-mouth existence is eloquently described by the ragpicker de Jesus in her diary.

The various techniques developed for the mobilization of limited resources can be viewed in a twofold manner. There are those responses which are so constrained by the situation that the behavior patterns appear to be forced, allowing no alternatives, for example, small, infrequent purchases of food and the use of usurers in extreme circumstances. There are also responses which can be viewed more as if they were chosen from a series of alternatives, for example, pooling mechanisms and pawning.[25]

Consumption Patterns

The consumption patterns of those in poverty are obviously related to the low levels of cash available to the individual or household unit. Basic items such as shelter, food, clothing, services (health, education, transportation and recreation) are normally part of the budgetary requirements of such units. However, there are variations depending on the region under discussion. Where squatting or street sleeping is widespread, housing costs may be nonexistent. Food seems to be a basic expense in all areas of the world although even this item may vary depending upon begging and scavenging. All other expenditures may be kept to a minimum, for instance, by walking to avoid transportation costs and using patent medicines instead of medical practitioners. The recreational activities of the poor are also kept to a minimum. A more precise view of actual consumption patterns can be obtained from some specific examples of household budgets (see Table 1, pp. 166–167).

Some marked differences in the expenditure habits of the "wealthier" slum-dwelling families and the poorer ones can be seen in the comparison of the family units from Hong Kong. Such items as life insurance and transportation are not found in the poorer family budgets. Life insurance can be viewed as investment capital and is only found in the budgets of the more affluent families. It should also be noted that any possibility of additional forms of saving are absent in the poorer households since they either spend their total income or else overspend their income and must borrow.

Wagatsuma and De Vos present the following budget data for a household in a special Japanese community (a slum of former outcasts):

A widow, with one daughter of school age, is 41 years old, is registered for government labor for the unemployed, and receives from this 6,500 yen monthly (about $18). Each month rice costs her 1,400 yen and other food 1,500 yen (a total of less than $10 a month); housing 1,000; her child's education, 500 yen; and allowance, 300 yen. She has for miscellaneous use per month a residue of 1,800 yen—approximately $5.[26]

A somewhat different view of the consumption patterns of the poor can be obtained from an analysis of their material possessions. Lewis is one of the few anthropologists to have taken the trouble and devoted the time necessary to establish a total inventory of the material possessions of a group of households living in a tenement in Mexico City. The fourteen households own goods valued at $4,730, or $338 per household. The poorest household owned goods valued at $119, while the "wealthiest" owned goods valued at $937. Lewis notes the high proportion of goods which are obtained on a second-hand basis. This is particularly true for household furnishings which are purchased from neighbors and relatives.

Table 1. Contrasting Monthly Household Budgets for "Poor" and "Wealthy" Slum Dwellers in Hong Kong

POOR FAMILY—WIDOW AND THREE CHILDREN

INCOME		EXPENDITURE	
Source	*Amount (H.K.$)*	*Source*	*Amount (H.K.$)*
Mother[1]	30	Rent	10
Charities[2]	20	Rice	10
		Other Food	5
		School[3]	17
		Capital Expenses	8
Total	50	Total	50[4]

[1] Mother works by taking in ironing
[2] Receives payments from local settlement house
[3] All members of the sample had school expenses because the sample was derived from school roles
[4] Capital expenses were for charcoal for her iron. No expenditure on cooked food (some provided by Social Welfare Department, cooking fuel (gathered from scrap wood), clothing (obtained second-hand from settlement house), or medicine (received treatment at local clinic)

POOR FAMILY—HUSBAND, WIFE AND THREE CHILDREN

INCOME		EXPENDITURE	
Source	*Amount (H.K.$)*	*Source*	*Amount (H.K.$)*
Main Earner[1]	120	Rent[3]	25
Other[2]	30	Rice	35
		Other Food	85[4]
		Fuel	8
		Electricity	5.50
		Water	2.70
		Clothing	4
		School	45.50
		Pocket Money	9
		Medical	2
		Cigarettes	6
Total[5]	150	Total	227.70

[1] Father works at miscellaneous repair jobs
[2] Mother makes paper bags at $1 per 1,000 bags
[3] Rent is for 6' x 7' cubicle
[4] Researchers tended to question this expenditure
[5] Mother admits that she frequently has to borrow $20 to 30 from neighbors

WEALTHIER FAMILY—HUSBAND, WIFE AND FIVE CHILDREN

INCOME		EXPENDITURE	
Source	*Amount (H.K.$)*	*Source*	*Amount (H.K.$)*
Main Earner[1]	420	Rent[3]	50
Others[2]	120	Rice	40
		Other Food	96
		Cooked Food	75
		Fuel	20
		Clothing	10
		School	88
		Medical[4]	0
		Transportation	12
		Pocket Money	15
		Life Insurance	23
		Entertainment	30
		Moon Cake *ooi*	3
		Daughter's expenses[5]	100
Total	540	Total	522

[1] Husband is a government worker
[2] Daughter is a tutor
[3] Total rent of $150 but part of apartment was sublet for $100. Family occupied one bedroom and one sitting room and obviously shared the kitchen facilities
[4] Medical services were provided free since husband was a government employee
[5] Daughter who worked as a tutor had expenses for job and entertainment which she received separately

When the goods owned by the poorest and "wealthiest" households are compared (Tables 2 and 3), a striking difference in ownership patterns can be seen. The poorest households not only own religious objects which constitute a much higher proportion of their total possessions, but these objects have a cash value which is considerably in excess of the corresponding objects owned by the "wealthiest" households. Another difference which might be expected is that furniture and house furnishings (including television sets owned by the "wealthiest") represent a much higher proportion of the possessions of the "wealthier" poor than the poorer poor. Still another major difference is the ownership of toys by the "wealthier" families and their total absence in the inventories of the poorest households.[27]

In Pauw's study of the second generation residents of East London in South Africa, analysis is also made of the material possessions of

Table 2. Percentage Distribution of Material Possessions
Owned by Fourteen Mexico City *Vecindad* Households

Possessions	Dollar Value	Percent of Total
Furniture	1468	31.0
Personal Clothing	1357	28.7
Tools	337	7.1
Household Equipment	313	6.6
Bedclothing	312	6.6
Kitchen Equipment	295	6.2
Religious Objects	211	4.5
Personal Adornment	139	2.9
Toys	134	2.8
Household Decorations	124	2.6
Animals	17	0.4
Plants	12	0.3
Medicine	12	0.3
Total	4731	100.0

Source: Based on Oscar Lewis, "The Possessions of the Poor," *Scientific American,* vol. 221, 1969, pp. 116–17.

the poorer and wealthier families and a typology of hierarchical consumption patterns is constructed.[28]

One important budgetary item is food. Diet is characterized by a high starch content and frequent ingestion of small quantities of food of poor quality. When food is produced by those in poverty through ownership of small animals (for example, chickens), the market value of the items produced is usually so high that the foods are sold to produce cash. When eggs and meat are sold, the proceeds are used for the purchase of larger quantities of poorer quality food as in the case of Jesus Sanchez and his pig-raising activities. Sometimes urban animal husbandry is used as a direct food input. Once again, differences in cultural style are found in each area. Food preferences are an area of cultural conservatism and anthropologists have long noted that people are reluctant to change their eating habits by adopting new foods. Food taboos are tenacious as well. Therefore it should not surprise us that the poor have a diet which is a modified version of the general dietary pattern of the society in which they live or have come from and are reluctant to tap new sources in their environment (for example, insects, rodents and

Table 3.   Percentage Distribution of Material Possessions Owned by Two "Wealthiest" and Two "Poorest" Households in a Mexico City *Vecindad*

Possessions	Two "Wealthiest" Households		Two "Poorest" Households	
	Dollar Value	Percent of Total	Dollar Value	Percent of Total
Furniture	635	44.3	37	15.4
Personal Clothing	222	15.5	52	21.6
Tools	207	14.4	6	2.5
Household Equipment	44	3.1	19	7.9
Bedclothing	81	5.6	25	10.4
Kitchen Equipment	43	3.0	18	7.5
Religious Objects	24	1.7	67	27.9
Personal Adornment	57	4.0	3	1.3
Toys	89	6.2	0	0.0
Household Decorations	27	1.9	10	4.2
Animals, plants	2	0.2	1	0.4
Medicine	3	0.2	2	0.8
Total	1434	100.1	240	99.9

Source: Based on Oscar Lewis, "The Possessions of the Poor," *Scientific American*, vol. 221, 1969, p. 118.

other high protein sources). The Japanese woman whose budget is described above, cooks 700 calories of rice and another 700 of gruel each morning. Her daughter eats half the rice for breakfast and half for lunch. The mother eats no breakfast and half the gruel for lunch. For dinner they share the remaining gruel and a side dish costing $0.10.[29] Whiteford describes the diet of the lower class in Queretaro, Mexico and Popayán, Colombia as much simpler than that of the upper class and almost devoid of meat, milk, cheese, coffee and vegetables.[30]

As we have mentioned before, much of the clothing of the materially deprived is second-hand and is acquired by cheap purchase or donation. As Whiteford points out in his description of the lowest segment of the lower class in two Latin American cities, if clothing appeared new or of current style, ". . . it was always safe to surmise that it was a gift from a patron, employer or charity." [31]

The housing of the poor is usually located in what is defined as a slum. There is little space per person (relative to the rest of the society), poor construction techniques and poor building materials are used. The settlement pattern is irregular and a lack of decoration, public service and private facilities (such as water, plumbing, sewage, electricity and paved streets) are characteristic. Frequently these conditions are linked to high rentals (relative to value) or threats of eviction.

Slums are to be found in all urban centers regardless of the degree of modernization. As Abrams has suggested, one of the most neglected areas in the modernization process is that of housing and it is such neglect which has led to the maintenance of slum communities.[32] This neglect can be traced to the low-profit margin provided by the low-income residential housing market. Based upon the available data, there appear to be three major types of physically substandard housing areas. These are the inner-city slum, the squatter settlement and the scattered substandard hovel. Inner-city slums are usually older residential or commercial sites which have deteriorated and have been converted into high density residential areas. Those living there are tenants not owners. Examples of this type are the *vecindades* in Mexico City described by Lewis, the *callejones* and *quintas* in the Andes, the *bustees* of Calcutta and Delhi, and the shophouse cubicles in Singapore. All such housing is characterized by extremely high-density population and lack of facilities such as plumbing and sewage. The examples found in Singapore, Hong Kong and Japan suggest the upper limit of density which can be found in urban dwellings. In a cubicle comprising little more than bedspace, a family of five or more can be found cooking, eating and sleeping. Sometimes upper and lower berths arranged in stairwells are rented as well.

There is a qualitative hierarchy even in slum housing. Lewis contrasts two *vecindades* in Mexico City indicating significant differences in the quality of building materials, structure, size of units, lighting, and so on. Consuela Sanchez also discusses the relative ranking of the inner-city slums with which she is familiar.[33] Patch says that in Lima, the *quinta* (a collective unit providing cooperative use of patio facilities), which is frequently constructed of brick and cement, is considered superior to the *callejon* (similar structures but frequently constructed of inferior adobe and earthen floors, and in poor repair).[34]

One particular form of substandard housing, not extensively found in the West, is the squatter settlement. Squatters are those who take over land to which they have no legal right. Shanty dwellings are built with cast-off materials such as scrap lumber, tin, cardboard, or straw matting. Although squatters are defined as "illegal" residents taking over public or private land, they frequently legitimize their rights to the land by petitioning the government or making nominal payments.

If security is established, residents tend to improve their houses and make them more permanent. They also obtain some municipal services such as water, electricity and sewage. After some time, housing can no longer be considered substandard and it is difficult for the observer to distinguish between a squatter settlement and any other section of the city. Some residents pay rent to the original squatter who now becomes a landlord. Squatters' rights are frequently sold to others. The impact of this opportunity for minimal cost housing on possibilities for upward mobility cannot be overestimated. Nelson cites this as a major difference in the contemporary transition (as compared to the West).[35]

There are other types of squatter dwellings which are not located in communities but are interspersed throughout the city. Aside from noting their existence, particularly in the case of street sleepers in India, no research has been done among these people. Thus we find references to "hovels" built alongside of modern hotels, along rivers, near golf courses, in old forts, parks and even on top of luxury apartment houses (as the rooftop dwellers in Lima (*azoteas*) and in Hong Kong).[36]

Furnishings in slum homes are frequently purchased second-hand. Decorations are surprisingly similar throughout the world. Lewis mentions the ubiquitous presence of family photographs, calendars and religious pictures as decor (in contrast to the austere use of home altars and religious symbols in the peasant village). Pauw's descriptions of South African homes are very similar, including the reliance on photographs and calendars.[37] Kitchen facilities in the home are minimal and frequently cooking and storage appliances are portable.

It should also be observed that some occupational categories of marginal careers lead to the individual spending some time attached to a non-poor household as in the case of domestics or watchmen who sleep where they work. Since careers are fluctuating, however, it is likely that these individuals have more or less permanent ties with households in substandard housing areas.

The consumption patterns relating to the purchase of medical and legal services, recreation and transportation differ from those of the larger society in both the frequency of use and the quality of services. There is a tendency to generate a separate body of quasi-specialists to perform medical, legal and entertainment functions. Thus, native curers, legal touts and less efficient transportation facilities are invented or perpetuated from an earlier tradition to serve the poor.

Inexpensive recreational activities such as the widespread use of pinball machines, cheap cinema, listening to the radio or paying to watch television in the home of an entertainment entrepreneur are frequently mentioned. Whiteford describes the minimal cost of such activities in two cities in Latin America and contrasts such patterns to those of the upper lower class whose recreational activities require a larger cash outlay.

The Formation of Basic Social Units

Those who are materially deprived by reason of their marginal occupations differ somewhat from the dominant classes in their basic social structure as demonstrated by patterns of sexual unions, marriage, household organization, child rearing and social networks. Some of the specific social traits can be said to be adaptations to the general forces of modernization and thus are distributed among all class segments of the population. For instance, the changing role of women, an effect of modernization, independently affects some of these patterns. However, they also seem to be specifically adaptive to the conditions of material deprivation and consequently will occur more frequently here than among the new bureaucratic, working and professional classes. These forms are also given less normative disapproval by the materially deprived and become neutrally valued rather than negatively valued behavioral alternatives. People whose experience paths or careers have differed from those locked into marginal occupations (for example, there are those who retain traditional aspirations or move upward) will also have had direct experience with the forms characteristic of the materially deprived through observing members of their own social networks. However, those enmeshed in cyclical marginal occupations tend to develop even more accepting attitudes toward these forms.

THE FUNCTIONS OF MARRIAGE AND THE FAMILY

If we examine the traits frequently found among the materially deprived against the background of the social scientists' approach to the functions of marriage and the family, we can see why the movement away from traditional forms can be considered a rational and coping response for the poor.

There seems to be general agreement that transitory and consensual unions as well as female-based households are associated with material deprivation. A consensual union involves marriage based on the mutual consent of the cohabiting pair without legal or ceremonial aspects. Such marriages are recognized by the members of the communities in which they are frequent and children of such unions are recognized as legitimate. Marriage and consensual union are primarily based upon individual choice among the materially deprived. As such, the union is not primarily viewed as the amalgamation of different kin groups which become related through marriage ties. This kin group amalgamation is one of the important functions of marriage in most societies. It seems to be somewhat less important to the urban poor.

In relation to family bonds usually created by marriage, in most societies there is an exchange of goods and property during courtship and at the time of marriage, such as the dowry in traditional European societies. These exchanges symbolize family unions and promote the stability of marriage, since contributing relatives have an economic stake in preserving the union. Among the urban poor, such economic exchanges occur less frequently.

The traditional economic functions of marriage are not as important to the materially deprived as they are for other sectors of society. This is largely because of the poor economic prospects of the male and the corresponding fact that the male is not economically indispensable in the family. If we compare industrial to pre-industrial societies, we see that the division of labor based upon sex is not as important a factor in the former. In non-industrial societies generally, men provide raw materials through hunting or agriculture. Women also provide some raw materials through food collecting and gardening. However, they also play an indispensable role in processing the materials provided for them by men. This specific division of labor makes it almost impossible for an adult male to survive without a female or a female to survive without a male and consequently marriage forms an important economic unit. In contemporary industrial societies, a man can survive economically without a woman and vice versa. This is primarily because processed goods and services can be purchased for cash by both men and women. What we are saying, in effect, is that in an industrial society, in economic terms cash is more important than a mate. Perhaps this would be most explicitly realized by those enmeshed in marginal occupations where the male's ability to provide cash is extremely limited.[38]

We have just suggested that two major traditional functions of the family, that is, amalgamation of kin groups and economic cooperation based on a division of labor, are not very important for the urban poor. It is generally recognized that another function of marriage, sexual gratification, can and frequently does take place outside of the marriage unit. In many societies, sexual experience before marriage is expected and sexual access to non-mates after marriage is permitted and sanctioned between particular individuals. Thus we find in some societies that a woman is "lent" by her husband to his brother, best friend or guest. For the urban poor, a pattern of premarital and extra-marital sexual gratification is also found. However, if we are to accept the data on contemporary sexual behavior in the United States this is common to all classes of society. The difference stems from the fact that such behavior is more public among the poor than among the dominant class.

What is perhaps more unique about the urban industrial poor when compared to other classes of society is the relative lack of concern with the legitimacy of offspring. An anthropological perspective on the question of legitimacy of offspring would indicate that where inheritance of property or totemistic identity and the conferral of status as a result of birth are important, great significance is placed upon the recognition of offspring as legitimate offshoots of a family unit.[39] For those in marginal occupations, who have neither property nor status, legitimacy is not of central concern. In other segments of an acquisitive industrial society, the family is still the basic unit of wealth, property and status conferral and this is one of the main reasons for its perpetuation among the dominant classes where the economic and kin group amalgamation functions are also attenuated.

Socialization and the care of children, particularly at an early age still remain concerns of the family in urban poverty circumstances. However, there is no firm evidence that the absence or presence of a male who is the biological father of the child seriously affects socialization. Anthropologists know of many societies in which the significant adult male in a child's life is *not* the biological father. Frequently male relatives of the mother play an important role in the socialization of her offspring. Furthermore, a resident mate who is not the father of a child is usually ascribed certain obligations to the children and frequently the non-resident father himself performs certain duties. Since the major relationship in the family unit is the mother–child bond, the ephemeral nature of the male's influence is not as significant as it might be in a unit where he is expected to play a major role.

The impact of the mother–child role and its importance in the de-prived setting can be seen in the expressive culture of the urban poor, that is, in their literature, music and art. In a number of studies, the grief displayed by adults over the deaths of their mothers is one of the most striking displays of affect.[40] Another piece of evidence indicating the differential relationship of adult males and females to children would be the degree of responsibility generally recognized. Males who abandon their offspring do receive relatively little negative sanction while females who do so become objects of gossip and other sanctions.

One typical family unit consists of a woman, her transitory mate and her children. Complementing this pattern is the development of household patterns for single men not permanently tied to mother–child household units. Sometimes the woman's parents reside with the woman and child. Where this is the case, it is usually only the mother of the woman who is present since the male mates of the mother are, like the mate of the central female figure, transient. Sometimes, sisters and their offspring also reside together during periods when they are not partners to consensual unions. Significantly, most households in a slum community at a given point in time, probably contain units with women, mates and offspring. However, if one follows a given household through time, one might see a series of consensual unions alternating with periods of time when the woman and her offspring reside alone or in households with the woman's mother or sisters and their offspring.

We have attempted to show in this discussion that some of the traditional functions of marriage and the family play a smaller part in an industrial society and supposedly an even smaller part for the poverty segment in such a society. The emergent patterns of marriage and the family for those in marginal occupations would be particularly adaptive to the social and economic conditions they live in.

A great deal has been said about the instability of marriage among the poor. Frequently the variant forms of marriage and household patterns developed by those in poverty are viewed negatively by observers and are thought to be indications of disorganization and cultural deterioration. The households are viewed as "weak" units, "broken homes," and a poor milieu for the socialization of adequate social actors. Illegitimacy is seen as a widespread evil. However, we see these forms as alternatives providing adaptive flexibility rather than instability. From both the man's and the woman's point of view, flexibility in marriage is desirable. The man does not want the financial responsibility of children. Since she *does* have financial responsibility, if it should present itself, the woman wants to be able to take advantage of a better economic opportunity. Such opportunity may be in the form of a mate with a higher income or an income opportunity for herself such as domestic service or prostitution. In addition, marriage is not only avoided because of the customary initial economic costs, such as gift exchanges mentioned above and the cost of the usual celebration which accompanies a formal ceremony in most societies, but also because of the costs of severing the relationship. In Catholic countries, formal dissolution of marriage is practically impossible. In other systems, divorce is a very costly affair. It is much easier not to marry in the legal sense, than to try to dissolve a marriage once it has taken place. Furthermore, in the eyes of the community, the offspring of these unions are legitimate. The dominant society's legal definition is of less importance when no property or status is transmitted. Thus, consensual unions are an adaptive solution. However, although we might find a high proportion of consensual unions which are not negatively sanctioned, it might be true that most people still prefer family units based on dominant norms which emphasize formal marriage.

MARRIAGE AND CONSENSUAL UNIONS

One of the difficulties in obtaining data on marriage patterns is pointed out by Gonzalez in her attempt to assess the frequency of consensual unions. She notes the tendency for investigators in Africa to record only those marriages which are formed in civil or church ceremonies or those ceremonialized according to native custom. In this way, they ignore a type of consensual union which is not ceremonialized in these formal ways, but is recognized as legitimate by the Africans in cities.[41] Freedman has also noted the development of several non-traditional, non-ceremonial types of marriage in Singapore which dispense with go-betweens and formal ceremonies, but it is doubtful whether many social surveys take into account these non-legal forms.[42] Thus we frequently find that non-legal marriages accepted by a community are not recorded as marriages by investigators or, conversely, that investigators accept the informant's simple statement that he or she is married or widowed without discovering the nature of the bond.

For much of Africa, bride price, usually in the form of cattle, was an essential component of marriage signifying the amalgamation of kin groups. Through the gift of cattle, given by the groom's family to the bride's family, the ties between the two sets of kin were emphasized. In twentieth-century Africa, cash has largely replaced cattle in the bride price. Where cash is in short supply, alternative marriage forms have either taken the place of the bride price, or have allowed for payment to be deferred until enough cash has been saved. In cases of deferred bride price, before bride price is paid, the commitment of the couple to the groom's family is minimal whereas, traditionally it has been important. Interaction and mutual aid activities with the groom's kin are restricted. The marriage also tends to be unstable and may dissolve at any time. Fathers do not gain rights to their offspring as they did when bride price was paid. Instead, these rights belong to the mothers, who retain the children if the marriage ties are severed. For patrilineal societies, this emerging pattern is the direct reverse of traditional patterns.[43]

In Lagos, the wedding ceremony has become a very elaborate affair, a form of conspicuous consumption.[44] In many cases, ceremonial costs far exceed the bride price and this often leads to an avoidance of ceremonial marriage. Southall points out that many of the Bantu groups in Kampala, in which the traditional gift exchanges have not taken place, are characterized by unstable marriages.[45] However, there has been no attempt to correlate these practices with low and sporadic income sources.

In a wider world context, the desire and necessity of avoiding cash gifts or costly ceremonies lead to consensual unions. In the Doya-Gai community in Tokyo, a significant proportion of marriages are classified as "illegal." [46] In other slum communities of Japan, a predominant form of marriage is referred to as "unregistered common-law marriage." [47] Taira refers to unions in a ragpickers community in Tokyo as consensual.[48] Peattie points out that in the Venezuelan slum community she observed, church and civil marriages are rare.[49] Pearse indicates that "common-law" unions were most frequent in the favela he studied in Rio de Janeiro.[50] Roberts notes that 87 percent of the unions of urban born residents in one shanty town were consensual.[51] Whiteford also points out that the consensual union is frequent in the lower-lower class (as opposed to the upper-lower) in two communities he studied, but that people were recognized as "married." He makes a special point of the fact that this frequently occurred to avoid the costs of traditional marriage.[52] De Jesus states that most of the women in the favela are married. However, at other times, she indicates that such unions frequently break down and the women "remarry." [53] Phillips notes that in the city of Witwatersrand in South Africa, most marriages are irregular unions with few partners able to produce certificates.[54] Verster found that 17 percent of the limited number of households which were male-headed in a Johannesburg slum were headed by a couple "just living together" and that a much larger number were concealing such an arrangement from the investigator (but not the neighbors).[55] Not only are consensual unions frequent, but there are many references to their acceptability within the norms of the poverty groups although formal marriage might still be the ideal.[56]

A corollary to the increase in consensual unions and the avoidance of traditional ceremonies is the growth of the individually contracted marriage with no family participation. Thus, the kin group or family is not involved in the formation of the union. This increases the tendency to marital instability, since there is little family pressure on the pair to stay together. Whiteford notes that in the lower-lower class in contrast to other classes, there were many cases of girls who had run off to marry without parental consent.[57] Marris notes that four-fifths of his sample in central Lagos were married to spouses they had chosen themselves without parental intervention.[58] The new marriage forms in Singapore tend to dispense with go-betweens.[59] While Whiteford's data are the only set that correlates this trend with class, we assume that the degree to which marriage is left to individual choice is higher in the real poverty segment.

A related pattern of mating behavior which is not marriage and does not serve to legitimize kin is the temporary or sporadic mating union. This form does have an effect on household and family structure. It differs from consensual unions in that the male may not reside with the female at all or may reside with her for a very short time and neither party views this union as permanent. Obviously, it is difficult in many cases where the male resides in the household, to distinguish between those temporary liaisons and true consensual unions. These two forms are not mutually exclusive since it is quite possible for a temporary liaison to become a consensual union. Textor refers to the frequent temporary liaisons engaged in by the pedicab drivers he studied in Bangkok.[60] In Japanese slums, it is stated by De Vos that "casual liaisons" are common.[61] Hunter notes that in East London, South Africa, there is what she calls a large class of "semi-prostitutes" or concubines made up of deserted or deserting wives, unmarried mothers and widows.[62] She refers to these women as "semi-prostitutes" because their lovers provide them with presents or temporary contributions to household expenses. Rather than confuse this pattern with professional prostitution which is usually defined as involving merely a commercial transaction and no affect or continuity,[63] we consider that these unions conform to our notion of sporadic mating unions. Verster, in her analysis of a "coloured" slum outside Johannesburg makes the point that sex and procreation seem to be increasingly divorced from marriage and family.

Sex rights in marriage are not precisely defined and maintained and conjugal bonds are viewed as dispensable.[64]

Even though these references do not include discussions of the nature of the marriage ceremony, the involvement of kin groups in the union, and so on, they are probably all referring to individually contracted consensual unions or sporadic mating unions. The fact that these unions may be viewed as within the approved normative structure of the group is only pointed out infrequently as in Rodman's work in Trinidad[65] and in the ethnographic study of a Japanese slum where it is stated that "a wife may leave her home to join another man without incurring negative sanctions."[66]

While social scientists have viewed these forms as promoting instability, informants' statements seem to indicate that such forms are viewed as providing flexibility—from both the male or female point of view— and in both cases are strongly affected by economic considerations. From the woman's point of view we have the following example. When de Jesus was asked, "Where does your husband work?," she said, "I don't have one, I don't want one." Her view of the role of men in the family can be seen in the statement about how hard the women in the favela have to work while their husbands ". . . remain home under the blankets. Some because they can't find jobs, others because they are sick, others because they are drunk."[67] Peattie indicates that the women she interviewed frequently commented that church weddings were undesirable since they made separation difficult in a situation where separations were frequently desirable, from the rational, economic point of view.[68] Marris notes the frequency of failed marriages in Lagos and lists financial reasons in many cases. One wife had deserted her husband when he lost his job and one man in financial trouble deserted two polygamous wives whom he left "to feed themselves."[69] Manuel Sanchez clearly states his perception of the economic factors of marriage and the consequences for the poor:

There is also the matter of being poor. If one begins to examine what a marriage comes to, a poor man realizes he doesn't have enough money for a wedding. Then he decides to live this way, without it, see? He just takes the woman, the way I did with Paula. Besides, a poor man has nothing to leave his children so there is no need to protect them legally. If I had a million pesos, or a house, or a bank account or some material goods, I would have a civil marriage right away to legalize my children as my legitimate heirs. But people in my class have nothing. That is why I say,

"As long as *I* know these are my children, I don't care what the world thinks." . . . And the majority of women here don't expect weddings; even they believe that the sweetheart leads a better life than the wife.[70]

Thus, from both the male and female point of view, marital instability can frequently be viewed as economically rational behavior when women have independent access to cash and males are in marginal positions.

Some of the anti-marriage tendencies may be found in all classes of a modernizing society. However, they are strongest among those in poverty. Certainly, consensual unions and publicly recognized temporary liaisons are not characteristic of the dominant classes. However, it is interesting to note that middle class students in the United States are presently making unions which resemble sporadic mating and consensual unions. In such cases, the motivations appear to be perceived psychological gratification rather than economic benefits. What will happen to this pattern as children are born and the problems of status and property conferral are confronted is still open to question.

A factor which may reinforce the tendency toward temporary or consensual unions among the marginally employed is government policy. Welfare systems in which unemployed, able-bodied men are not eligible for assistance are generally considered to reinforce the pattern of marital instability. Not only is this true in the United States, but parallel examples can be found elsewhere. In Japan, where public work programs have been instituted to help the unemployed, no more than one member of a family unit is eligible for such work. There is evidence that in many cases, husbands divorce their spouses and physically move out of the household while they continue to support the family. This enables both adults to gain government-provided employment.[71] In South Africa, labor laws force women and children to reside separately from male workers, and this frequently results in marriage severance or the establishment of temporary liaisons.[72]

The economic factors in class differences involve not only the scarcity of cash resources for ceremonies, gift exchanges and dissolution or the lack of property which decreases family interest and intervention, but the difficulties of securing sufficient and steady cash resources for the maintenance of the household unit. With the growing possibility of female employment in begging, petty trade, domestic service and prostitution, the non-working male is a household liability. Much of the discussion of the nature of the female-based household in the Caribbean emphasizes this point.[73]

THE MOTHER-CHILD BOND

One of the most significant factors related to poverty household units is the comparatively greater emphasis placed on the mother-child bond in relation to the other bonds (father-child, sibling, and ties to other related and unrelated co-residents). This emphasis contrasts with that in both the dominant class in the urban society and the traditional agrarian household. In the modern household in which the nuclear family is largely an affective and recreational unit, the emotional bonds extend to other ties. In the traditional family, which served important economic and social control functions, even if the father did not have a warm spontaneous relationship with the child he had an important authority role.[74] However, both Pearse and Peattie note a tremendous emphasis on the mother-child bond in their respective communities.[75] Verster notes the decline in the importance of the husband-father role in the Johannesburg slum in which she worked.[76] With the increasing instability of marital bonds, a larger number of household units will consist of a "single parent" and children. However, in spite of traditional notions of rights to offspring, there is a tendency for the mother to retain control of the children rather than the father or father's female relatives. Even in those societies where children were formerly viewed as members of the father's kin group this tendency occurs. Thus in Lagos, where children are living with only one of the parents, despite the patrilineal tradition of many groups, twice as many children are residing with their mothers as are residing with their fathers.[77] In Kampala, where Ganda women constitute the major segment of the female population, they almost invariably retain control of the children.[78] Again, in the once strongly patrilineal Chinese communities in Hong Kong and Singapore, where mother and father do not live together, children remain with the mother. The mother's obligation to children is stronger than the father's as indicated by the attitude of slum dwellers in Venezuela that "a father should care for his children, but a mother *has to* care for them." [79] In addition, the child's obligation to the mother later in life is intensified. This is also true in Lagos where women who used to fall back on their husband's kin in old age no longer relate to these relatives but rely on their children.[80]

HOUSEHOLDS

The frequency of matrifocal (female-based) household units has often been noted among the materially deprived. Obviously this is related to the more flexible marital arrangements and the mother-child bond previously discussed. In addition, we have previously noted the tendency by respondents to reply to a question regarding marriage that the co-habiting unit is a married one. A counter-tendency which we have also noted is to report the absence of a male adult in those societies where welfare and charity are given only to those families in which no adult male is reportedly present. All of this simply means that statistics describing the frequency of female-centered household units must be carefully evaluated.

Another factor which will distort the view of such households relates to the time dimension. In all societies, households of like individuals move through phases. Many households now including a male, at other points in time would have been or will be female-based. If we find a large proportion of individuals who have directly experienced such households or who, as kinsmen, have been on the periphery, then we assume that the attitude toward these households among people of this class is more accepting than it is among other population segments.

Female-based household units can result from many events; for example, women with offspring from transitory mating unions, or consensual or formal unions which have been dissolved voluntarily, through some enforced migration or from death. Thus mothers may be separated by agreement, abandonment, death or temporary male migration for economic reasons. The distinctions are seldom made in the literature and perhaps they are not important since the household structure and needs are the same in all cases; that is to say, the woman is alone and responsible for the children. As a type, this unit is frequently encountered in the experience of the marginally deprived in their families of orientation, procreation and the families of their kin.

Many such household units are to be found throughout Latin America and the Caribbean. Aside from Lewis's data, Safa notes the high proportion of such household units in Puerto Rico.[81] Peattie discusses the frequency of households made up of mothers and children or mother-child units grouped together in a community in which only 50 percent of the families at that point in time comprised the dominant, stable, nuclear type. The notion here was that the woman "owned" the house and "husbands" attached themselves peripherally for long or short times.[82] Whiteford studied the lower-lower class in two Latin American cities and found that, particularly in Colombia, the predominantly free unions (consensual) were unstable, leaving women alone to support their children.[83] Hammel found a relatively high frequency of such households in a coastal Peruvian slum. He notes the increased solidarity of the matricentric (mother-centered) core in this structure and cites this as a response to marital instability. He particularly notes that, in contrast to the poor rural dweller, the urban man lacks property to tie him to his offspring and he tends to circulate among resident women. [84] Mangin notes that 30 percent of the households in one squatter settlement were made up of mothers and children with "temporary and easily replaceable males." Other squatter settlements have fewer such households because the community tenant councils keep single women out of the community.[85] Gonzalez has done a major review of the distribution of such households in the Caribbean and finds them to be widespread.[86]

When we move to other areas of the world, this particular form of household—made up of a woman and her children—is found, but perhaps less extensively. The frequency of such household units is the subject of current research in Kampala, Uganda.[87] Verster also found that one-fifth of the households in her Johannesburg slum survey were female-headed, and almost half of these were stated to be results of sporadic mating (20 percent) or separation (22 percent). In addition, many of the extended households which included more than one generation contained unmarried or separated daughters and their offspring.[88]

In a later reconsideration of his study of Lagos, Marris states, "So, besides the bourgeois and more or less traditional conceptions of life, there emerges an emancipated household of mother and children, in which the children's fathers play a casual and intermittent role. . . . This kind of household does not seem to face serious social disapproval in Lagos." [89] Such households may also include the mother's mother who had also adopted this pattern. Marris describes one such household as a woman and her daughter and grandchild who make their living by hawking loaves of bread for a few pounds a month.[90] The data on the incidence of consensual unions, marital instability, transitory unions and the emphasis on the mother-child bond implies the development of the female-based household even though direct references to it are few.

Pauw has recently described such household patterns for second-generation urban Bantu households in East London, South Africa.[91] Kay reports a case of an area in urban Tahiti (Papeete) where 46.5 percent of the households in one section contained no complete nuclear family and tended to be dominated by women. (These included separate mother-child units, as in the Venezuelan case.) Such household structures were related to the economic insecurity of males.[92] Belshaw suggests the likely emergence of this pattern in other Pacific towns where urban wage labor has increased in importance since World War II.[93] Calley notes similar households in New South Wales among mixed bloods.[94] It might be asserted that in these instances such unstable marriage patterns and households were products of "deculturation" due to racial discrimination. However, much of the discussion concerning household forms these days is moving in the direction of stressing economic variables and de-emphasizing cultural and historic variables.[95] Hannerz looks at this type of household among blacks in the United States as an adaptive structure for pooling and redistributing resources more efficiently.[96]

As Harris has recently stated:

Like all domestic arrangements, the matrifocal family arises under specific and known material conditions and represents an adaptive achievement that is no more or less "pathological" than any other family form. The conditions in question are (1) males and females lack access to strategic resources, that is they own no significant property; (2) wage labor is available to both males and females; (3) females are paid as much or more than males; (4) male wages are insufficient to provide subsistence for a dependent wife and children.[97]

He goes on to point out that while everyone strives for a traditional or formal union, men sometimes personally prefer temporary unions because they realize their inability to support a family. On the other hand, if the woman has the backing of a "strong matrifocal unit," she may be more resistant to formal marriage since she views the male as a free-loader draining the household income.

The prevalence of consensual unions and transitory liaisons in the Japanese special communities also implies the existence of these forms. Japanese social workers paralleling their American colleagues write articles about the problems of the single-parent (mother) household.[98] In Upper Nankin Street in Singapore, 28 percent of the households (excluding single person households, one-sex households, and multi-generational households) were mother-child households. It is possible too that some of the multi-generational households listed in other categories included several mother-child units. In addition, there was significant correlation between the mother-child household types and the lowest level unskilled occupations in this geographic area (which contained both skilled and unskilled workers).[99]

One area where the existence of sporadic mating, consensual unions and female-based households is infrequently mentioned is the Middle East. As a matter of fact, Gulick states that an "unwed" mother in the Middle East is much more severely sanctioned than in the United States and is thus likely to be forced into prostitution.[100] It is hard to tell whether the lack of data for this area reflects empirical reality or a gap in the information.

ALTERNATIVE PATTERNS OF CHILD CARE

In spite of the importance of the mother-child bond, because of the circumstances of life such as the nature of the mother's work activities, many surrogate child care arrangements are made. One cannot focus exclusively on the mother-child household or the household made up of several mother-child units. In many cases, especially cases in which children disrupt the economic opportunities of the mother, the care of children may be given over by the mother to her own relatives. For prostitutes and domestic servants, the burden of keeping children is particularly onerous (although Peattie does note one case in which a prostitute maintains a houseful of seven children during the day and works in a brothel at night).[101] In Hong Kong, one particular household is noted where the mother is engaged in prostitution and has turned the care of her child over to her mother.[102] In Singapore, Kaye mentions the "coolie-fong," a household in which domestic servants share a room which they use between jobs after they have given the care of their children to their kin.[103] Verster notes the frequency of grandparents raising grandchildren in her Johannesburg slum survey.[104] This pattern of using the female's kin for child care can be either informal and temporary or more formal and permanent adoption. One example of the latter is the Puerto Rican institution of *hijos de crianza* or "children for raising" (that is, children defined as members of the household by virtue of their being raised there, although not born to any member). According to Peattie, the adoption of children by a mother's mother or a mother's sister is frequent in La Laja.[105] Mangin notes one case of a mother "depositing" a daughter with an older daughter for semi-permanent rearing.[106] The Japanese *buraku* (former outcast) community is characterized by frequent adoptions by siblings,[107] and grandparent-grandchild households are frequent in Lagos and Singapore. Some of this data is precise, but the rest merely provide us with potential inferences as to other ways in which females can adapt household structure to poverty conditions and marital impermanence.

MALE HOUSEHOLDS

One important effect of the foregoing on social structure is the new residential patterns for males in systems characterized by household units built on the mother-child bond. In Japan, among the Doya-Gai residents exclusively male units are common.[108] In Singapore, the *kongsi*, a term used for a household of unrelated adults of the same sex, is predominantly male.[109] In a squatter settlement in Buenos Aires, Germani refers to the *convivencia* or households of unrelated males.[110] Calcutta is also characterized by a high frequency of exclusively male households.[111] Textor describes this pattern of male lodgings for the pedicab drivers in Bangkok. Raum describes the frequency of the "common mess" in New London, South Africa. Sometimes male lodgings are concentrated in particular zones as in the market distinct in Lima described by Patch or in the Doya-Gai district in Tokyo described by Caldarola. In other regions, room rentals are found distributed throughout a low-income area. For example, in Port Said and Cairo, many households are found to rent rooms to non-kin male lodgers and such rental income is also frequent in Pauw's description of East London. The existence of such multi-male households or single-male lodging house patterns is not merely to serve ex-partners of unstable marriages and mating unions. In some cases, they are serving males who have left their wives and children in the rural areas while they have migrated temporarily for wage labor. Their commitment to their family in terms of cash contributions and frequent visits is strong. In other cases, the men in these households have not yet married. However, it is likely that a third category would include men who have left wives (either legal or consensual) and children. In any case, where male lodging areas comprise a particular geographic zone a single male lifestyle seems to develop which has certain implications for various aspects of behavior.

Where such single-sex household units are found, some outlet for sexual activity is needed. One such outlet is the use of prostitutes. In Calcutta, Bombay and Lahore, for example, the recent growth of prostitution is marked.[112] Another response to this situation is the establishment of sporadic mating activities such as those previously described. These can lead to offspring who remain in the mother's household. Textor indicates this latter pattern in a study of *Samlormen* (pedicab drivers) in Bangkok. He indicates that many of the men in the pedicab drivers' lodging house have wives and children in the Northeastern provinces of their origin. They visit their families several times a year and return to the village for harvests and ceremonies. They also return for periods of several years and then come back again to the city to raise cash. However, some migrants become committed to wage labor and urban life. Their visits home decrease and there is a marked tendency to cohabit with "informal spouses" in the city. He tells of one driver who has had five "Bangkok" wives and is no longer interested in his village.[113] Mayer refers to the South African men with rural and urban households as the "double-rooted."[114] In India, it is assumed that most male migrants to the cities retain strong ties to their wives and the village. However, we would suggest that if depth studies of the life of these migrants were made, similar patterns of cohabitation might be found.

Another way to satisfy sexual needs is through homosexuality. Although evidence for such activities is lacking in most studies, it is explicitly mentioned in the Doya-Gai in Tokyo.[115]

CHILDHOOD

Cross-cultural studies of the patterns of child-rearing and attitudes toward this stage in the life cycle have shown great diversity. Some societies view the child as a miniature adult, while other societies view childhood as a special status unrelated to the roles of adulthood. In some societies children are encouraged to be independent, while in others they are viewed and treated as dependent. In different societies children are encouraged to be assertive, passive, aggressive, competitive, cooperative, and so forth.

The materially deprived are believed to have developed particular modes of behavior and attitudes toward children. According to Lewis, lack of concern with childhood and rapid initiation into adulthood are characteristic of the urban poor. This is partially reflected in an earlier initiation into sexual activity. Children are not perceived as extremely vulnerable, and therefore to be protected from harsh experiences. One observable indication of this is the large number of children who are abandoned by their parents at an early age and left to care for themselves.

This is in direct contrast to the attitudes toward childhood characteristic of the dominant class in urban industrial society. In part, this may be viewed as a direct response to the requirements of the social system which emphasizes a long period of formal education for the development of skills to place the individual at a high level. Since those in poverty do not acquire these high-level skills, such an emphasis is not needed. An additional factor in the early initiation into adulthood is the lack of available resources. Children who remain children require maintenance. For the middle-class reader of Lewis's *La Vida,* Fernanda's apparent lack of concern for her children, the apparent neglect of them at almost all times unless they were obviously hurt or hungry, the lack of concern with their whereabouts and their coming and going are all indicative. Alternatively, it might be argued that this pattern is an early training for independence rather than neglect. If, at an early age, Fernanda's children do not learn to take care of themselves most of the time, then their chances of survival would be that much lessened. Children are not perceived as vulnerable individuals to be protected while they learn their appropriate roles through formal education, but as future adults who must learn the expected behavior pattern of adults through early experience.

Another way of looking at childhood among the poor is possible if we remember that young children spend much of their time away from home with children of their own age. The house in a slum community is a setting hardly conducive to play activity. It is a place to sleep and eat. The physical environment is such that even young children are anxious to leave the house for long periods of time. Bearing in mind the definition of parental responsibility and the perception of the child as a small adult, we see that the network of a child's street relationships becomes an important element in the formation of attitudes, beliefs and behavioral patterns. This point is frequently made by social scientists in the literature of poverty but it should not be assumed that there is an absence of socialization or the prevalence of deviant learning. After all, in many societies in the world the family is not the only significant agent of socialization.

One result of the early initiation into sex which affects family structure may be the intensive competition between mother and daughter or father and son for sexual partners. In a setting of early initiation to sexual activity, with child-bearing beginning at fifteen or earlier, it is quite possible to find a thirty-year-old woman and her fifteen-year-old daughter seeking male companionship. This could produce strain between the two. An example of this situation is found in the play and film, *A Taste of Honey,* Shelagh Delany's drama set in urban industrial Britain today. In the *Children of Sanchez,* similar competition exists between Jesus Sanchez and his sons.

The Views of the Dominant Classes

As we have seen, it is not so much one household form which is characteristic of the poor, but a range of varying forms all of which differ from the ideal of the dominant class as well as from the traditional rural pattern. What is striking is that all of these variant forms have a widespread distribution among those who are materially deprived. These forms indicate the flexibility of response patterns where cash resources are very limited. As they develop, they become acceptable to the poverty segment although they are still viewed as deviant by the dominant class. Thus Whiteford notes that the elite Ladies of Charity, a lay church group, are giving instruction to the lower-lower class on the importance of legality and stability in marriage.[116] Similarly, social workers in Venezuela and Japan are concerned with "weak family structure" and mother-centered households. In Lagos, Marris tells us of the morality play social workers have staged in the streets telling of the difficulties that follow if one just "takes the girl" without the ceremony.[117]

In stressing the adaptive nature of such marital and household patterns, we are not implying that such structures are not without stress-producing features. Hammel talks about the tensions generated by ambiguity about legitimacy, and so on.[118] However, to some degree, all social units produce strains and tensions.

Cross-Cultural Comparisons

As with all the other adaptive structural traits, the particular cultural tradition in which the poverty group is located will have an effect on the way in which the structural feature develops. In regard to the consensual union, for instance, many effects of cultural tradition and style can be illustrated.

In Latin America and the Caribbean, consensual unions are frequently acceptable forms of marriage in rural tradition. (There is some question as to how long this pattern has existed, and this too seems to be related to economic deprivation.) [119] Thus, the development of this type of union among the urban poor in Latin American and Caribbean cities is not as drastic a contrast to tradition as in other parts of the world. However, the consensual union is just as stable in the rural areas as the formal marriage is there. It becomes less stable under conditions of urban industrial poverty. Furthermore, the consensual union is not approved by the dominant classes in the urban setting, and we suggest that if it increases and/or persists as a norm over time, this increase and/or persistence is likely to be related to economic not historical variables. In a traditional Peruvian village, Hammel observes that there are significantly fewer households of this type than there are in an urban slum.[120] The form does appear to be strengthened by the increasing economic independence of women in the Caribbean.[121]

Africa provides an intriguing example of the way in which traditional forms have been modified in the development of consensual unions. Where polygamy was a preferred form of marriage, now a traditional marriage can be contracted in the rural area with spouse and children remaining there while consensual unions are formed in the city. These latter units are relatively unstable as men abandon their "wives" when they migrate from one city to another in search of cash.[122] For overseas Chinese communities, the traditional institution of concubinage (inferior wives) can be modified to encompass a unit which fits our notion of a short-term consensual union.

Kinship and Networks

As we move away from primary social units, it becomes less possible to generalize about the materially deprived in urban industrial society. This is in part a result of the intervention of many new non-economic variables in the formation of social units and in part a result of great confusion and misunderstanding in the literature.

An area with which we can begin is the nature of the kinship structure in which the household is embedded. On the one hand it is assumed by many writers that the urban poor are somehow more "traditional" in their use of kin than their upwardly mobile counterparts. Thus, they will continue to emphasize the traditions of kinship in social interaction and neglect the formation of more "modern" associations based on neighborhood, workplace, and so on. On the other hand, some analysts assert that since the poor cannot take care of their end of the reciprocal obligations in a kinship relationship, such relationships become weak and tend to rupture easily.

KINSHIP

There are two basic types of kinship systems. In a unilineal kinship system, relationship is traced either through the male line in which case the kin group formed consists of a man, his sons and daughters and his *sons'* children, and so on; or, through the female line, in which case the kin group formed consists of a woman, her sons and daughters and her *daughters'* children. In contrast, a bilateral system like ours is one where kinship is reckoned through both male and female lines. Most of the world's cultures have been characterized by unilineal systems. Where unilineal systems are found, they frequently lead to the formation of bounded kin groups such as lineages or clans which include members of all generations. These groups are usually structured, corporate in nature, and they give the individual a basic source of identity and integration. Bilateral kinship systems do not lend themselves to this kind of kin organization. If any Western reader has had the experience of sending invitations to a wedding or other social occasion, he will appreciate the difficulties of deciding who should and who should not be recognized as key relatives. The presence of a bounded kin group makes this task easier.

As a society industrializes, the highly structured, corporate kin groups tend to break up. This would remove one potential kind of social organization. Such corporate kin groups perhaps disappear earliest in transitional societies among the materially deprived whose careers consist of alternating marginal occupations. It is only in the ethnic enclaves discussed in Chapter 4 that such kin groups are retained. Such enclaves are socially insulated from the influence of urban industrial society. Traditional exchange and sharing institutions are maintained, and an urban standard of living or comfort level is not a relevant aspiration for them.

NETWORKS

In industrial urban areas as a whole, the maintenance of traditional corporate group structures is rare. Instead, an individually *chosen* personal-centered network of people becomes an important social unit. An individual develops reciprocal relationships with many others. An individual's network is a constellation of such reciprocal relations. For the poor, it is especially important to extend one's ties because of the necessity of assuring crisis aid. For women raising children, sources of cash loans are necessary for medical or legal emergencies. Loans of goods and services (such as substitute child care or domestic duties) are also frequently needed. For men, cash loans and services in securing employment form the basis of many reciprocal relationships. Such ties are often defined by a set of mutual obligations, familiarity in terms of address, trust, intimacy and frequent and/or intense interaction.

Individually chosen networks constitute a basic social unit in all classes in urban industrial society. However, for the dominant classes, there are many alternate sources for recruitment to one's network. The social "worlds" in which one operates such as the workplace, occupation, neighborhood, voluntary association and recreation group are important source groups. People live next door to non-related individuals from different ethnic groups who practice different types of occupation. The number of separate "social worlds" of the poor person, however, is restricted by the nature of his unstable career and his lack of resources. Frequently, there is no stable workplace group nor any core of formal voluntary associations from which to select a variety of individuals with which to establish meaningful social relationships. Instead, sources such as kin and neighborhood remain most significant. Kinsmen are therefore still an important source of meaningful ties, probably more so than for the dominant classes. However, obligations are not automatically in effect with a relative unless the individual is selected for the network. Furthermore, ruptures with kinsmen are permissible and frequent. Finally, such kinship ties are different from their traditional counterparts. Often a bilateral extension of kin obligations replaces a unilineal tendency. Relatives by marriage who may have been less important in the traditional system may assume strategic roles. What is perhaps most important is the overlapping of the "social worlds" of kin, neighborhood and workplace. Among the materially deprived especially, one's kinsmen are more apt to be one's neighbors and one's co-workers.

Since mothers and children form a basic household unit, mother's kin become important even in a traditionally patrilineal society. Male kinsmen of the mother and even the kin of a former mate no longer in the household may enter into important reciprocal relationships. Frankel suggests that among the black poor in Philadelphia, while a man may be referred to as a "boy friend" by a woman, his parents are called "mother-in-law" and "father-in-law," and act as grandparents to their son's offspring even when the son no longer resides with the woman.[123]

Thus kinsmen remain important but they do not retain their traditional importance. A blood tie does not automatically create obligations unless validated through recruitment to the network. Not all kin enter the effective network of the individual. Moreover, there are great stresses and strains placed upon kin relationships and they rupture frequently. Plotnicov stresses the tendency for trust to break down between kin who are geographically distant. In contrast to most of the other writers on African migration who stress the retention of ties with the rural area, Plotnicov indicates that the very process of migration dislocates the individual from his kinship network. There are mutual suspicions which emerge. Rural kin suspect that the urban migrant is not sending back enough money to the village, while the migrant feels that the money he sends back, "bush money," is being dissipated. Plotnicov notes that this is a major source of conflict for the poorer migrants who feel acutely that they are trapped between the mutual demands of expensive urban living and the requests made by kinsmen in the village.[124]

In the city, friends and neighbors may take over some of the functions previously reserved for kin. In two African cities Gutkind has shown this basic shift from kin to friends as sources of support for those who are long-term unemployed. He indicates that much of the kinship system is based upon reciprocal obligations. It is quite apparent to the successful migrants that their poorer kinsmen cannot reciprocate favors. It is also apparent to the unemployed individual that his welcome is wearing thin and that he ought to take over responsibility for his own welfare. Such individuals begin associating with friends acquired in the urban setting and use them as sources of welfare and job opportunities. Gutkind notes that the expansion of an unemployed individual's social network beyond his kin allows him to obtain more information about potential work opportunities.[125]

In a Hong Kong slum, although friends, neighbors and relatives are mentioned as sources of loans, a number of individuals stated that they preferred to borrow from friends and neighbors rather than kinsmen because they shared a common way of life and realized the need to lend small amounts to one another. There also is a tendency among the Hong Kong population to retain close ties to those kinsmen who are in the same economic circumstances, frequently residing in close proximity to each other.[126] Lewis notes the same tendency in the study of a *vecindad* (tenement) in Mexico City where many of the families were related to each other.[127] Bryce-Laporte indicates that such kin networks located in one neighborhood are essential in the structure of the San Juan slum he studied and even are transposed with difficulty to public housing projects.[128] Similarly, in a study of a slum community in Manila, many of those interviewed said that they would be unwilling to move out of the community to public housing because they would be moved away from their relatives.[129] Thus, people use both kin and neighbors as sources of aid and support, whether financial or emotional. Kin *of the same socio-economic status* seem to be preferred in many places. Because of strains in the relationships between kin of different economic levels, some movement to non-kin friends and neighbors is noted. Kinsmen and neighbors are often one and the same since kin of similar levels settle near one another.

There is some conflicting evidence which appears to indicate that some of the more economically successful urbanites maintain ties and provide support for their poorer kin in the city. Lewis observes that the poorest families in his Mexico City sample wear only second-hand clothing given them by their relatives.[130] Peattie indicates that many of the poorer households (members unemployed) in her community are being supported by more successful kin and that these obligations are interfering with the upward mobility of the latter.[131] Where there is mobility, we assume that in time the economically successful detach themselves from these obligations. According to Gutkind, this trend is common to all the tribal groups he studied in two African cities. While the trend is consistent, the rate of breakdown varies between tribes.[132] Marris noted that the white-collar workers he interviewed in Lagos (who had left the dense central city area for a suburban housing development) were happy to have left their poorer kinsmen behind so they were not pressured by them.[133]

While neighbors become important sources of aid, the whole neighborhood is never one cohesive social network. People select from among their neighbors those with whom they wish to develop reciprocal material and emotional obligations. For example, Maria de Jesus, who has no kin in the favela in which she lives, has many different kinds of relationships with her neighbors. From an analysis of the patterns of social relationships which Maria has established in her favela, we find several alternative modes.[134] She has a subordinate relationship with some, particularly with those from whom she is consistently borrowing food and money. There is no reciprocity in this relationship and she notes that she never returns these favors. There are others at her own level with whom she has reciprocal relations, they entertain one another

with stories and gossip at the water tap. With some other favela dwellers, Maria has open conflict relations frequently based upon the activities of her children. There are also some neighbors in the favela with
whom there are no relationships at all. It should be obvious that an
individual cannot select all members of his community to be incorporated into his network.

PATRON–CLIENTAGE

People who are superordinate in wealth, power and prestige to the
materially deprived are commonly found in an individual's network.
In these situations, we are dealing with patron–client relationships. The
obligations of the two parties to each other are not the same. The patron
provides material aid or social intervention (with authorities, and so
on) in return for deference and menial services on the part of the
client. Maria de Jesus has several patrons, especially the entrepreneurs
to whom she sells scrap who often extend her credit. It is very common
to find hawkers developing special relationships with their suppliers.
Laborers in small-scale enterprises also can develop a tie with their employer. Such ties are strong in the lives of the *Children of Sanchez*
where almost all the jobs are in small-scale enterprises. However, except
for the tie between Jesus, the father, and his boss, the restaurateur, none
of the other ties are stable nor is the employment itself stable. Manuel
is very perplexed by the reversals in his relationships to his employers
who behave like sponsors one day and fire him the next. Obviously the
transition from the traditional mode of patron–client ties (which in
many ways were quasi-kin relationships) to more commercially oriented
employer–employee relationships has created new strains and tension
points. When such ties are stable, they can be instrumental in changing
the nature of the career. Peattie provides us with the example of Leo-
nardo who was sponsored by a family for whom he worked and later
was sent to school by them so that he became a trained bookkeeper, a
white-collar worker with considerable job and income security. Dietz
also describes the role of a North American social scientist as the patron
of one of his subjects.

In general, the social structure of the urban poor differs from that of
traditional society. In such stable societies, one is an ascribed member
of a corporate group whose members frequently share residential location, occupation and even kin ties as well as a common heritage. The
network of the urban industrial individual includes personally selected

individuals from heterogeneous groups. The difference between the networks of the poor and those of the dominant classes in urban industrial society lies in the restricted arenas from which members are recruited. Ties based on a common occupation or common interests as represented in voluntary associations are less frequent for the poor. On the other hand, kinship and neighborhood remain more significant for the poor than for the dominant groups. Not all kinsmen are members of one's network nor are all neighbors. The trend is toward relationships with kin and neighbors who are also materially deprived. This is partly due to the strains of differential mobility on the demands of reciprocal obligations. Kin who are also neighbors are also preferred because contact does not necessitate the expenditure of time or money.

Integration into the Larger Society

When we move outward from the individually-based social network, we are entering an area of significant independent variables and the relationship between social structure and material deprivation becomes much less obvious. Much has been said by social scientists about the integration of the poor into the larger social system, that is, the urban industrial system, in which they are located. There have been attempts to generalize about the political participation of the poor both in conventional terms (political parties and elections) and in terms of the potential for revolutionary action. Lewis suggested that the non-participation of the poor was the key variable in his "culture of poverty" formulation. Such primacy was unfortunate, for it is in this area that a clearcut relationship between poverty and behavior is lacking. Much of the discussion on this topic has led to a controversy involving diametrically opposed positions. In order to discuss this area of behavioral responses, we shall have to look at both the behavior of the poor and the explanations offered for this behavior.

INSTITUTIONS

Lewis alleges that the poor do not actively participate in the institutions of the larger society, such as financial institutions (banks and investment), educational–cultural institutions (schools, museums, and so on), political institutions (interest groups and party organizations), and organized religion (church). While this generalization is probably valid, the explanations of non-participation in terms of attitudes are not. Many view the lack of patricipation as derived from *apathy, alienation* and *withdrawal* all resulting from a fatalistic feeling of helplessness. Others view this as evidence of active hostility to the larger society, a potentially anti-social force. Still others regard the poor as *anomic,* that is, confused about appropriate behavior and unable to act.

In fact, the reasons for resistance to institutions are many and are usually results of forces generated by the dominant classes rather than the belief structure of the poor. Participation is limited by the lack of material resources, and furthermore, there is a realistic recognition that many institutions, for instance, those related to the judicial system, are designed to control the behavior of the poor. In the case of many membership associations like labor unions, political parties and the like, forced exclusion through formal or informal membership policies can be the most significant reason for "non-participation." Finally, the alternative institutions set up by the materially deprived themselves such as curers, legal touts, worship groups and vigilantes often are preferred and sometimes function more efficiently. In addition, feelings of alienation and/or hostility to bureaucratic institutions are strong among many segments of the non-poor. As Nelson points out, the more successful working-class groups in the developing nations are more likely, through their common work experience, stable contacts and mutual anti-management attitude to develop conscious, anti-establishment political attitudes.[135] The supposed attitudes of the poor used to explain the presumed avoidance behavior are not confined to the poor and, in fact, it may even be incorrect to attribute such attitudes to them as a class.

ORGANIZATION

Another aspect of the non-participation attributed to the poor is their alleged incapacity to organize interest groups via the voluntary association. In this case, empirical evidence can again be mustered to indicate that such a description of behavior has some basis in fact. However, as critics of this particular view have pointed out, there are many community-based organizations which are devoted to community improvement. There are migrants' associations based on region or tribe of origin, mutual aid associations based on pooling resources, recreation groups such as sports clubs and church associations, all of which can be found among low-income populations. The range, form and nature of these organizations are based on the cultural traditions of the region as well as the features of urban life. Thus African associations differ from those of Latin America, and so on. The existence of these groups per se indicates that the poor have a capacity to organize.

Although voluntary organizations can be shown to exist among the materially deprived, thus giving the lie to those who say that the poor have no organizational ability, it is generally agreed by most observers that the membership of such organizations is small and the participation at a low level.

In the literature dealing with overseas Chinese communities, considerable attention is paid to the widespread associational activities found in such communities. However, a study of a Chinese inner-city slum in Singapore showed that only 17 percent of the study population were members of *any* association. In addition, 97 percent of those who belonged had never attended meetings.[136] In spite of the degree of *barriada* organization in Lima, Dietz indicates that most of the members of the community he studied did not know about the existence or aims of the local group, the Fathers of Families El Mariscal.[137] Peattie also notes that while named community organizations exist in La Laja, there was a low level of participation.[138] Whiteford studied slum communities in two Latin American cities. He found only one lower-class neighborhood with a community organization.[139] He also found that while *upper-lower* class segments in the cities occasionally joined church associations, there was virtually no participation on the part of the *lower-lower* class. The American social science literature and Dotson's work in Guadalajara, Mexico also show that membership patterns vary with socio-economic level and that the materially deprived are the least likely to become members of voluntary associations.[140]

We might tentatively accept the proposition that participation and membership in voluntary associations is low. However, we must look at some of the reasons for this. Once again, we would suggest the exclusion of attitudinal or value components such as apathy, hostility and alienation, and focus our attention on structural and functional components. Among the sample of the unemployed in Africa which he studied, Gutkind found that there had been several attempts to organize the unemployed as an interest group. Since this group had a locational focus (the national Employment Exchange), the logistics of organization were simplified. However, the organizations were not successful. The obstacles were *not* the crippling ideology, apathy or hostility of the unemployed, but on the one hand a lack of financial resources and on the other a strong loyalty to ethnic-tribal groups which proved divisive.

The unemployed competed with each other in terms of tribal membership and thus were unable to form a cohesive group.[141] Mangin states that in general organizations among the poor in Latin America will attract participants if they are at all successful in achieving their goals. However, given the nature of the political systems to be found in most of Latin America, this rarely occurs, and the groups lose their pull.[142]

From the studies just described it can be suggested that some of the reasons for non-membership in voluntary associations are the heterogeneity of the materially deprived which introduces a divisive factor, the lack of financial resources which are frequently vital to the membership and maintenance of an organization, and the inability of some of the established organizations to realize their goals. Basic to the functional definition of voluntary groups is the limited nature of the activities and goals of these organizations. Where the specific goals cannot be met because of the constraints placed upon the organization by more powerful segments of the society, membership and participation are meaningless.

Furthermore, Bott, in her discussion of networks in urban-industrial society, has suggested that, for those individuals who have "tightly knit" social networks, formal organizations are not required to reaffirm social ties to provide social norms for the individual and social control for the group. A "tightly knit" network is one which is long-term and intimate and contains a limited number of individuals who are known to each other. This small group is a constant source of reinforcement and solidarity for its members who do not have to have the "do's" and "don't's" listed for them. On the other hand, individuals with "loosely knit" networks need reaffirmation and explication of norms, and thus need formal organization.[143] It is probable that networks among the materially deprived based on limited and overlapping "social worlds" (kin and neighborhood) are more likely to comprise a small mutually known group. Thus, the poor are less reliant on formal associations to preserve norms than are the middle class whose networks are recruited from more diversified sources. It might also be added that even the political goals of the community are often achieved by the informal groups and associations which lack formal titles, rules and structure.

DIFFERENTIATING FACTORS

The attitudes toward the larger society ascribed to the poor, for example, apathy, withdrawal, suspicion, distrust, hostility, and anomie, are

believed to be reactions to the frustrations of relative material deprivation. However, such simplistic generalizations are useless and dangerous. Some further precipitating factors must be responsible for producing the particular and variable responses among the poor. The most
suggestive differentiating variables which seem to warrant further investigation are the nature of one's occupational career, the nature of the
community of residence and the "lifestyle" of one's personal group.
One's career refers to the different paths one may take; either away from
marginal occupations (through upward mobility or a return to tradition), or engagement in cyclical marginal activities. The nature of the
community of residence refers to the significant differences found in the
composition and degree of organization within different types of "slum"
communities. The third variable is the most difficult to describe, but it
refers to certain types of lifestyle groups which seem to emerge in urban
industrial society and are independent of occupation and neighborhood.

We have already discussed the different occupational sequences and
experience paths which are found among those who enter the urban
industrial society at a marginal level. Obviously, the different career
experiences may encourage different attitudes to the larger society and
different political behavior, since the contact with the larger society is
of a different nature for different types. The relationship between these
two factors needs further examination.

THE NATURE OF COMMUNITY

The nature of the urban community where the materially deprived
live has been directly investigated as a variable which affects political
attitudes and behavior. For a long time it has been assumed that slums
could be characterized as having certain social features in common.
Now it appears that slums which are defined by the physical criteria
used in Chapter 4 (in the discussion of housing) are extremely diverse
in social characteristics. Before this point became apparent to social
scientists, low-income communities were described by them as full of
conflict and social pathology on the one hand or having extreme cohesiveness and internal order on the other. Seeing low-income communities as transplanted peasant villages, some noted high rates of gregari-
ousness, gossip and local control.[144] Others claimed that the communities
were extremely disorganized, riddled with conflict and that no means
for control existed. Neighbors would call in outside law enforcement
agencies to resolve conflict.[145] Roach and Gursslin go as far as to

say that the poor do not interact frequently with their own kind.[146]

Often there is disagreement about the nature of community between different observers of the same area. Lloyd Rogler, in his article, "Slums in Latin America," based primarily on his experience in Puerto Rico, emphasizes the conflict and disharmony between neighbors.[147] Lewis's work on the slums of Puerto Rico also emphasized a lack of cohesiveness.[148] On the other hand, Safa has described the slum community she studied in Puerto Rico in almost romantic terms reminiscent of the traditional folk society. She describes a squatter settlement in San Juan, Puerto Rico, as extremely well integrated and characterized by cooperation and mutual aid networks. Old men are fed by their neighbors in return for which they "contribute little or nothing." She views the sharing and mutual aid as a wealth leveling device which she likens to those of the stable, traditional peasant community. Safa says, "Relationships between residents of the shanty town are reciprocal, highly personal and largely non-utilitarian." Informal social control is strong. Adjustment of newcomers is easy. This community is characterized by great differences in the wealth of its inhabitants as are most so-called slums. It seems as if in order to refute the negative beliefs about urban slum life, the author has presented a slightly exaggerated view of harmony and friendliness in the community.[149]

More recently, it has been acknowledged that slums differ in these very characteristics and cannot be generally described.[150] Moreover, the differences are not based on cultural tradition but on other variables. At first, rather gross differentiations along the lines of "slums of hope" and "slums of despair" were made,[151] but it now becomes possible to isolate some of the more significant variables.

One of the most significant variables in differentiating slums relates to the class homogeneity or heterogeneity of the community. Because of the tremendous rate of rural–urban migration in developing nations, the urban housing shortage presents a phenomenal problem. Thus, many slum areas are inhabited by a large number of the non-poor, that is, by people who have moved away from marginal occupations and by others who were born into the lower-middle class. Furthermore, certain inexpensive housing alternatives such as the squatter settlement are used by the upwardly mobile even when there is a choice because non-rent or low rent permits a high degree of saving. A recent example of this process of mobility is the case of a Tokyo slum dweller, Shinsaku Takeda, who was able to move out of a wooden tenement because he won the right to a public housing apartment through a lottery.[152] Ever since they were married, seven years before, the Takedas had lived in a single room measuring nine feet by nine feet. For this room they were paying $20 a month out of a combined income of $350 per month, $70 of which comes from Mrs. Takeda's sewing activities. From their one-room cubicle which housed Mr. and Mrs. Takeda and their two children, came a television set, a washing machine, a small refrigerator, a chest of drawers, a toy automobile big enough for the six-year-old son, a sewing machine, and chest after chest of clothes. It should be obvious that the Takeda family stayed in their single room while accumulating goods. It is also probable that they would still be there if they had not been fortunate enough to win the public housing lottery since rents which have been high in Tokyo are continuing to increase rapidly. This means that an area which is physically defined as a slum can contain a heterogeneous mix of social classes and the impact of class heterogeneity on political behavior is great. Households with marginal income located in a slum with a high proportion of non-poor or upwardly mobile inhabitants may become politically socialized by the more experienced groups.

The greater experience of the non-poor slum dweller is based upon his command of financial resources, his social ties with potentially powerful elites and the likelihood of his having learned the basic skills of manipulation and organization rather than his attitudes. The likelihood of the existence of community organizations is increased and the opportunities for membership are enhanced.

Some communities can be characterized as ethnic enclaves. It is here that those individuals who retain their traditional attitudes and behaviors dwell. They are not really part of the urban industrial system as such and will have many autonomous social and political attributes which are different from those in other communities.

There are a number of other factors which influence the degree of organization of slum communities. These are the length of time the community has existed and the stability of the population, the degree to which the community is physically bounded and set off from others and the existence of certain symbolic representations of the collective identity of the community such as a name, a patron saint or a separate ritual cycle. Thus Siddiqui indicates that the highly organized inner-city slum which he has described in India is over a century old.[153] In this slum there is a *panchayat* (community-wide governing unit) and a headman. Where physical boundaries such as waterways, canals, remnants of old walls or gates and separate names exist, there is a higher degree of internal organization. Units built around their own mosque as the *kampongs* in Djakarta have a symbolic identity of their own.[154]

One type of slum community which has often been regarded as having a high propensity for organization is the squatter settlement. It was this type of community which Mangin and Leeds used as examples to refute Lewis's thesis of non-organization. Because of the housing shortages in newly expanding cities, squatter settlements which are found all over the world can comprise a high proportion of the total number of households in the city. It is estimated that 62 percent of the households in Lima, 45 percent in Ankara, 33 percent in Karachi and similar large proportions in Caracas and Manila are located in squatter settlements.[155]

Squatter settlements do seem to have high degrees of organization. One reason for this is the need to organize to protect the members of the community from attempts to dislodge them from the area to which they have no legal right. Another reason is the necessity to form groups to petition the municipality to provide municipal services such as water, electricity, sewage and so on. Squatter settlements are also characterized by hopefulness since the individual is usually a de facto homeowner and independent of an exploitative landlord. The population tends to be stable and interested in voluntary community improvement activities. Furthermore, the squatter settlement is characterized by a very high degree of class heterogeneity since, for a variety of reasons, many young university graduates and other members of the middle class live there. Thus, professionals, white-collar workers and the skilled working class live cheek by jowl with marginal groups and the political socialization of the marginal groups is affected.

Abrams notes the presence of lawyers and physicians in a number of such settlements.[156] McGee lists teachers, police, office workers and professionals in a Djakarta settlement.[157] Mangin and others have listed similar middle-class occupations in Latin America.[158] Laquian found 4.5 percent of the residents in the Manila community he studied were college-educated. He also found a great range in income.[159] McGee has indicated that squatter communities in Rangoon and Djakarta often are organized under a "headman" who serves to negotiate with municipal authorities.[160] Laquian describes the development of a very complex organization in one Manila squatter settlement. The community itself is broken into several neighborhoods which are physically bounded units. Each neighborhood has its own association primarily concerned with protecting the land rights of the inhabitants. Each association selects representatives to a larger council which represents the total community.

The headman of that unit negotiates with the municipal authorities.[161] Mangin has discussed the high degree of organization for Latin American squatter settlements in general.[162] Matos Mar noted that thirty of fifty-six *barriadas* in Lima had associations.[163] Roberts notes the proliferation of betterment organizations in many shantytowns in Guatemala City. Such groups both perform labor services on community projects and lobby for community improvement. He notes a weak relationship between individual income and individual local or electoral participation. However, the less wealthy communities are often more actively organized than the more wealthy because of spatial and ecological factors.[164] In other areas of Latin America where squatter settlements have been extensively studied, the organized nature of some communities has also been described. Ray discusses some of the specific features which promote or discourage organization in the *barrios* of four Venezuelan cities.[165]

Not all squatter settlements are organized. Harrison describes a *bidonville* in Tripoli, Libya, as extremely disorganized. Municipal attempts to set up *"sheikhs"* or headmen have been unsuccessful.[166] Recent studies, which have taken a longer time perspective have shown the breakdown or weakening of these organizations even where they once existed.[167] In many cases, this is the result of the fulfillment of organizational goals; for example, the legitimization and official recognition of the community. It is also mistaken to infer from the existence of community organizations the participation of all residents. In the light of available statistics on organizational membership, it would be unfair to assume that the proportion of active members is large.

LIFESTYLE

It seems that in many slum communities in the urbanizing and industrializing societies of the world, several distinct lifestyle groups appear to be emerging. These lifestyles correspond neither to economic differences nor to community differences. They seem to emerge in the urban industrial society and to recruit from different age groups among the people entering the system. Thus people who migrate to the city as unmarried young adults tend to be recruited into certain groups while the elderly migrant with a growing family moves into others. Once established, these peer group networks reinforce the subculture of a given group through selective interaction and significant similarities in dress, slang and beliefs within the group.

One of the most obvious lifestyle types is the "tough." The content of this subculture is probably first developed by urban adolescents, and is related to the nature of entry into the labor force in industrial society. After development, adherents to the behavioral style expand to include recently arrived unmarried migrants and males who are past adolescence. Such groups have their own dress patterns, language, recreational activities and so on. Gambling, physical contests and drinking are characteristic of this group, as are casual illicit activities and challenges to authority. The similarities between the *tsotsi* lifestyle among young males in South Africa described by Pauw,[168] the *hampon* subculture and the gangs (*galladas* and *colleras*) in Lima described by Patch,[169] the adolescent group in the Doya-Gai in Tokyo described by Caldarola,[170] the peer group of Manuel Sanchez [171] and the streetcorner men described by Hannerz [172] in the United States are striking.

Another lifestyle group consists of the extremely pious sect groups found among the poor all over the world. These groups are strongly temperance-oriented and anti-hedonistic. Such groups are described by Pauw in Africa and they are found in non-Christian groups in African cities as well. The Protestant sect groups found throughout Latin America (Pentecostals, Seventh Day Adventists, and so on) are also of this type. Even before World War II, Drake and Cayton differentiated styles of life in a low-income community in Chicago and described one group as the "church folks" who "despite their verbal protests, must live in close contact with the world of Sin . . ." [173] Hannerz finds a similar group in his study as well.[174] They recruit from both the stable blue-collar groups and the unstable laboring class.

As Cayton and Drake mentioned, and as Hannerz illustrates, it is possible for individuals with diverse lifestyles to live side by side within the slum maintaining social boundaries reinforced by differences in dress, slang and recreation patterns. Ellis and Newman suggest that, even within the young "tough" category in the area they studied, there were six distinct roles which differed in dress, language and values.[175] An individual's network contains mostly like members and excludes other elements so that each type achieves social isolation in spite of geographic proximity. The effect of a lifestyle subculture on attitudes to authority, the larger society and to the efficacy of political action may be extremely important, and may be only tenuously related to the nature of one's career or community.

Because of the variation in career patterns, the nature of community and the lifestyle groups among the urban poor, there are many variables which intervene between the direct effect of material deprivation on political attitudes and political behavior. All of these variables need further investigation especially in regard to their impact on political organization. Furthermore, other forms of deprivation such as prestige deprivation and political deprivation (powerlessness) may occur independently of material deprivation, and may have a greater effect on political attitudes and behavior. This is true in the case of the Chinese in Southeast Asia, a wealthy but despised and politically powerless group who do not engage actively in political life. It is certainly nonproductive at this point to attempt to generalize about political attitudes and behavior in relation to poverty.

Behavioral Responses and Culture

As we move away from the concrete area of economic responses, it becomes more difficult to generalize about the behavior of the poor. It seems that all over the world, there are many behavioral responses to cash shortage and insecurity which are adaptive in that they maximize the amount of cash available at any one point in time. Most of these behaviors are in no way counter-productive for the poor in their circumstances.

When we look at the formation of basic social units, we again find similar types of households among the materially deprived around the world. In this instance too, the behavior can be shown to be adaptive to material deprivation. Although the dominant classes are moralistically judgmental in this area of behavior, the concern seems unwarranted. These behavioral responses do not, in and of themselves, help to perpetuate poverty and the plight of the poor nor do they present a moral threat to the rest of society.

Finally, as we move away from the above areas it becomes increasingly difficult to generalize about the behavior of the poor. One cannot make definitive statements about the relationship between poverty and apathy, poverty and anti-social behavior or poverty and political action. In all of these areas which are related to integration and participation in the larger system, the behavior of the so-called poor is affected by many nonmaterial variables which are perhaps more important in affecting behavior than is simple material deprivation. Thus, while Lewis was wrong in attributing a crippling ideology to the poor, his pinpointing of various coping responses was extremely perceptive.

While it is obvious that the poor in many urban industrial societies develop similar coping behaviors in response to a resource-poor environment, can we call this a culture or subculture of poverty? Such a term *cannot* be used if by subculture we mean a bounded group of individuals who share a common way of life which is consciously taught to successive generations. If it is implied that a subculture is an internally consistent set of traits systematically related to each other, such a subculture does not exist among the poor. If it is asserted that the world view and values of the poor are significantly different from those of the dominant classes, there is no evidence to support such an assertion. If it is believed that such values are autonomously perpetuated by an insulated, closed group of individuals who are born in the group, socialized in a unique culture and remain there due to an engrained internalized commitment to such values, then the notion of a culture or subculture of poverty is incorrect and dangerous. It is impossible to demonstrate a direct relationship between poverty and a consistent world view, an area influenced profoundly by other than ecological variables.

If, however, we assume that in a mobile society of the complex urban industrial type, the traditional notion of culture no longer applies, then we cannot generalize about the behavioral responses of the materially deprived to their resource-poor environment and impute all the attributes of culture to these behaviors. We *can* say that only certain aspects of the behavior of the poor, those related most directly to survival and the maximization of resources are likely to be similar. Furthermore, since the individual in such a society has many possible career alternatives which may remove him from marginal occupations and consequent material deprivation, survival behavior is flexible and less strongly internalized. Thus, it is meaningless to talk about a bounded group of deprived individuals who are born and socialized into a self-perpetuating culture of poverty. Sources of socialization in urban industrial society with its multiple segmented status categories are many: age, occupation, ethnicity, membership in a residential community, membership in voluntary associations, and so on. The behavior of an individual or a group is not determined by a single factor such as his class or ethnic group, but by a complexity of social positions. Furthermore, the very fact that in many cases status in urban industrial society is not ascribed makes a change of status possible.

Some areas of behavior are more clearly affected by material deprivation. In other areas, material deprivation is overshadowed by ethnicity, nature of community or age grade. Furthermore, as the individual changes status he acquires new behavioral guides. One's early childhood socialization is not fixed. As one changes status, one's effective social network or peer group also changes and it is through this network that new behavior is learned. Thus, as material deprivation is overcome, the former coping responses are replaced by responses which are appropriate to the new circumstances.

The inapplicability of the term "culture" to the shared behavioral responses of the poor does not negate the similarities in such behavior. It is possible that when the notion of subculture has been refined for the analysis of complex society, that it will be used to signify the abstract behavioral guides that are characteristic of particular status categories or combinations of them. The different norms which operate for the poor in economic behavior and the formation of household units would be important in describing the class subculture of the poor. Such different behavioral guides develop in adaptation to the social setting and are perpetuated by selective interaction among similar peoples. If precisely defined in this way, then it might be possible to refer to a poverty subculture, but given the present confusion, it is misleading, and even dangerous to use this concept.

It should also be noted that the mixed nature of the empirical evidence used in the discussion of the behavioral responses of the poor are such that we must assert the *hypothetical* nature of such generalizations. The universality of these behavioral responses still needs careful testing before definitive statements can be made.

Notes

1. William Mangin (ed.), *Peasants in Cities* (Boston: Houghton Mifflin Company, 1970, p. XVII.
2. *Ibid.,* p. XVII.
3. Julian Steward, *The Theory of Culture Change* (Urbana: University of Illniois Press, 1955).
4. *Journal of the Hong Kong Institute of Social Research,* vol. 1, 1965, 126 pp.
5. Peter Gutkind, "The Energy of Despair: Social Organization of the Unemployed in Two African Cities: Lagos and Nairobi," *Civilizations,* vol. 17, 1967, pp. 186–211.
6. Oscar Lewis, *Five Families* (New York: Basic Books, Inc., Publishers, 1959).
7. Anthony Leeds, "The Concept of the Culture of Poverty: Conceptual,

Logical and Empirical Problems with Perspectives from Brazil and Peru," in E. B. Leacock (ed.), *The Culture of Poverty: A Critique* (New York: Simon & Schuster, Inc., 1971), p. 250.

8. For a discussion of capital expansion groups, see O. F. Raum, "Self-Help Associations," *African Studies,* vol. 28, pp. 119–141.

9. *Ibid.,* p. 134.

10. Carolina Maria de Jesus, *Child of the Dark: The Diary of Carolina Maria de Jesus* (New York: The New American Library, Inc., 1962), pp. 34, 46.

11. *Journal of the Hong Kong Institute of Social Research, op. cit.*

12. Joseph Lelyveld, "Kishan Babu," in Mangin (ed.), *Peasants in Cities,* pp. 135–137.

13. Oscar Lewis, "The Possessions of the Poor," *Scientific American,* vol. 221, 1969, pp. 114–124.

14. Raum, *op. cit.*

15. Lewis, *The Children of Sanchez* (New York: Random House, Inc., 1961), p. 139.

16. Carlo Caldarola, "The Doya-Gai: A Japanese Version of Skid Row," *Pacific Affairs,* vol. 41, 1968–9, pp. 511–525.

17. Henry Mayhew, *London Labour and the London Poor* (London: Frank Cass and Co., Ltd., 1967), vol. 1, p. 4.

18. Lelyveld, *op. cit.*

19. De Jesus, *op. cit.*

20. *Journal of the Hong Kong Institute for Social Research, op. cit.*

21. Lee Taylor, *Occupational Sociology* (New York: Oxford University Press, 1968), p. 570.

22. B. A. Pauw, *The Second Generation* (Capetown: Oxford University Press, 1963).

23. Richard Patch, "La Parada: Lima's Market," *American Universities Field Staff Report, West Coast of South America,* vol. 14, 1967, Part I.

24. Valentine mentions the distribution system for "extra-legal bonanzas of goods" which he has observed in a lower-income community in the United States. This trait may also be present elsewhere. See C. L. Valentine and B. L. Valentine, "Ethnography and Large-Scale Complex Sociocultural Systems" (mimeo), 1969, p. 28.

25. This same point is made in Leeds, *op. cit.*

26. G. De Vos and H. Wagatsuma, "The Ecology of Special Buraku," in G. De Vos and H. Wagatsuma (eds.), *Japan's Invisible Race* (Berkeley and Los Angeles: University of California Press, 1966), p. 126.

27. Lewis, "The Possessions of the Poor."

28. Pauw, *op. cit.*

29. De Vos and Wagatsuma, *op. cit.,* p. 127.

30. Andrew Whiteford, *Two Cities in Latin America* (Garden City: Doubleday & Company, Inc., 1964).

31. *Ibid.*, pp. 169–170.

32. Charles Abrams, *Housing in the Modern World* (London: Faber and Faber, 1964).

33. Lewis, *The Children of Sanchez.*

34. Patch, *op. cit.*

35. Joan Nelson, "Urban Poor: Disruption or Political Integration in Third World Cities," *World Politics,* vol. 22, 1970, pp. 393–414.

36. *Journal of the Hong Kong Institute of Social Research, op. cit.*

37. Pauw, *op. cit.*

38. Every study of poverty groups or slum communities indicates the male's inability to provide major cash resources either because of a limited job market or limited skills. See the extended discussion in Chapter Four and general volumes such as Michael Harrington, *The Other America: Poverty in the United States* (Baltimore: Penguin Books, Inc., 1962); Louis Ferman et al. (eds.), *Poverty in America* (Ann Arbor: University of Michigan Press, 1965); Margaret S. Gordon (ed.), *Poverty in America* (San Francisco: Chandler, 1965).

39. E. A. Hoebel, *Anthropology: The Study of Man* (New York: McGraw-Hill, Inc., 1966, pp. 332–3); Robin Fox, *Kinship and Marriage* (Harmondsworth, Middlesex, England: Penguin Books Ltd., 1967).

40. See descriptions of grief in L. R. Peattie, *The View from the Barrio* (Ann Arbor: University of Michigan Press, 1968), and E. Liebow, *Tally's Corner* (Boston: Little, Brown and Company, 1967).

41. Nancie L. S. Gonzalez, *Black Carib Household Structure* (Seattle: University of Washington Press, 1969), p. 95.

42. Freedman, cited in Barrington Kaye, *Upper Nankin Street, Singapore* (Singapore: University of Malaya Press, 1966), pp. 97–100.

43. P. Bohannon and G. Dalton (eds.), *Markets in Africa* (Garden City: Doubleday & Company, Inc., 1965), Introduction, and Peter Marris, *Family and Social Change in an African City* (London: Routledge and Kegan Paul, 1961), p. 47.

44. Marris, *op. cit.*

45. Aidan Southall, "Urban Migration and the Residence of Children in Kampala," in Mangin (ed.), *Peasants in Cities*, pp. 150–59.

46. Caldarola, *op. cit.*

47. De Vos and Wagatsuma, *op. cit.,* p. 132.

48. Koji Taira, "Ragpickers and Community Development: Ant's Villa in Tokyo," *Industrial and Labour Relations Review,* vol. 22, 1968, p. 11.

49. Peattie, *op. cit.,* p. 45.

50. Andrew Pearse, "Some Characteristics of Urbanization in the City of

Rio de Janeiro," in Philip Hauser (ed.), *Urbanization in Latin America* (New York: UNESCO, 1961), p. 198.

51. Bryan Roberts, "The Social Organization of Low Income Families," in R. N. Adams (ed.), *Crucifixion by Power* (Austin: University of Texas Press, 1970), pp. 479–515.

52. Whiteford, *op. cit.*, p. 174.

53. De Jesus, *op. cit.*

54. R. E. Phillips, "The Bantu in the City: A Study of Cultural Adjustment on the Witwatersrand," in *Social Implications of Industrialization and Urbanization in Africa South of the Sahara* (Geneva: UNESCO, 1956).

55. Joan Verster, "Social Survey of Western Township, 1964," *African Studies*, vol. 26, 1967, pp. 175–246.

56. This theme is constant in Gonzalez' description of such patterns both in Honduras and the world in general. See Gonzalez, *op. cit.*, and also Peattie, *op. cit.*, p. 46.

57. Whiteford, *op. cit.*, p. 174.

58. Marris, *op. cit.*, p. 44.

59. Kaye, *op. cit.*, pp. 97–100.

60. Robert Textor, *From Peasant to Pedicab Driver*, Southeast Asia Studies Cultural Report Series No. 9 (New Haven: Yale University Press, 1961), pp. 12–13.

61. De Vos and Wagatsuma, *op. cit.*, p. 132.

62. M. Hunter, "An Urban Community in East London," in *Social Implications of Industrialization and Urbanization in Africa South of the Sahara, op. cit.*

63. S. Khalaf, *Prostitution in a Changing Society* (Beirut: Khayats, 1965), pp. 3–5.

64. This theme pervades the articles by Phillips, Hunter, and Schapera, in *Social Implications of Industrialization and Urbanization in Africa, South of the Sahara,* and can be seen more recently in Verster, *op. cit.*

65. H. Rodman, "Lower Class Attitudes toward Deviant Family Patterns: a Cross-Cultural Study," *Journal of Marriage and the Family*, vol. 31, 1969, pp. 325–31.

66. De Vos and Wagatsuma, *op. cit.*, p. 132.

67. De Jesus, *op. cit.*, pp. 27, 39.

68. Peattie, *op. cit.*, p. 45.

69. Marris, *op. cit.*, p. 51.

70. Lewis, *The Children of Sanchez, op. cit.*, p. 59.

71. De Vos and Wagatsuma, *op. cit.*

72. Marvine Howe, "Under Apartheid It Is the Black Women Who Suffer Most," *The New York Times*, October 20, 1970, p. 8.

73. Gonzalez, *op. cit.*, pp. 118–134.

74. For a description of the traditional father-child role see R. Levine, N. Klein and C. Owen, "Father Child Relations and Changing Life Styles in Ibadan Nigeria," in H. Miner (ed.), *The City in Modern Africa* (New York: Praeger Publishers, Inc., 1967), pp. 215–257.

75. Pearse, *op. cit.*, p. 197, and Peattie, *op. cit.*, pp. 41–44.

76. Verster, *op. cit.*

77. Marris, *op. cit.*, p. 56.

78. Southall, *op. cit.*

79. Peattie, *op. cit.*, p. 43.

80. Marris, *op. cit.*, p. 52.

81. Helen I. Safa, "From Shanty Town to Public Housing," *Caribbean Studies*, vol. 4, 1964, pp. 2–12; and "The Female-Based Household in Public Housing," *Human Organization*, vol. 24, 1965, pp. 135–140.

82. Peattie, *op. cit.*, p. 46.

83. Whiteford, *op. cit.*, p. 197.

84. E. A. Hammel, "The Family Cycle in a Coastal Peruvian Slum and Village," *American Anthropologist*, vol. 63, 1961, pp. 346–354; and "Some Characteristics of Rural Village and Urban Slum Populations on the Coast of Peru," *Southwestern Journal of Anthropology*, vol. 20, 1964, pp. 346–358.

85. Mangin, "Urbanization Case History," in Mangin (ed.), *op. cit.*, pp. 47–54.

86. Gonzalez, *op. cit.*, pp. 118–134.

87. Mary Jane Aerni, "Contributions to Lewis Review Article," *Current Anthropology*, vol. 8, 1967, pp. 492–493.

88. Verster, *op. cit.*

89. Marris, "Methods and Motives," in Horace Miner (ed.), *op. cit.*, 1967, p. 45.

90. Marris, *op. cit.*, p. 69.

91. Pauw, *Xhosa in Town, Studies of the Bantu-Speaking Population*, Cape Province No. 3, Cape Town, 1963.

92. P. Kay, "Aspects of Social Structure in a Tahitian Urban Neighborhood," *Journal of the Polynesian Society*, vol. 72, 1963, pp. 325–71; and "Urbanization in the Tahitian Household," in A. Spoehr (ed.), *Pacific Port Towns and Cities* (Honolulu: University of Hawaii Press, 1963), pp. 63–74.

93. C. S. Belshaw, "Pacific Island Towns and the Theory of Growth," in Spoehr (ed.), *op. cit.*, pp. 17–24.

94. M. Calley, "Economic Life of Mixed Blood Communities in New South Wales," *Oceania*, vol. 26, 1956, pp. 200–213.

95. See in particular the discussion in the Introduction to N. Whitten and J. Szwed (eds.), *Afro-American Anthropology* (New York: The Free Press, 1970), pp. 40–43.

96. Ulf Hannerz, *Soulside* (New York: Columbia University Press, 1969).

97. Marvin Harris, *Man, Nature and Culture* (New York: Thomas Y. Crowell Company, 1971), p. 367.

98. Kimi Hara, "Problems Related to One-Parent (mother) Families in Miraka City," *Journal of Social Science,* vol. 7, 1968, pp. 347–348.

99. Kaye, *op. cit.,* pp. 32–39.

100. J. Gulick, "Village and City: Cultural Continuities in Twentieth Century Middle Eastern Cultures," in I. Lapidus (ed.), *Middle Eastern Cities* (Berkeley: University of California Press, 1969), p. 139.

101. Peattie, *op. cit.,* pp. 45–48.

102. *Journal of the Hong Kong Institute of Social Research, op. cit.*

103. Kaye, *op. cit.,* p. 241.

104. Verster, *op. cit.*

105. Peattie, *op. cit.*

106. Mangin, *op. cit.*

107. DeVos and Wagatsuma, *op. cit.,* p. 140.

108. Caldarola, *op. cit.*

109. Kaye, *op. cit.,* p. 34.

110. Gino Germani, "Inquiry into the Social Effects of Urbanization in a Working-Class Sector of Buenos Aires," in Philip Hauser (ed.), *op. cit.,* p. 214.

111. S. N. Sen, *City of Calcutta: A Socio-economic Survey* (Calcutta: Firma Mukhopadhyan, 1960).

112. Dom Moraes, "Bombay: Wealth, Shanty-towns, Speakeasies, Intellectual Ad Men and Death on the Train," *New York Times Magazine,* October 11, 1970; and N. A. Razvi, "Extent and Avenues of Prostitution," *Pakistani Review,* vol. 13, 1965, pp. 6–7.

113. Textor, *op. cit.,* p. 12.

114. Phillip Mayer, *Townsmen or Tribesmen: Conservatism and the Process of Urbanization in a South African City* (Capetown: Oxford University Press, 1961).

115. Caldarola, *op. cit.*

116. Whiteford, *op. cit.,* p. 206.

117. Marris, *op. cit.,* p. 46.

118. Hammel, *op. cit.*

119. This theme runs through most of the community studies of Latin American peasantry; see, for example, Lewis, *Life in a Mexican Village* (Urbana: University of Illinois Press, 1951).

120. Hammel, *op. cit.*

121. Gonzalez, *op. cit.*

122. Southall, *op. cit.*

123. Barbara Frankel, "When Systems Collide: Ambiguous Marital Status Reporting Among Low Income Negroes in Philadelphia," unpublished paper.

124. Leonard Plotnicov, "Nigerians: The Dream Is Unfulfilled," in Mangin (ed.), *Peasants in Cities,* pp. 170–174.

125. Gutkind, *op. cit.*

126. *Journal of the Hong Kong Institute of Social Research, op. cit.*

127. Lewis, *Five Families.*

128. Roy Bryce-LaPorte, "Urban Relocation and Family Adaptation in Puerto Rico: A Case Study of Urban Ethnography," in Mangin (ed.), *op. cit.,* pp. 85–97.

129. Aprodicio Laquian, *Slums Are for People* (Phillipines: Bustamante Press, 1968).

130. Lewis, "The Possessions of the Poor."

131. Peattie, *op. cit.*

132. Gutkind, *op. cit.*

133. Marris, *op. cit.,* pp. 39–55.

134. De Jesus, *op. cit.*

135. Nelson, *op. cit.*

136. Kaye, *op. cit.,* p. 275.

137. Henry Dietz, "Urban Squatter Settlements in Peru," *Journal of Inter-American Studies,* vol. II, 1969, pp. 353–370.

138. Peattie, *op. cit.,* pp. 54–71.

139. Whiteford, *op. cit.,* p. 204.

140. Floyd Dotson, "A Note on Participation in Voluntary Associations in a Mexican City," *American Sociological Review,* vol. 18, 1953, pp. 380–386.

141. Gutkind, *op. cit.*

142. Mangin, *op. cit.*

143. Elizabeth Bott, *Family and Social Network* (London: Tavistock Press, 1957).

144. Safa, "The Social Isolation of the Urban Poor: Life in a Puerto Rican Shanty Town," in I. Deutscher and E. J. Thompson (eds.), *Among the People: Encounters with the Poor* (New York: Basic Books Inc., Publishers, 1968), p. 347.

145. For example, see the work of Peattie, *op. cit.,* and the article by Lloyd Rogler, "Slums in Latin America," *Journal of Inter-American Studies,* vol. 9, 1967, pp. 507–528.

146. J. Roach and O. Gursslin, "An Evaluation of the Concept of Culture of Poverty," *Social Forces,* vol. 45, 1967, pp. 383–391.

147. Rogler, *op. cit.*

148. Lewis, *La Vida: A Puerto Rican Family in the Culture of Poverty* (New York: Random House, Inc., 1967).

149. Safa, "The Social Isolation of the Urban Poor," pp. 335–351.

150. For a critical review of the general areas of social disorganization among the poor, as well as their lack of interaction, see Thomas Gladwin, "The Anthropologist's View of Poverty," in *The Social Welfare Forum* (New York: Columbia University Press, 1961).

151. C. Stokes, "A Theory of Slums," *Land Economics,* vol. 38, 1962, pp. 187–197.

152. Takashi Oka, "Tokyo Housing Shortage Persists Amid Affluence," *The New York Times,* January 5, 1971, p. 8.

153. M. K. Siddiqui, "The Slums of Calcutta: A Problem and Its Solution," *Indian Journal of Social Work,* vol. 29, 1968, pp. 173–182.

154. T. J. McGee, *The Southeast Asian City* (New York: Praeger Publishers, Inc., 1967).

155. Charles Abrams, *op. cit.*

156. *Ibid.*

157. McGee, *op. cit.*

158. Mangin, "Latin American Squatter Settlements: A Problem and a Solution," *Latin American Research Review,* vol. 2, 1967, pp. 65–98.

159. Laquian, *op. cit.*

160. McGee, *op. cit.*

161. Laquian, *op. cit.*

162. Mangin, "Latin American Squatter Settlements: A Problem and a Solution."

163. José Matos Mar, "Migration and Urbanization: The Barriadas of Lima," in Hauser (ed), *Urbanization in Latin America,* pp. 170–190.

164. Roberts, "The Social Organization of Low-Income Families."

165. Talton Ray, *The Politics of Venezuelan Barrios* (Berkeley: University of California Press, 1969).

166. R. S. Harrison, "Migrants in the City of Tripoli, Libya," *Geographical Review,* vol. 57, 1967, pp. 397–423.

167. Roberts, "Urban Poverty and Political Behavior in Guatemala," *Human Organization,* vol. 29, 1970, pp. 20–29; Daniel Goldrich et al., "The Political Intergration of Lower-Class Urban Settlements in Chile and Peru," *Studies in International Development,* vol. 3, 1967–8.

168. Pauw, *op. cit.*

169. Patch, *op. cit.,* Part I.

170. Caldarola, *op. cit.*

171. Lewis, *The Children of Sanchez.*

172. Hannerz, *op. cit.*

173. Hylan Lewis, *Culture, Class and Poverty: Three Papers from the Child Rearing Study of Low Income District of Columbia Families* (Washington, D.C.: Cross-Tell, 1968), p. 17.

174. Hannerz, *op. cit.*

175. H. C. Ellis and S. M. Newman, " 'Gowster,' 'Ivy-leaguer,' 'Hustler,' 'Conservative,' 'Mackman' and 'Continental': A Functional Analysis of Six Ghetto Roles," in E. B. Leacock (ed.), *op. cit.,* 1971, pp. 299–315.

Chapter 6

Poverty and the
American Scene

THE American capitalist system is at present in a state of advanced industrialism. This economy can be compared and contrasted in several ways with the systems which have been described in the preceding chapters. At this moment in time, it is difficult to distinguish between those features which are characteristic of this stage of development, and therefore, universal, and those which are peculiarly American.

Advances in production have been made at such a rapid rate that the problem of poverty is, for the first time, exclusively one of distribution. Perhaps this can best be demonstrated by indicating the per capita national income for the United States in 1971 which is $3,780.

Much of the productive capacity of the United States economy can be traced to a particular set of historical and ecological conditions. Although the early colonization of America occurred in the seventeenth century, the major movements began at much the same time as the Industrial Revolution in Western Europe, in the eighteenth century. Another significant circumstance was that the British, rather than the French or Spanish, became the primary power in colonial America and exported their emergent productive techniques as well as certain basic ideological commitments which set the stage for the rapid growth of capitalism and industrialism. Although the "open frontier" theory of American development has recently been challenged, there can be no question about the major potential for development of a massive, largely unexploited, sparsely populated continental area. During the eighteenth and nineteenth centuries, large numbers of people migrated to the United States and became part of the labor force necessary for the capitalist, industrialist expansion of that time. If mass production and the standardization of parts are key factors in industrial development, then the United States can be seen as one of the leaders in this process.

Advanced Industrialism

The early period of the Industrial Revolution can be characterized as one in which man harnessed new sources of energy and developed machines which could outproduce human and animal energy. On the other hand, the present stage of development can be seen as one in which machines themselves run other machines. This latter development is subsumed under the term "automation." A truly automated industry is one requiring very little human labor input, that is, infrequent human operation of machines and even infrequent direct supervision of machines, since many of them have self-correcting devices. Unskilled and semi-skilled laboring occupations are particularly vulnerable to the inroads of automation. Harrington notes the impact of this phenomenon on one phase of the meatpacking industry, sausage making. Unemployment has been significantly high since the introduction of new machinery which can cut casings, stuff them and pack the finished product without human intervention. The previous technology involved a great deal of direct human manipulation in the various phases.[1]

From a long-range economic point of view, the displacement of laborers by machines is a temporary disruption of the system and, in the future, will cease to have any significance. Ideally, those displaced will filter into alternative occupations in the burgeoning service/clerical sector. The new jobs created by a need for designing, implementing and controlling automated production will outnumber the jobs presently being taken over by machines. While it will be hard to retrain those already in the labor force, the new generations will acquire greater skills for these higher skilled jobs.

Alternatively, as production increases and manpower needs decline, the system will respond by developing new institutions to distribute work within the labor force. Among these are a shorter working week, increased vacation periods, later entrance into the work force through prolonged education and training, as well as earlier retirement.

The entire history of industrial development is related to basic changes in the occupational structure. In some ways, these changes can be viewed as cyclical in nature. In the early phases of mechanization, machines were relatively crude and required large quantities of unskilled operators. At the same time, skilled artisans were no longer needed and were in fact undermined by mass production, thus losing their previous place in the system. More recently, the trend in mechanization has diminished the need for unskilled or semi-skilled machine operators while increasing the demand for skilled personnel in technical and clerical fields involving administration, coordination and information storage. This is quite obvious from an analysis of the present occupational structure in the United States where increasing numbers of those gainfully employed are engaged in skilled technical, managerial, clerical and professional activities with decreasing numbers in semi- and unskilled manual labor.

Another significant trend has been the increase in leisure time with a corresponding decrease in work time. At present, the five-day, forty-hour week is common. While this seems short in comparison to the six-day, sixty to seventy-hour week which was quite usual in the early part of this century, there is now considerable pressure to shorten the working week. One thrust in this direction is to maintain the number of hours, but to decrease the number of days from five to four. Another way might be to decrease the number of hours, from forty to thirty-two, and the number of days, from five to four. The trend to rationalize legal holidays to provide spaced three-day weekends as well as to extend vacations are also adding to the amount of leisure time at a worker's disposal. These trends are creating a need for ways in which to use leisure time, and as a by-product, the growing recreational industries provide new occupational opportunities.

Another trend in the contemporary American industrial economy is the emphasis upon immediate gratification in consumption of material goods and services. To a certain extent, this is related to the needs of a productive system continually increasing in capacity and thus requiring an expanding consumer market. This perspective on the relationship between high levels of demand and expanding productivity first appeared in the economic theories of John Maynard Keynes. These views repudiated the earlier virtues of thrift and saving of the classical economists whose thinking was applied to the early phase of capitalism.

To facilitate rapid satisfaction of demands, financial innovations have been made in the area of credit. Several novels as well as surveys of American life have illustrated the current American tendency to overspend, a repudiation of the former values of American society which emphasized the accumulation rather than the consumption of wealth.

Although Veblen, as early as 1899,[2] characterized the American people as conspicuous consumers, the consumption was striking only among the upper classes. As the American's spending power has increased through such devices as personal loans, credit cards, and checking accounts which allow automatic loans to cover overdraughts, so has conspicuous consumption spread to all classes of society.

THE EXTENT OF POVERTY IN AMERICA

During the Great Depression of the 1930s, which was a massive disruption of the economy, poverty as indicated by the high unemployment rates was a widespread condition. General estimates for that period suggest that one-quarter of the labor force was unemployed. As America emerged from this period primarily with the advent of World War II, the problem of poverty became submerged under the notion that almost everyone was sharing in the unprecedented prosperity of the 1940s.

The bubble burst with the publication of Michael Harrington's *The Other America*,[3] which exposed the existence in the United States of widespread poverty. Harrington argued that the elimination of poverty in the United States could no longer be expected as a result of natural economic growth; despite the growing affluence of many people in the system, material deprivation was still the lot of between 20 and 25 percent of the population. This, of course, is less than the one-third alluded to by Roosevelt in 1933 as the ill-fed and ill-clothed. However, Harrington demonstrated that the decline in the proportion of the population living in poverty, in large part, was due to the prosperity of the war era and that little change in the proportion of the poor had resulted from the advances of the 1950s.

WHO ARE THE POOR?

If there is one major difference between the contemporary American poor on the one hand and the poor in the developing areas or in the early Western transitional phase on the other, it is the nature of the groups affected by material deprivation. In the developing societies, historic and contemporary, poverty was dispersed. The poor were comprised of all age categories, all ethnic groups and were located in all regions. At present, in the United States, the poor are largely located in particular target groups in the population—the aged, ethnic minorities and the residents of particular areas. Traditionally, the poor have been those employed in the marginal occupations which were part of the economic structure of transitional societies. At the present time, these occupations are declining in importance in the occupational structure and thus account for a relatively smaller section of those who are materially deprived. However, those marginal occupations which remain account for a surprisingly large number of the poor.

Among those who can be considered as part of the traditional poverty groups are those who are physically incapacitated. Within this category we find the blind, the crippled, the mentally retarded, and so on. This group constitutes a shrinking proportion of the population because of advances in preventive and rehabilitative medicine. The incapacitated poor are supported by federal programs and aside from further advances in prevention and rehabilitation, the only policy for this group, and one which is popularly approved as well, is state support.

All those concerned with estimating the extent and distribution of poverty in contemporary America point to the significant number of the aged in this group.[4] One of the striking demographic features of contemporary America is the increase in the over-sixties. Medical knowledge has progressed to the point where the average life expectancy is over seventy. This has been accompanied by a breakdown in traditional mechanisms for care of the aged, that is, extended family residence and corporate mutual aid groupings. Although certain programs have been initiated to take care of the elderly, they are still inadequate. Social Security has remained minimal, although from time to time, there have been increases in the allocation. In addition, the elderly are most prone to illness which is a major drain on meager resources resulting from fixed incomes and inflation. Medicare has only recently been introduced. It should also be recognized that Social Security was designed for those with a history of employment in a large but categorically limited group of occupations (for example, self-employed marginal workers and domestics are usually not covered). Obviously the problems of this category of poor are specific and require different solutions.

Technological displacement has been characteristic of the entire period of the industrial era. However, as previously noted, the entire occupational structure is changing once again and the ability to shift from one occupation requiring minimal skills to a similar semi-skilled position has declined. Therefore, those displaced in this way face long-term unemployment or employment in marginal occupations—both circumstances leading to material deprivation. One way of avoiding technological displacement is by strong union organization, as in the railroad and stevedore industries. The union movement has, in effect, created a real dichotomy in the American laboring class. Those belonging to strong unions which can control the supply of labor and their conditions of work have been able to make increments in real income which separate them from the others.

Although we have previously noted the displacement of meat-packers, this process is more vividly portrayed by the plight of the farm laborer. Rural-urban migration described as occurring in the period of early industrialism in both the West and the contemporary developing world has been related to technological displacement in agriculture. However, the situation is exacerbated in advanced industrialism. American agriculture has been characterized by a heavy emphasis upon mechanization and large-scale commercial enterprises. There have been marked increases in production, while the number of those employed in production has declined both relatively and absolutely. In the United States, certain minorities, Blacks, Mexican Americans, American Indians and Puerto Ricans, have traditionally been engaged in non-mechanized farm work. As the demand for such activities decreases, even those fully employed at such work are materially deprived. The Southern (rural) to Northern (urban) migration of twentieth-century American blacks can thus be seen as agricultural displacement.

Unfortunately, much of this migration has taken place at a time when the need for unskilled labor in the industrial cities of the North has decreased, leaving little aside from marginal occupations. Furthermore, discrimination and racist attitudes have further attenuated the opportunity structure as they affect employer policy as well as union recruitment. This experience has led to the disproportionate representation of minorities among the poor. Black Americans, for instance, constitute approximately 10 percent of the total population, but 40 percent of the defined poverty segment.[5] This can be viewed as the result of large-scale reliance on marginal occupations among this segment of agriculturally displaced people. It is only this segment of the American poor, participating in urban marginal occupations, which is analogous to the majority of the urban poor in the developing world. In the American case, racial discrimination is a major factor in determining who will be pushed into marginal occupations. In many transitional societies active discrimination also plays a selective role; but since poverty is so pervasive the role is not as significant.

Another industry which has been heavily affected by displacement and decreased demand is coal mining. One of the major *geographic* pockets of poverty, Appalachia, owes its unenviable position to this decline. Deprived mining communities in Western Pennsylvania and West Virginia are overt evidence of this phenomenon.

The Nature of Marginal Occupations. One fact that continually surprises analysts is that a large proportion of the poor are employed on a full-time basis. Obviously this employment is of a marginal nature, although in America today, jobs in this category are somewhat different from those in transitional societies. In part, this is because the process of economic development has eliminated many of the previous occupations or changed the nature of work so they are no longer marginal in the amount or security of income.

Much heavy work disappears as machines are introduced. Time-consuming jobs are also affected. Technological changes in food storage and transportation has in many cases affected the marketing cycle, replacing daily shopping with longer range purchases. Thus, the hawker of food is replaced by a large-scale retail establishment. In this instance and in the case of other individual hawkers, these economic activities are replaced by those which are more highly organized. Large-scale organizations like supermarkets and department stores, using specialized personnel and timing transactions to take advantage of market conditions, replace the vendor who could not, from his vantage point, understand the market price-setting mechanism. Petty scavengers are replaced by large-scale junk dealers and resource regeneration is less emphasized. Manpower resources are allocated more systematically in other services; nightwatchmen are replaced by public and private security forces.

In this brief description we have emphasized some generalized economic shifts which have been and still are taking place in American society. Obviously these tendencies have not quite permeated the present system. Remnants of an older system or counter-trends are also observable. It should be apparent to anyone who shops in a supermarket that some of his fellow shoppers are not buying large quantities. It should also be obvious that street vendors still exist in urban areas. However, petty retail activities do not constitute a significant distributional force in contemporary America. Incidentally, it is worth noting that two pretzel vendors in New York City have very different incomes. A pretzel seller at City College earns $18,000 a year, while his counterpart at a subway station in another section of New York earns $2,600. Petty vending activities in contemporary America do not necessarily lead to material deprivation.[6]

The major negatively valued occupations such as beggars, prostitutes, thieves and gamblers are also affected by modernization, but not in a simple or straightforward way. We have already indicated that modernization first brings more people into these occupations. Instead of facing shrinking opportunity as the heavy energy, heavy time, redundant occupations do, these occupations can expand. Although the potential for begging may increase in a developed society, there is usually a move toward social welfare schemes which displace the more personal almsgiving to individual beggars. This too can be seen as the result of a more systematic attempt at human resource utilization. Despite such attitudes, beggars do not disappear entirely. In New York and Philadelphia, beggars are found in the downtown sectors where large numbers of people congregate. They are also found at major transportation points; subways, train stations and bus terminals. Physically handicapped beggars resemble those found in developing areas. However, the ubiquitous mother with infant found begging in many developing areas is absent. One intriguing aspect of the recent expansion of begging is the number of young people (under twenty-five) who choose begging as a source of income.

It is difficult to estimate the total activity of prostitutes and thieves. Statistics relating to theft of all types show an increasing rate. However, these statistics have been challenged on the basis of the data collection process and the short time period used for comparison. Since theft is not usually an occupation which one lists on a census form, the actual number of those who participate in this occupation on a full-time or part-time basis cannot be determined. However, the fact that more and more business establishments are hiring security forces and are attempting to prosecute shoplifters is an indication of growth in this sector. The incidence of prostitution, which is sometimes referred to as the oldest profession in the world, is equally difficult to determine. We have previously noted that attempts to eliminate prostitution in many transitional societies have been unsuccessful and there is no indication that it is decreasing, either as a full-time or part-time activity, in the United States. In addition to the inability to measure the extent of both of these activities, it is also difficult to determine the ratio of amateur to professional practitioners. To a degree, these activities are more inclined toward large-scale organization, but organized crime does not yet have a monopoly.

The inventory of the remaining marginal occupations in today's economy is quite different from that of transitional societies. The bulk of these jobs are those of institutionally employed service workers performing menial tasks for hospitals, restaurants and the like. Many others are located in residual pre-mechanized heavy labor and sweatshop manufacturing.

Liebow provides an excellent description and classification of the marginal (irregular and poorly paid) activities of the streetcorner men in *Tally's Corner*. Work activities are classified as inside work, outdoor work and hustling (illicit activity). Inside jobs consist of work as stock clerks, delivery boys, busboys, dishwashers, car washers, janitors (mopping floors, "pulling" trash and cleaning toilets at night). These jobs in hotels, restaurants, offices and apartment houses are very low in social value and are poorly paid. However, as essential services they do not depend on the business cycle to as great a degree as do others. They are always available; they are indoors (not dependent on the weather) and they are less taxing in energy than the outdoor jobs. They also provide an opportunity for petty pilferage which is almost encouraged, since it is expected by the employer and considered in wage setting (that is, wages are lower to take into account the expected thievery).

Marginal construction is a significant source of outdoor work which pays more than indoor work but has serious disadvantages. Transportation costs to most sites are high. The work is seasonal and depends on the weather. The energy expenditure required by pre-mechanized pick and shovel digging is too high for many of the men. Furthermore, slightly higher education and a clean police record are often required.[7] Liebow describes how the demand for this kind of labor has declined in the United States.

Heavy, backbreaking labor of the kind that used to be regularly associated with bull gangs or concrete gangs is no longer characteristic of laboring jobs, especially those with the larger, well-equipped construction companies. Brute strength is still required from time to time, as on smaller jobs where it is not economical to bring in heavy equipment or where the small, undercapitalized contractor has none to bring in. In many cases, however, the conveyor belt has replaced the wheelbarrow or the Georgia buggy, mechanized forklifts have eliminated heavy, manual lifting, and a variety of digging machines have replaced the pick and shovel. The result is fewer jobs for unskilled laborers and, in many cases, a work speed-up for those who do have jobs.[8]

The third work alternative for the streetcorner man is hustling. The hustler buys and sells sex, liquor, narcotics and/or stolen goods.

Bluestone presents a detailed analysis of why low-paying industries still exist in American society in his examination of the "working poor." According to him the working poor are made up of manufacturing operatives (sweatshop type), practitioners of personal services, laborers and farmers, as well as some segments of those in sales work, clerical work and private household work. He says, "In general the skill requirements for working poor jobs are below average, yet are the same as the requirements for many high wage industry jobs." [9] The reasons for the differences in the two types of industry are related to unionization, product demand, the productivity of the industry itself, capitalization and profits. In discussing the plight of the working poor, he says,

For many of the working poor the trials of poverty must indeed be oppressive. To toil at a sweatshop job, reminiscent of the Nineteenth Century, for up to 60 hours a week every week of the year is the cruel fate of many working poor. For their meager reward the working poor spend nearly half of their waking hours at jobs often arduous, numbingly repetitious, and devoid of opportunity for occupational mobility. In the best of times, when the economy is booming all around them, they can hope for full work weeks and wage increases which may keep pace with inflation. In the worst of times, the fear of losing their pittance of a wage constantly haunts them. Whether the economy comes up heads or tails, the working poor always lose.[10]

AMERICAN VIEWS OF THE SIGNIFICANCE OF POVERTY

Popular views of the significance of poverty in America can be related to the previous discussion of the extent of material deprivation. During the two decades between 1940 and 1960, it was generally assumed that material deprivation was disappearing from the United States. With the wide circulation of statistical data on hunger and medical deprivation, some sections of the population began to clamor for programs which would give priority to the elimination of these conditions. One response in the legislative arena was the War on Poverty.

There have been sporadic reform movements in the past, especially when the urban poor became visible and "troublesome." However, once it was recognized that poverty had not been eliminated as a result of general prosperity, for the first time in American history, a full-scale program at the federal level became the legitimate enterprise of all political parties. Such programs had as their goal the direct intervention in both the economy and the lives of the poor to permanently eradicate material deprivation; they were not merely designed to maintain the poor through charity or public assistance. Implicit in all the anti-poverty measures was the belief that poverty was destructive both psychologically and physically, and that its existence weakened the whole system. This, of course, ran counter to the traditional notions of the ennobling nature of poverty and its inevitability.

In order to show just how new the federal legislation was, it is necessary to contrast this program with earlier types of reform. One of the basic difficulties with many programs, governmental as well as private, which deal with the poor, is the confusion between maintenance and eradication. Most private charities and early welfare legislation focus upon the maintenance of the poor rather than the permanent eradication of material deprivation throughout the system. Charity for the good of the donor has persisted as an important value in America as well as in transitional societies. However, in America there has been a basic shift away from personal charity to systematic, large-scale charitable organizations. The United Fund campaigns are a good example of this effort. Many of the agencies which are part of the United Fund help support the poor through the provision of material aid and social services, but do not intend to "lift up" the poor. The relationship between the goodness of charity in its own right (the good derived by the donor) can also be seen in campaigns associated with holidays such as the "One Hundred Neediest Cases" campaign run by the *New York Times* at Christmas and other campaigns timed to coincide with Christmas and Easter. Many governmental programs can be seen as direct parallels to the notions of maintenance. Aid to Families with Dependent Children, a basic program developed with the early social security legislation of the 1930s, is a program designed to ensure the survival of children in households with no working male head. More recently, surplus food distribution, food stamp programs, public housing and the general package subsumed under the notion of public assistance are all designed to ensure survival rather than eradicate the causes of material deprivation.

The programs in the War on Poverty, however, have had as their stated goal the elimination of material deprivation through the elimination of unemployment, underemployment and through the redistribution of wealth. Still other programs in the recent antipoverty legislation attempt to redistribute access to power thus ideally further facilitating the movement of the poor into the middle class.

At the present time, there appears to be a popular reaction against expanding the War on Poverty at the expense of public funds. Many people feel that the existing programs, primarily those which are maintenance programs, are adequate or "too good" for the poor. It is felt that the poor should "pull themselves up by their bootstraps." Despite all of the evidence to the contrary, there appears to be a reemergence of the belief that the economic system will provide opportunity for upward mobility for everyone and that public responsibility is limited to ensuring the *survival* of the poor. It is apparent that the previously mentioned confusion between traditional maintenance and modern eradication has influenced public acceptance of government policy. Despite the fact that eradication programs are justified by the assumption that they will eventually increase economic expansion, this message has not been perceived or accepted by a large proportion of the population. The economist's assumption is that by incorporating the poor into the economic system as both producers and consumers, the economy will expand. However, the non-poor perceive the poor as recipients of more than their share. Eradication programs are seen as increasing charitable largess above the survival level without any long-term gains for the total system.

Social Science Views. Contributing to the emergence and elaboration of programs designed to eradicate poverty, a large body of American social science literature has developed which has been influential in determining the scope and direction of these programs. Within this literature, there appear to be three major reasons suggested for eliminating material deprivation: (1) poverty leads to a drain of economic resources as well as an inefficient use of manpower; (2) poverty leads to public danger through producing high rates of deviant behavior; and (3) poverty in a productive society is manifestly unjust.

The first argument has two basic elements, the popular and the social-scientific. It is popularly believed that since maintenance programs siphon off a significant amount of the nation's wealth, the elimination of poverty will be healthy for economic growth. This argument can be seen emerging as a minor theme, in England, as early as the 1700s.[11] However, *popular belief* is one thing, social science analysis another. Analysis shows that poverty itself directly depresses economic growth in more ways than producing a welfare drain. By depressing the total demand for goods and services and preventing the effective use of manpower resources, poverty adversely affects growth. We have previously noted the surprising fact that many of those who live in poverty are employed full-time. However, as redundant labor they are not contributing to the growth in Gross National Product and the income they derive is too low to make them effective consumers.[12]

For those who are not employed, underemployed or partially employed, their contribution to measurable production is low or nonexistent and the level of their income keeps them from becoming an economically significant part of the consuming population.

Other social science literature has atttempted to show the relationship between material deprivation and a high incidence of social problems or deviant behavior such as juvenile delinquency, crime, drug addiction and mental illness.[13] Once again, this is a position which can be traced back to intellectual belief in the eighteenth century,[14] and one which has been readily accepted in popular belief. However, the implications are once again different for the social scientist and the layman. Rather than build more jails and institutions, social scientists suggest that the elimination of material deprivation should be the primary goal of social policy for this will lead to a decline in those social problems which relate to material deprivation. In addition, social scientists are more cautious in stating a direct causal relationship between poverty and social deviance, since correlation doesn't necessarily imply cause. Such phenomena as political oppression or racism may be indirect causes of both poverty and social deviance in American minority groups. This is especially true in the area of political violence. Civil disorder and political revolution are frequently perceived threats from the poor. In this context, the two variables of objective material deprivation and subjective feelings of relative deprivation have been combined. It has been suggested that the widespread existence of *relative* deprivation in an affluent society may lead to sporadic violence or organized efforts to overthrow the political system. The writings of Banfield and Franz Fanon have contributed to this belief. However, the relationshiip between objective *material* deprivation and political instability has not been clearly demonstrated. Despite the lack of evidence, there is a persistent belief in this additional potential threat from the poor in both the popular and academic traditions.

Many social scientists coming out of a liberal tradition perceive material deprivation as an anomaly in America's highly developed industrial society. Social justice is served by the eradication of poverty. The United States Bill of Rights and the Constitution have been interpreted as guaranteeing the social and economic rights of the individual as well as his juridical rights. The continuance of poverty due to the circumstances of birth and the remnants of ascription in a supposedly open social system is unjust since these are accidents beyond the control of the individual. Liebow, Valentine, Rainwater and Gans emphasize race and job discrimination.[15] These writers maintain that the elimination of ascribed deprivation must be a major social goal for ideological as well as pragmatic reasons. They point to the limited life chances of those born to poverty and suggest that if there is no intervention to equalize opportunity and destroy inherited privilege, then poverty will be perpetuated.

However, in not all social science literature, is the same significance given to the problem of poverty in the United States. Walter B. Miller, for instance, suggests that poverty in America is not a question of material deprivation, but of subjective relative deprivation.[16] According to Miller, compared to the poverty of other times and places, the poverty in America today is not a major problem. Miller also claims that there is no proven relationship between feelings of relative deprivation and social problems and that such concern about relative deprivation is unnecessary. Banfield has also indicated that the problem of poverty has been overemphasized.[17] This overemphasis, he says, has resulted from raising the standards for measuring poverty. If present trends continue, according to Banfield, real material deprivation will soon no longer exist. To a certain extent, this may be seen as related to the position which states that the American poor are the best fed, housed and clothed poor in the world, or alternatively, have the highest comfort level. While there is some truth in this position, it does not take account of the state of our productive capacity in relation to other times and places. Given the nature of our consumer society, and stimulus of the mass media, the accepted standard of living is indeed higher and in fact has an effect on survival itself. When describing material deprivation in the United States we must recognize that many of those who are materially deprived are above the survival level but well below the generally accepted minimal comfort level, or what is frequently referred to as the adequacy level. In addition, there still exist a number of the poor who are very close to the basic survival level. Even if they constitute a rather small proportion of the American population they must not be "swept under the rug" by statistical generalizations proving their insignificance.

Contemporary American Policy.   As we have seen, American social scientists have attempted to understand poverty and to make suggestions about anti-poverty policy. Poverty does seem to be a significant problem and the elimination of poverty has become a major goal of American policy. It seems evident that continued growth of the Gross National Product alone will not solve the problem. On the basis of some of the social scientific research, two basic approaches have been developed and implemented. One aims to change the opportunity structure and give the poor access to resources. The other approach seeks to change the behavior and lifestyle (or "capacity") of the poor.[18] Actually, many programs combine both approaches. Thus, job training programs which can be seen as modifying behavior by "correcting" attitudes to dress, time and language also intervene in the opportunity structure when they train skills and place those whom they have trained in jobs. However, many educational programs emphasize resocialization and broadening experience to "compensate" for deprivation; such programs proceed on the assumption that the system is one of equal and adequate opportunity. Community action programs also give weight to both behavior and opportunity. Programs aim to change behavior by dissipating apathy and promoting indigenous organization, so that the poor as a group can create their own opportunities. However, as many analysts have noted, these programs have failed because the power structure has refused to permit expansion of opportunity.

Recent legislation has brought about some further attempts to increase opportunity and access to resources. A larger segment of the working population has been brought under minimum wage coverage. The minimum wage itself has been raised. Income maintenance programs and the Nixon Administration's proposal for minimum guaranteed incomes are recent attempts to redistribute income and eliminate poverty through intervention in the economic system. However, the Nixon program, through its emphasis on the willingness to work (regardless of the nature of the job, and the rate of pay), is a hangover of the old moralistic and paternalist attitudes to the poor. This was made especially clear in Nixon's Labor Day Speech of September 5, 1971.

BELIEFS ABOUT THE BEHAVIOR OF THE POOR

A major concern of social science is explaining the behavior of the poor and analyzing the implications of such behavior for the persistence of poverty and the potential for its eradication. It is popularly believed that the poor are lazy, violent and have loose morals, and such behavior is considered an important factor in the maintenance of poverty itself.

To a certain extent, this can be seen as consistent with the Western view that the individual has charge of his own destiny and is personally responsible for his position in society. Traditional prejudices against the poor are thus reinforced, and the poor as a social category are condemned to be the moral lepers of society. Characterizing as immoral the lifestyle of the poor serves to heighten the morality of the rest of society. The existence in a complex society of some such déclassé group seems to be essential for the respectable classes.

The literature of social science is itself divided. There are analyses which support popular belief about the character of the poor by stressing the need to change their behavior in order to eradicate poverty and those which discount behavioral differences. The second type of literature concentrates on the fact that the individual is affected by forces beyond his control. Even in a system in which man has achieved technological mastery over natural forces, he has yet to harness the economic and political forces to which he is subject.

One approach focuses on the behavior of the non-poor to the poor, which is primarily exploitative and contributes to the continuation of poverty. An example of this approach is Caplovitz' analysis, *The Poor Pay More,* which shows the degree to which poor people are victimized by local businesses which charge higher prices for poor merchandise and provide minimal service or shoddy goods. The exploitative credit mechanisms used are also described. (It should be noted, however, that many of the local businesses are victims, as well. They are faced with high rates of defaulted loans and transients. They also pay higher wholesale prices because of the small volume of their enterprise.) The result of these processes is that those who are poor, but do not renege on their indebtedness, are the true victims.[19] Another example of this approach is found in Ten Broek et al., *The Law of the Poor.* This volume demonstrates the variety of ways in which the United States legal system operates against the interests of the poor.[20]

Many other writings focus on the behavior of the poor in an attempt to discern whether or not the poor behave differently from the non-poor. If their behavior is different, the question to be asked is whether differences are responses to exploitative forces and limited opportunities, or whether they constitute a different "culture" or set of values. The policy implications of the two perspectives are very different. If one believes that the poor have an autonomous deeply internalized commitment to a set of values different from those of the dominant class, then by pursuing the "wrong" goals the poor are perpetuating their own lack of success and behavioral intervention is necessary. However, if behavioral differences exist, not as the result of separate norms but as responses to macrostructural forces, then only the forces need to be changed.

Those who look at the actual behavior of the poor in the light of exploitative forces imply that the social position of the poor forces them to behave differently from the non-poor in spite of their having the same goals as the other social segments. The social situation in which the poor live limits their access to the means to achieve societal goals, so that alternative, modified means or behaviors are developed to achieve them. An example of this approach can be seen in Rodman's work where the poor are seen as aspiring to the same goals as the middle class with respect to marriage and child-rearing. Since their economic position limits access to desired patterns, the poor stretch the notions of legitimate means to achieve these goals to include consensual unions and the legitimacy of some children born out of wedlock. They thus declare to be normative the behavior which the middle class views as deviant, while still aspiring to middle-class ideal patterns. While formal marriage and children born in wedlock are preferred, the alternate forms are acceptable.[21] Rainwater's work on marriage and the family also indicates that while the poor in America aspire to the same forms of legal marriage and legitimate offspring, they feel no guilt or loss of self-esteem if they do not achieve these goals.[22] Hylan Lewis says in regard to some of his informants, ". . . many low income families appear here as the frustrated victims of what are thought of as middle-class values, beliefs and aspirations." [23] Liebow sees the poor he studied as having "shadow values" or modified middle-class values.[24] Valentine has taken a similar position.[25] In all these instances, the inability to achieve the goals of mainstream society leads to a behavioral pattern which is viewed by the middle class as a direct reversal of appropriate behavior. While Rodman states that stretching values alleviates the discrepancy between ideal and achievable patterns, it is often implied that psychic conflict is generated by the failure to achieve those goals. Therefore, it would seem that if there were sufficient economic opportunity to achieve aspirations, the behavior of the poor would be middle class.

A somewhat different approach points out that in many areas, the actual behavior of the poor itself is the same as that of the middle class, but because of difference in context and due to the general attitude to the poor, their behavior is considered different. An outstanding example can be found in the work of Miller, Reissman and Seagull on the de-

ferred gratification pattern. It is generally assumed that the behavior of
the poor is characterized by a lack of planning and the inability or unwillingness to defer immediate gratification in either material or sexual
consumption. As Miller and his co-workers have pointed out, the middle
class in contemporary America appears to be no more willing to defer
immediate gratification for future rewards.[26] Certainly the growth of
consumer credit is not confined to the poorer section of the community.
In addition, the early work of Kinsey may be read as a key to the increased freedom of the sex lives of the middle class, and certainly the
current sexual revolution is essentially middle class.

As Miller and his co-workers have pointed out, it is the actual behavior, not the ideal norms, of the poor which are compared to the ideal
norms, not the actual behavior of the middle class. Furthermore, the
authors show that if one measures the degree of sacrifice and the likelihood of eventual reward and compares them within the context of the
life of the poor and the middle class, then the propensity to defer is the
same. For instance, you cannot compare the sacrifice of saving $10.00
for a person whose income is low and unstable and who has learned
that his goals have little probability of achievement with the sacrifice of
saving $10.00 for a middle-class person. For those who assert that the
behavior of the poor is essentially the same as that of the non-poor—
but is perceived differently because of the context—there is an implied
need to change the popular *perception* of the behavior of the poor rather
than the behavior itself.

Hylan Lewis and S. M. Miller, among others, have pointed out the
extreme variability of the lifestyles and attitudes of the poor.[27] Hannerz also discusses the heterogeneity of lifestyles among the ghetto residents he studied for the ethnography of a black community, *Soulside*.[28]
However, Hannerz sees that all of the residents of the community regardless of the lifestyle they act out behaviorally are aware of the
alternatives of the other subgroups. They can also use behavioral norms
of the other subgroups when appropriate. He refers to the larger set
of behavioral guides known by the whole community as a cultural *repertoire* from which the individual selects appropriate behavior. In the
cultural repertoire of the residents, regardless of the primary lifestyle
they act out, are many elements taken directly from mainstream culture,
some additional modified norms or guides (as in Rodman's thesis of the
"value stretch") and a few outright substitutes for mainstream cultural
items. The residents, as an interacting community, also develop a nas-
cent collective world view and idiomatic expressive techniques. Signifi-

cantly, Hannerz does not see these differences as providing an impediment to change if those macrostructural variables producing material deprivation are changed. It is obvious that as more ethnographic research is done, the description of the behavior of the poor becomes more complex.

Finally we must turn to those writers who feel that the behavior of the poor does reflect significantly different values and beliefs. Two anthropologists have taken this position. In all fairness, it should be be stated that to a great extent they have done so in an attempt to counteract the prevailing view of the behavior of the poor as pathological, chaotic and random. However, these analysts have concluded that the the behavior of the poor reflects a completely separate, coherent set of values and goals. To a large extent, Lewis's work on the subculture of the poor falls into this category. Lewis suggests that in adapting to poverty, the poor develop patterned behavioral responses which become coherent, self-perpetuating cultural systems. Lewis implies, as a result of his analysis, that intervention should be made in both the social system which generated the subculture of poverty and directly in the behavior of the poor. Walter B. Miller is perhaps the strongest champion of the idea that the poor have a separate value system. In his view, the culture of the unstable laboring class is founded on a different set of focal concerns or value emphases, and he goes so far as to say that they prefer their goals and would not change their lifestyle even if they had an alternative. If Miller's observations are valid and his conclusions accepted, the solution to the problem would appear to be through behavioral intervention, that is, by resocialization.[29]

Another approach to the behavior of the poor which emphasizes the differences is one which proposes that the poor have been inadequately socialized with the result that they are "culturally deprived." This point of view is most commonly to be found in the area of education. The children of the poor are seen as cognitively incapacitated because they have not been exposed to "normal" life experiences and are alleged victims of parental neglect. An example of this point of view can be seen in the following statement based on interviews with slum children:

What strikes us most in these interviews is a seeming malfunction of emotional or cognitive processes. . . . What confronts the interviewer is not so much the impression of a thinking human mind but something like the floor of a mountain lake covered with the sedimentation of different pebbles, algae, pieces of wood and debris which have no other connection but the fact that they happened to come to rest in the same locality.[30]

As an example of the evidence used for such "inconsistent" thought, a Puerto Rican child in New York is asked who cared about him. He replied, "God, my father, my mother, my parents, my cousins," and later revealed that his cousins lived in Puerto Rico and his only contact with them had been many years ago. Anyone familiar with Puerto Rican migrant culture would know that even if there is no direct, frequent interaction, kinsmen play a significant role economically and emotionally. Also, in the Puerto Rican kinship system, it is appropriate to call several sets of people "my parents" or "mother" or "father." All too often, an ethnocentric approach to other cultures produces an incorrect definition of "deviant" behavior.

Moynihan in his controversial study blames the behavior of the Black poor in America on weak family structure and poor socialization.[31] Roach and Gursslin call the poor "inadequate social actors." [32] Those who have alleged that the poor cannot control their impulses or defer gratification are saying, in effect, that they have been poorly socialized. To these analysts, direct behavioral intervention seems appropriate. However, unlike the "positive" interventionists, Lewis and Miller, these people consider that they are working with "cultureless" people with random, purposeless behavior.

As we have seen, much of the controversy in the American poverty literature is over the validity of the concept of a *culture* of poverty. In fact, Hylan Lewis and Charles Valentine have amassed much documentation showing that the terms culture and sub-culture have been greatly overused and misused in American social science.[33] Are all generalizations about the American poor true about the poor everywhere? This entire discussion about culture and the poor in the American poverty literature has taken place without any attempt at cross-cultural or historical comparisons, such as those which we have attempted in the previous chapters.

Few people question that some of the behavior of the poor is different from some of the behavior of the non-poor. However, many balk at the use of the concept of culture with its implications of integration and intergenerational transmission. When we recognize that a complex society like America provides dozens of alternative behavioral guides for the individual then we see that it is best to avoid the trouble-fraught notion of culture.

However, this does not mean that we should move to the other extreme of assuming that all the behavioral responses of the American poor are random, idiosyncratic responses invented by individuals. They are transmitted and they are shared. This point is underscored by the analysis which we have previously made of the comparative materials. As Gans and Hannerz have pointed out, all behavioral responses, even those which, collectively, are traditionally called cultures, at some point emerge from adaptation to a natural or social setting.[34] These responses are then transmitted to those with whom meaningful social interaction takes place and are to some extent perpetuated. Hannerz asserts, in relation to the poor, that although some lag might occur between macrostructural change and behavioral change, behavioral change is inevitable. It is thus not inconsistent to see the behavior of the American poor as in some ways different but to see the differences as adaptations to a setting rather than obstacles to change. Perhaps it would be best to avoid using the notions of culture and subculture until these terms have been adequately modified for use in urban industrial society.[35]

We shall shortly examine the arguments about the behavior of the American poor in a broader perspective and it will then be possible to tell what is unique in urban industrial poverty and Western poverty and what is not.

The Implications of an Historical and Cross-Cultural Perspective

An historical perspective in which to view poverty in the advanced industrial society of the United States, which takes account of developments in other parts of the world, makes it possible to assess policies for dealing with poverty. Traditional attitudes toward the poor are no longer tenable if poverty is to be eliminated. Some of the older views of the significance of poverty are characteristic of the different socioeconomic phases of cultural development in general, while others are particular to the development of early capitalism in the West. While some analysts have argued that these attitudes are determined by the facts of life in a developing capitalist industrial system, our survey indicates that they are not inevitable. Some attitudes, because they are obsolete, are dysfunctional while others have been overelaborated in Western tradition and are not necessary to economic growth.

THE WORK ETHIC

Perhaps the most significant exaggeration in American culture is the view that work is intrinsically good. In primitive societies, work is viewed as a necessary and pervasive aspect of life directly related to survival. While some kinds of work are often more highly valued than others, for example, hunting and herding may be preferred to house-building and firewood collection, activities are valued for the *extrinsic* rewards they produce and not as worthwhile in themselves. Where little division of labor exists, everyone participates in the same work. Motivation is strong because of the need to survive, but work is not glorified. During slack seasons, enforced leisure is free from guilt.

In most traditional agrarian societies, one's work is related to his birthright. Each occupational group attaches a positive value to its metier. Work is viewed as inextricably bound to a person's identity, place of residence, beliefs, and so on. Status is derived from the social evaluation of the work done. While elites are concerned with avoiding activities directly productive of goods and services, that is, manipulating matter or money, the system of values still attaches some worth to all manual and commercial activities. Only the defiling activities of the underclass are void of moral worth. Since mobility is limited, there is no notion that harder work and greater productivity will better one's social position. In fact, the notion of a closed system of resources makes it a social liability to achieve higher material success because in doing so one "takes away" resources from one's fellows. Thus, the ideology supports and rationalizes the real limits in resources and technology, as well as the existing maldistribution of wealth, power and prestige.

In the study of early Western capitalist society, the notion that work is good in and of itself becomes obvious. This is related to the expanding productive system which required a flexible pool of labor circulating between industries and activities. However, now that the technological revolution has reduced the need for intensive work input, this view is no longer essential. In fact such a work ethic is not necessarily characteristic of other societies undergoing the transition today. However, it continues strongly in the West and results in negative self-evaluations among the unemployed and the failure of the middle class to utilize their increasing leisure time. It is not surprising that achieving guiltless enjoyment of leisure is a major social problem of our time. The maintenance of a belief in the intrinsic value of work prevents leisure activities from being considered intrinsically worthwhile. Leisure time is viewed as a way to prepare oneself for resuming work or doing better work. Moreover, it is often directly productive itself as in do-it-yourself home improvement activities. Some modification of these attitudes toward work and leisure appears to be necessary in the changing technico-economic system in the United States.

It is perfectly feasible to maintain the work incentive necessary for production by stressing and upgrading the *extrinsic* rewards rather than the *intrinsic* "nobility" of such activity. The overemphasis on the work ethic when coupled with the overemphasis on individual responsibility and the persistence of moralism has led to the negative evaluation of the poor and has contributed to the failure to eradicate poverty.[36]

INDIVIDUAL RESPONSIBILITY

Another belief characteristic of Western capitalism is that the individual is an independent agent. Several aspects of the developing social system were related to this particular belief. One factor was the belief in an open society in which an individual could move from one class to another. A second factor was the emphasis placed upon competition. A third factor was the growing belief that man could understand and control his environment (including those social aspects which controlled his destiny). Emphasis upon individual responsibility can be seen as the complete negation of the notion of divine causation of stratification and moves the system from a perceived basis in ascription to a basis in achievement. A major point of the preceding discussion has been that the realities of social life did not and do not substantiate this view. Individuals are subject to the man-made forces of the socioeconomic system over which they have minimal control, and inherited privilege is still significant. While laissez-faire economic theory was intensely believed, awareness was slow to develop. However, such laissez-faire beliefs are not necessary prerequisites for successful economic development.

Today, the overemphasis on individual responsibility has been avoided by many developing nations which look to the "system" for causation and not to the individual. This is especially true for systems with socialist and communist ideologies where the capitalist distribution system is viewed as the cause of poverty. If we accept the idea that overemphasizing individual responsibility is no longer useful, then the responsibility of the social and economic system can be stressed. Therefore a greater attempt should be made to manipulate this system rather than the personality of the individual.

Another unique attribute of poverty in the United States comes from the limited extent of material deprivation in the system relative to the extent of the rest of the world. Because the poor are proportionately a more limited group, there is perhaps more social pressure on them to move into the middle class. This is further exacerbated by the mass media in the United States which disseminate a universal standard of living. Thus the American poor are pressured to share the goals and aspirations of the rest of society perhaps more than the poor in the Third World. As Mangin has stated:

I suggest that in efficient, tightly controlled industrial states such as Russia and the United States, diversity and autonomous behavior on the part of groups of people, especially poor and relatively powerless people, is much more difficult than in politically unstable "developing" societies.[37]

BELIEFS ABOUT THE UNDERCLASS

Confusion of immoral behavior with poverty can be seen as a vestige of earlier agrarian views about the underclass. As we have previously noted, the underclass in agrarian society consisted of those who followed lowly or negatively valued occupations and lifestyles. The work done was immoral or menial in society's definition and the lifestyle was immoral as well. The traditional underclass in the West was replaced by the poor or materially deprived as capitalistic development took place. It was no longer a fall from grace or the intervention of the divine that ascribed lowly status but lack of economic success. The notions of immorality imputed to the former lowest status class were transposed to the emergent group. A large segment of the new "poor" practiced the same work activities as those of the underclass in the old system. The core of illicit and menial activities remained the same and to them were added other lowly and unstable work activities such as street vending. The "unemployed," a new category in the new occupational structure, were defined as poor because of explicit lack of economic success. This category too became tainted by the allegation of immorality.

SOCIAL POLICY

Another implication of the historical perspective relates to social policy. The maintenance of the poor, primarily through private and public charity, has been a major theme in Western history. In most traditional agrarian societies, support for the poor was primarily the concern of the corporate groups which made up the basic social structure. Charity had intrinsic value for the donor as well as the value it possessed in maintaining those who were dependent on others. In the

Western tradition a clearcut distinction between the deserving and the undeserving poor emerged. The deserving were those who were viewed as temporarily dislocated by economic forces while the undeserving included those confused with the morally tainted underclass.

At present, the thrust for the elimination of poverty is not one which emphasizes the old notions of charity as an implicit good. Instead the permanent eradication of material deprivation is viewed as both possible and beneficial for the social system as a whole. Unfortunately, however, the distinction between charity which is good for the soul of the giver, programs focused on traditional maintenance at a subsistence level, and the new large-scale programs designed permanently to eradicate material deprivation are not always explicitly or consciously recognized. This leads to public views which misunderstand the long-range goals of public policy. It also permits a belief in the appropriateness of a moralistic distinction between the deserving and undeserving. Based upon this distinction, "charity" is administered so that it does not exceed the maintenance level.

OCCUPATIONAL STRUCTURE

One of the most intriguing conclusions which can be drawn from a survey of poverty in the developing nations is the similarity of the conditions which induce poverty and the similarity of responses to these conditions. Early industrial development would seem to favor the emergence of a large pool of unskilled practitioners of marginal occupations. Such activities are rewarded at such a low level and under such conditions of insecurity that material deprivation must occur. For the group of materially deprived who remain in this condition, certain common response patterns can be seen. It should be noted, however, that in most developing societies, some individuals, albeit a lesser proportion, move out of the stratum of material deprivation back to a traditional setting or up into a higher level of affluence.

A major source of recruitment to the materially deprived segment of urban industrial society is the rural hinterland. Migrants to urban areas who frequently lack the skills necessary for secure, high paying blue-collar jobs and who also lack the capital to become entrepreneurs in the new commercial centers, frequently form the basis for the pool of unskilled practitioners of marginal occupations. This, of course, is still apparent even in the industrially advanced United States where rural migrants (from the South, Appalachia, Mexico, Puerto Rico, and so on) form a significant segment of the marginally employed materially deprived.

The same historical and cross-cultural perspective helps us to see the relationship between the occupational structure and the poverty segment. As the United States has moved into the position of an advanced industrial nation, much of the persisting material deprivation derives from the survival of marginal occupations important in earlier periods of development but no longer rational. The demands for the unskilled in the labor force has been diminishing while the demand for skilled, technical/clerical/managerial segments has expanded.

Despite this shift, marginal occupations still exist, and are characterized by low and unstable income and demeaning reputation. As a result, these "temporary" positions offer no career opportunities. They exist to be filled by the unskilled so that they can "work" and avoid the stigma of unemployment. In addition, such activities serve to form a modern underclass which provides psychic and social rewards to the less marginal groups. To a very large extent, the flow of labor in and out of these activities is related to the poor extrinsic rewards (money and reputation) of such jobs. This in turn is related to a lack of organization (in the union sense) which could raise wages, improve conditions of work and regulate the flow of labor to follow trends of supply and demand in a rational way. The continuation of these occupations maintaining marginal characteristics necessitates the continuity of a materially deprived segment of able-bodied but unskilled workers in the system. Such work activities should be converted into better-paying, organized positions with stable opportunities for advancement. This will produce upgraded income, prestige, and career directions. Some could be eliminated through mechanization and the residual work force redistributed to less marginal occupations.

Certainly, the continuation of such jobs and the continued allocation of new segments of the poverty population to these jobs (for example, forcing the unemployed who cannot work because of technological displacement, recessions or age to do this work for its "intrinsic" value) will only serve to perpetuate "the poor" in this country. As Bluestone says:

> The vogue solution to the poverty of those able to work, but either unemployed or low-paid, has been to inject a dose of retraining and subsequently place the individual back into the labor force presumably now equipped to function in America's high speed economy. Yet it should be

clear that for many of the working poor (and many of the unemployed) the problem is not so much due to a lack of preparation on the part of the individual, but due to the inability of a section of the economy to furnish an adequate wage for what is adequate work. Manpower retraining is needed for those who can benefit by progressing to better paying occupations. But it cannot attack the root causes of low-wage jobs, which given their existence, will inevitably fall to those least able to take advantage of the affluent sectors of the economy.[38]

He advocates government intervention in minimum wage legislation and further unionization.

There is a tendency to view the problem of poverty in America as stemming from the unemployment and underemployment (or marginal employment) of unskilled able-bodied men. This was precisely the case in the early stages of industrialization and is the case in the contemporary developing world. For these nations and for the limited segment of such able-bodied poor in America, changes in the occupational wage structure have meaning. However, certain other large segments of the American poor, such as the aged, will not benefit at all from such policies. In our stage of advanced capitalism we have to refine our analysis of the causes of poverty so as to prescribe appropriate cures to different target populations.

One aspect of the contemporary American social system which has not been given adequate attention is that of planning for future manpower needs. Despite the vast increments in knowledge about the economic and social system, very little attention has been paid to the development of realistic plans for future occupational needs, possibilities of technological displacement and the generation of new work opportunities. Most planning efforts are piecemeal and frequently based upon straight line projections of the present into the future. A recent example of the negative effect of the lack of planning can be seen in the overproduction of teachers and engineers. One of the great problems related to the elimination of poverty in contemporary American society is that much of the effort is present-time oriented rather than future-oriented! Even if all our programs were fully implemented at the present time, there seems to be little recognition that without long-range planning the reemergence of material deprivation in the future is likely. For a nation with an ideology that emphasizes the control of natural, social and personal worlds, to disregard control of this aspect negates the possibility of success.

COPING RESPONSES

We have already seen in Chapter 5 that the widespread similarity in coping responses to poverty occurs because of the adaptiveness of such behavior. We cannot any longer look at such behavior in the United States as evidence of character flaws, moral weakness, social disorganization and pathology. As Gans has pointed out, most of the norm violations of the poor are not behaviors which block success, but they do irritate and threaten the non-poor.

A striking, although not unexpected common response is a set of behaviors which are geared to maximizing limited cash resources. Maximization can be seen in the institutionalized use of pooled resources as well as in consumption patterns which minimize the need for cash. Frequently, however, the easy-going informal lending of money to friends or the use of pawn shops or loan sharks is seen by the middle classes as the self-indulgent, extravagant and careless use of money.

One response pattern which becomes closely linked with the moral judgments of the dominant population is the propensity of the materially deprived to develop flexible patterns of sexual unions. A related phenomenon is the household composition of families of the marginally occupied. Mother–child units, sometimes alone and sometimes combined, transitory male presence and complementary male residential zones are commonly found. A widespread condemnation of the poor arises from their alleged propensity to have children out of wedlock whom they cannot maintain. It can be argued that morality has nothing to do with procreation, and in this case, even if the woman were faithfully married to a man who was marginally employed, the same children would be born and subsequently suffer material deprivation. However, many moralists would feel better were the situation legalized.

Another cluster of social variables related to the marginal occupational structure consists of the widespread arrangements for care of children away from the mother for long or short periods of time. These arrangements become necessary for the woman in certain marginal occupations. In the United States where we have emphasized the role of the mother in child-rearing practices, the alternative child-care arrangements made by the poor contrast starkly with those of the middle class and become a source for the negative evaluation of the mother in poverty. Tightly knit social networks, however, are an adaptive mechanism of the poor throughout the world. By establishing meaningful relationships with a limited number of friends, neighbors, and poor kinsmen, the poor are able to withstand the crisis aspects of their material deprivation.

Many of the alleged impacts upon the psychology of the individual who is reared in a "broken" home with an "absent" father, or "rejected" by his mother have not been proved to be universal human responses. The variety of familial forms operating successfully in many societies which have been described by anthropologists would indicate that alternative forms do not necessarily cause ego damage. Where such alternatives are normatively accepted by the subgroup itself, which seems to be the case here, any negative effect should be minimal. Any direct attempt to manipulate the behavior of the poor as in the "social work solution" would result in an actual loss of adaptation. The interventionist approach which would have the greatest impact on these institutionalized response patterns would be to affect the materially deprived conditions of life, the low and unstable income, and so on, rather than the behavioral responses.

Writers on American poverty have paid less attention to the coping or maximizing responses of the poor than they have to the more difficult area of ideological differences in world view and values. Yet in Chapter 5 we saw that it is largely in the area of economic behavior and the formation of basic social units that the poor develop different behavioral responses. Such areas as attitudes toward society, and so on, are not so precisely related to material deprivation since many other variables affect them strongly. Perhaps writers on American poverty ought to differentiate between maximizing behavior and the less precise area of values and aspirations. Moreover, if they continue to be concerned with ideological differences, greater care must be given to differentiating the complex variety of ideologies among the poor.

RACE, ETHNICITY AND POVERTY

While many common response patterns occur among all the urban poor in the United States, they are often attributed to the black population rather than the poverty segment. A classic example of this mode of analysis is that provided by Moynihan's study of the black family. Moynihan, following Frazer, argues that the black female-centered family unit is a heritage of slavery.[39] Many of the problems of the blacks in the United States today, according to Moynihan, derive from this circumstance. However, it is clear from the findings of our cross-cultural investigation that the phenomenon of the female-based household unit is a characteristic of poverty rather than a trait of any racial or ethnic group and that its adaptive features relating to flexibility in the face of unstable economic resources are numerous.

Some of the other supposed elements of black behavior related morally to impulse gratification and the inability to save for the future can also be seen as analagous to those behavioral responses found all over the world which help to maximize limited cash. Some specific examples are the purchase of expensive appliances and the use of take-out food and snacks. The first activity is thought to be a result of the irrational desire for status symbols among the poor, but can in fact be related to the purchase of pawnable items as forms of saving. Obtaining prepared foods is a characteristic shared by the poor all over the world and is related to inadequate kitchen facilities and the saving of time in a work schedule comprised of time-intensive and irregular activities. Thus, families are successfully fed even when all members are engaged in different petty remunerative activities with different schedules. Exchange relationships between networks of individuals involved in the transmission of second-hand and illicitly obtained goods also exist in black America and they are parallel to similar features found among the poor in other parts of the world.[40]

In a volume highly critical of the work of Moynihan, Lewis, and others who attempt to explain the behavior of the poor, Charles Valentine, an anthropologist, still concentrates on black America in his discussion. In his volume he treats literature on the poor in America as interchangeable with literature on black America.[41] The confusion engendered by the ready transposition of Afro-American culture and the behavior of the poor are widespread and it is hoped that this volume will help clarify which behavioral characteristics are widespread among the poor in urban industrial society and those which are an ethnic phenomenona. One attempt at trying to sort out the two behavioral sets can be found in Hannerz's work. He attempts to isolate behavioral traits which are adaptive to resource deprivation from those characteristic of Afro-American culture such as the soul complex (food, music, and so on) and the style of expression and self-presentation.[42]

The tremendous confusion between the influence of ethnicity and race on the one hand and poverty on the other is characteristic of much of the present social science literature. We have previously noted the high rates of minority representation in the American poverty group. From our perspective, the basic point is that these minority segments have entered the urban labor force recently and at the lower ends of the spectrum through much the same process as rural–urban migration in the developing world. This has occurred during a period when the demands for unskilled labor have been decreasing. Thus it is the nature of manpower needs in the economic system which exacerbate the unemployment and marginal employment of the minority population. The major input to those behavioral differences we have been discussing are primarily economic in origin rather than ethnic or racial.

It is intriguing to note that many of those taking an overtly antiracist position, as well as those who have been characterized as explicitly racist, both see race rather than poverty as accounting for all differences in behavior. Racists suggest that these negatively evaluated behaviors are inherent in the racial group and that the ultimate solution lies in the control or disappearance of the race. The anti-racists are trying to associate the negatively evaluated behavior of the minority poor with racial discrimination. For them, the elimination of racism in America should be the most important aspect of social policy. This seems to be the conclusion of the work of Johnson and Sanday.[43] They find that the black poor and white poor have different beliefs and explain this as the result of the black experience of discrimination. The policy implication in this case is to eradicate discrimination. It would seem to us that certain beliefs and attitudes would be directly related to racial discrimination while others, particularly those related to resource conservation, would be more properly related to economic conditions. Although we can analytically distinguish between the psychological impact of racism and the economic exploitation of *all* the poor, it is difficult in the real world to separate the two. Thus, any overall solution to poverty in America would have to focus on both the elimination of racist attitudes and a restructuring of economic opportunity.

Since many of the negatively evaluated behaviors associated with blacks and other minority groups, especially those associated with consumption and family structure, are the same as those associated with the marginally employed and unemployed in both the historical Western and non-Western transitional society, it seems unproductive to try to associate these behaviors with specific races or ethnic cultures. Racial characteristics are unrelated to this behavior, racial discrimination may be somewhat related in that it produces location at the bottom of the stratification system, but certainly low and unstable income is most strongly related.

There is a growing body of literature devoted to the question of the significance of racial or ethnic subcultures as opposed to social class subcultures in the determination of behavior. One of the early attempts to determine the significance of these two variables was the study of child-rearing patterns among lower- and middle-class blacks and whites.[44] Some recent studies have been more sophisticated in design and in a number of cases have specifically focused on the poor. One of the difficulties with much of this literature is that the emphasis has been upon an either/or approach. Many studies of poverty behavior among different ethnic groups have come up with the notion that each ethnic group has its own different "culture of poverty." [45] On the other hand, when a long time perspective is introduced as in Schneiderman's work on long-term white welfare recipients, the similarity between this group and non-white minority poor was found to be great.[46] One recent analysis of nonverbal behavior among the poor of many ethnic groups indicated that poverty overrode ethnic differences and produced similarity.[47] In fact, an attempt has recently been made to view the literature on the behavioral patterns of Mexican-Americans as the result of poverty not Hispanic tradition.[48]

One way of resolving this apparent contradiction in findings is to distinguish between different categories of behavior. Some of these are more responsive to class position while others are more responsive to ethnic tradition. Those aspects of life which appear to be directly related to class structure are such items as job patterns, sources of cash, the nature of the household unit, patterns of consumption, and the nature of one's social network. The relationship of the poverty segment to the larger socio-economic system of which it is a part would induce these responses as patterned ways of dealing with their lack of resources in a social system in which access to money is basic to the acquisition of all socially valued goods.

Some aspects of life which would seem to be more related to the regional/ethnic variable (culture of origin) would include verbal and nonverbal symbol systems of communication, aspects of clothing such as color and style, food preferences and preparation techniques, leisure time preferences, preferred kinsmen, and music and art styles. In all of the above areas of choice, there are limits established by the class parameter. For example, diets of the poor usually contain high proportions of starch and correspondingly low proportions of protein. However, the particular form of starch foods and the ways in which they are prepared will vary. One striking example of the interrelation of ethnic and class patterns can be found in the examination of house usage. Anyone who has seen a film of Japanese life will have been struck by the multiple uses of a single room. With a portable hibachi, the use of matting for sleeping and the very light, portable living room and eating furniture, a room may be at different times a kitchen, living room, dining room and bedroom. In contrast to the Japanese example, the Western European use of living space is inflexible, with separate rooms or areas of rooms given special uses. The implication of these ethnic style differences should be obvious. For both Japanese and Western European poverty groups, housing space will be extremely limited, of poor quality and lacking in aesthetic elaboration. However, the specific uses of living space would differ according to ethnic style and the flexible-use pattern of the Japanese would lessen the constraints of limited space when compared with the European situation.

GLOBAL PERSPECTIVE

One of the inescapable conclusions to be drawn from all of the preceding analysis is that unless we can do something to solve the problems of poverty in the United States, where it is limited to restricted segments of the population, then there is little hope for eradicating the more pervasive and deeply embedded material deprivation in the rest of the world. As has recently been stated:

It is reasonable to anticipate, however, that the present, weak international orientation in the new philosophy of poverty will be strengthened in the decades ahead. After all, even those now classified as below the domestic poverty line are far above the average in most parts of the world—and the differential is widening.[49]

This point is made even more clear when we compare the number of nations with per capita incomes of under $300 to the United States figure of $3,810 (see Table 1 in Chapter 4). Material deprivation in underdeveloped countries affects all ages and ethnic groups. Marginal occupations comprise a significant proportion of the urban labor force and even more important, the problem of material deprivation in these systems is not merely one of distribution but of production as well.

In a truly worldwide economic system, resource-poor areas would be offset by rich areas, technological innovations would be rapidly diffused and competition for limited resources would cease. In addition, new techniques for the distribution of goods and services would have to be developed which would eliminate the present inequitable distribution system. However, one despairs of seeing this utopian economy translated into reality within the near future. If the United States, with all its resources, does not develop an adequate solution to these basic problems, then the possibility of this happening on a worldwide basis is minimal.

Some would suggest that the continued existence of a capitalist system in the United States makes solutions both here and on the larger world scene impossible. We are not convinced that capitalism is the monolithic and unchangeable ideological and economic system projected by many critics of the system. Nor do we see a capitalistic conspiracy as the basic deterrent to real solutions in the United States or the world. One of the characteristic trends of recent history has been the degree to which ideologies have been able to accommodate themselves to changing social and economic conditions. As a result of this trend it is difficult at the present time to find a "pure" socialist or capitalist society.

Policy makers concerned with poverty in the United States must become less parochial and more concerned with the external distribution of resources as well as the internal. In a sense, we as a nation need to serve as a model to demonstrate that poverty *can* be eradicated successfully, but we cannot do this at the expense of interfering with the productivity in the developing nations.

The developing world is moving directly from a traditional agrarian system to a post-industrial era. While this accelerated process has its disadvantages, the excessive concern with certain ideological notions such as the work ethic will not restrict the *official* anti-poverty commitment in these areas as it did for so long in the West. However, the overriding impediment to implementing the social goals is restricted productivity. If real and large-scale growth is not made, then material deprivation will not merely remain with us, it will spread.

Notes

1. Michael Harrington, *The Other America: Poverty in the United States* (Baltimore: Penguin Books, Inc., 1962).
2. Thorsten Veblen, *The Theory of the Leisure Class* (New York: The Viking Press, Inc., 1945). It was published first in 1899.
3. Harrington, *op. cit.*
4. For example, see Mollie Orshansky, "Counting the Poor, Another Look at the Poverty Profile," *Social Security Bulletin*, 1965; and Harold L. Sheppard, "The Poverty of Aging," in Louis Ferman et al. (eds.), *Poverty in America* (Ann Arbor: University of Michigan Press, 1968), pp. 176–189.

5. Orshansky, in Ferman et al., *op. cit.*, pp. 67–115; and Herman P. Miller, "Poverty and the Negro," in Ferman et al. (eds.), *op. cit.*, pp. 160–176.

6. *New York Magazine*, May 1, 1972, vol. 5, no. 18, p. 31.

7. Elliot Liebow, *Tally's Corner: A Study of Negro Streetcorner Men* (Boston: Little, Brown and Company, 1967).

8. *Ibid.*, pp. 45–46.

9. Barry Bluestone, "Lower-Income Workers and Marginal Industries," in Ferman et al. (eds.), *op. cit.*, pp. 273–303.

10. *Ibid.*, p. 274.

11. Dorothy George, *England in Transition* (Baltimore: Penguin Books, Inc., 1953), pp. 150–151.

12. For example, see Arthur Ross, *Unemployment and the American Economy* (New York: Wiley, 1964).

13. As examples of some of the major works: Richard A. Cloward and Lloyd Ohlin, *Delinquency and Opportunity* (New York: The Free Press, 1960); Frank Reissman, Jerome Cohen and Arthur Pearl, *Mental Health of the Poor* (New York: The Free Press, 1964), and the following works of Walter B. Miller: "Lower Class Culture as a Generating Milieu of Gang Delinquency," *The Journal of Social Issues*, vol. 14, 1958; "Violent Crime in City Gangs," *The Annals*, vol. 365, 1966.

14. Frances Fox Piven and Richard A. Cloward, "The Relief of Welfare," *Trans-Action*, vol. 8, no. 7, 1971, pp. 31–39, 52–53.

15. For example, see Liebow, "No Man Can Live with the Terrible Knowledge That He Is Not Needed," *New York Times Magazine*, pp. 28–9, 129–133, n.d. 1970; Liebow, *Tally's Corner;* Charles Valentine, *Culture and Poverty: A Critique and Counterproposals* (Chicago: University of Chicago Press, 1968); Lee Rainwater, "Problem of Lower-Class Culture and Poverty-War Strategy," in Daniel Moynihan (ed.), *On Understanding Poverty* (New York: Basic Books, 1968), pp. 229–269; and Herbert Gans, "Culture and Class in the Study of Poverty: An Approach to Anti-poverty Research," in Moynihan (ed.), *op. cit.*, pp. 201–228.

16. W. B. Miller, "The Elimination of the American Lower Class as National Policy: A Critique of the Ideology of the Poverty Movement of the 1960's," in Moynihan (ed.), *op. cit.*, pp. 260–316.

17. Edward Banfield, *The Unheavenly City* (Boston: Little, Brown and Company, 1970).

18. For a discussion of how the war on poverty developed a two-prong focus on capacity and opportunity, see James Sundquist, "Origins of the War on Poverty," in Sundquist (ed.), *On Fighting Poverty* (New York: Basic Books, Inc., Publishers, 1969); and Adam Yarmolinsky, "The Beginnings of the OEO," in Sundquist (ed.), *op. cit.*

19. David Caplovitz, *The Poor Pay More* (New York: The Free Press, 1963).

20. Jacobus Ten Broek (ed.), *The Law of the Poor* (San Francisco: Chandler Press, 1966).

21. Hyman Rodman, "The Lower Class Value Stretch," *Social Forces,* vol. 42, 1963, pp. 205–215; also Rodman, "Lower Class Attitudes to Deviant Family Patterns: A Cross-Cultural Study," *Journal of Marriage and the Family,* vol. 31, 1969, pp. 315–321.

22. Rainwater, *op. cit.*

23. Hylan Lewis, *Culture, Class and Poverty: Three Papers from the Child Rearing Study of Low Income District of Columbia Families* (Washington, D.C.: Cross-Tell, 1968), p. 11.

24. Liebow, *op. cit.*

25. Valentine, *op. cit.*

26. S. M. Miller, F. Reissman and Arthur Seagull, "Poverty and Self-Indulgence: A Critique of the Non-Deferred Gratification Pattern," in Ferman et al. (eds.), *op. cit.,* pp. 416–432.

27. Hylan Lewis, *op. cit.;* S. M. Miller, "The American Lower Class: A Typological Approach," *Social Research,* vol. 31, 1964.

28. Ulf Hannerz, *Soulside* (New York: Columbia University Press, 1969).

29. W. B. Miller, "Lower Class Culture," and Miller and William Kvaraceus, *Delinquent Behavior: Culture and the Individual,* National Education Association, 1969; and W. B. Miller, "Implications of Urban Lower Class Culture for Social Work," *The Social Service Review,* vol. 33, 1959.

30. Deborah B. Offenbacher, "Cultures in Conflict: Home and School as Seen through the Eyes of Lower Class Students," *The Urban Review,* vol. 2, 1968, p. 6.

31. Moynihan, *The Negro Family: The Case for National Action* (Washington, D.C.: United States Department of Labor, 1965).

32. James Roach and O. Gursslin, "An Evaluation of the Concept of Culture of Poverty," *Social Forces,* vol. 45, 1967, pp. 383–391.

33. Hylan Lewis, *op. cit.;* and Valentine, *op. cit.*

34. Gans, *op. cit.;* and Hannerz, *op. cit.*

35. W. B. Miller's new approach is in this direction, but there is still too much emphasis on strong internalization of values and inflexibility. See W. B. Miller, "Subculture, Social Reform and the Culture of Poverty," *Human Organization,* vol. 30, 1971; and a paper presented at the Conference on the Implications of the Culture of Poverty Concept, Temple University, October 1969, reprinted in J. Winter (ed.), *The Poor: Culture of Poverty or Poverty of Culture* (Grand Rapids: Eardman, 1971).

36. Hannerz points out the confusion between culture and structure as cause of behavior when he discusses Oscar Lewis's confusion about unemployment. Lewis in stating that unemployment was a behavioral aspect of the culture of poverty was asserting that the poor were unemployed because of their values (that is, voluntary unemployment)

and not because of the macrostructure, a point which is well in line with popular beliefs about the poor! (See Hannerz, *op. cit.*)

37. W. Mangin, *Peasants in Cities* (Boston: Houghton Mifflin, 1970), p. XXIII.

38. Bluestone, *op. cit.,* p. 301.

39. Moynihan, *The Negro Family.*

40. See note 24 in Chapter 5.

41. Valentine, *op. cit.*

42. Hannerz, *op. cit.*

43. N. Johnson and P. Sanday, "Subcultural Variations in an Urban Poor Population," *American Anthropologist,* vol. 73, 1971, pp. 128–144.

44. Allison Davis, *Social Class Influences Upon Learning* (Cambridge: Harvard University Press, 1952).

45. Lola Irelan et al., "Ethnicity, Poverty and Selected Attitudes: A Test of the Culture of Poverty Hypothesis," *Social Forces,* vol. 47, 1969, pp. 405–443; Report of Research by Hugh P. O'Brien at the University of Notre Dame Center for the Study of Man in Contemporary Society which studied poverty pockets of Puerto Ricans, blacks and "Southern whites" as well as Johnson and Sanday, *op. cit.*

46. L. Schneiderman, *The Culture of Poverty: A Study of the Value-Orientation Preferences of the Chronically Impoverished,* unpublished doctoral dissertation, University of Minnesota, 1963.

47. Report of Paper delivered at the 55th Annual Meeting of the American Speech Association in 1970 by Stanley Jones.

48. Terry A. Caine, "Class, Culture and Ethnicity in a Northern Mexican-American Community," paper delivered at the 1971 meetings of the Society for Applied Anthropology.

49. W. Willard and H. Padfield (eds.), "Poverty and Social Disorder," *Human Organization,* vol. 29, 1970, p. 115.

Chapter 7

Summary and Conclusions

MATERIAL deprivation has been a persistent factor in the social development of man. Throughout history its implications have been variously understood. In earlier cultures with less sophisticated technologies, while material deprivation was pervasive there was less explicit concern. In agrarian societies, where there was great poverty, a system of beliefs was fashioned which justified its existence. Furthermore, money did not then have the value it has today in urban industrial society. While social ranking did occur, differences in wealth between elites, respectable non-elites and defiled underclasses as groups were less marked than differences between social classes today. However, the members of deprived groups were perceived as significantly different in spiritual qualities which were based on birthright and reflected in legal rights and occupational activities. Wealth came to an individual as a result of high birth, but his higher social evaluation did not derive from wealth. While social class was ideologically related to the possession of non-material qualities, the conception of the materially rich and poor was only peripheral to the ranking system. The poor were conceptualized as an amorphous nondescript group and were considered necessary to the system and to the elite donor of alms. By allocating some of their worldly goods to the poor the elite obtained spiritual blessings. The existence of poverty was further rationalized by assertions that the virtuous poor would be rewarded in the next life. The structure of society depending as it did on corporate groups based on kinship (clans and lineage), occupation (guilds) or territoriality (corporate villages and hamlets) ensured the individual mutual aid and support in times of stress.

Analagous to the "poor" as conceptualized in urban industrial societies were two groups of people. First, there were those who were more than momentarily dislocated from their corporate groups by natural calamities which were not within the control of the limited technology. These people were initially viewed as temporarily in trouble and deserving of aid through local alms and charity. If not rehabilitated, they were looked upon less favorably. At the bottom of the stratification system were the underclasses, the practitioners of defiling occupations with imputed immoral and disreputable lifestyles. These groups were not totally comprised of people who were materially deprived, for some members were wealthy. However, as a group, they were viewed as spiritually and morally deprived. Moreover, there was a high correlation between material deprivation and underclass membership. There also seems to have been a relationship between the dislocated and the disreputable in that, over time, the permanently dislocated would be recruited to underclass activities which offered a better livelihood. Such activities as begging (a complement to institutionalized almsgiving), prostitution, petty theft, and so on, were fed by the dislocated.

In agrarian societies, as long as the "poor" category included the materially deprived but respectable peasant and artisan, unique behavioral traits were not attributed to the "poor." A peasant, artisan or outcast, whether rich or poor, behaved primarily like a peasant, artisan or outcast. His perceived behavior and lifestyle derived from his inherited social position, not his level of wealth.

The Extent of Poverty

In the Western transition to urban industrial society, poverty persisted. A significant proportion of the total population could be characterized as materially deprived. However, this proportion must have been less than the proportion of materially deprived in agrarian feudal times. The impression which one receives from the literature that poverty became a problem under industrial conditions is related to the growing belief that material deprivation was not an inevitable or virtuous condition in the human experience. Lack of perception of poverty as a problem in earlier times is not only related to its perceived inevitability (an accurate perception given limited productive capacity) but also to the stability of a social system which fixed every man in his place and provided support for him. The increased dislocation of the early periods of the commercial and industrial transition and the increased visibility of the poor in urban centers led to the impression that poverty as a condition was more widespread than in previous periods.

In contrast to the probable decrease in the extent of poverty in the West, it is quite likely that the extent of material deprivation is growing or at least not declining in many of the non-Western nations of the world, currently undergoing an economic transition. This is a result of several differences in the nature of the contemporary non-Western and Western historical transitions.

One obvious difference is demographic in nature. In the entire developing world, a major demographic characteristic is that of population growth. In the Western development, high rates of infant mortality and epidemic disease depressed the rate of growth. In the developing nations, modern medical knowledge has been diffused prior to industrialization which has depressed mortality rates, resulting in large increases in population. In Asia, the population picture is most striking because of the large population base now exacerbated by the population explosion. There are those who might suggest that the present growth in population is a result of a continuation of the capitalistic demand for a pool of surplus labor. However, it seems to us to be somewhat strained to suggest a kind of capitalist conspiracy to stimulate population growth, particularly in a number of nation-states which are primarily out of the capitalist system, for example, China, India, and Ceylon. Since China and India constitute such a significant segment of the total world population, approximately one-third, any major shift in population trends in these two countries will have a great impact upon total world population growth.

Another significant factor is that much of the developing world has been economically constrained in the past as it served the Western colonial powers. Colonial exploitation which contributed substantially to the industrialization of the West relegated the developing territories to the role of sources of raw materials and markets. The developing world has no such context in which to operate. Formerly undeveloped nations must build industrial enterprises rapidly and compete with advanced nations in the world market. It should also be noted that many of the newly created nations which are classified as underdeveloped were and in some cases still are under the political as well as economic control of the more industrially developed nations.

For any analysis of the extent of poverty, there would seem to be a number of basic factors which determine whether material deprivation is increasing or decreasing within a given society. These factors are population growth or decline, resource expansion or decline and the utilization and distribution of available resources. As we have seen above, population is increasing, resource utilization is showing some gain, but large-scale gains are precluded by population growth. There seems to be no basic change in the distribution of wealth in developing areas of the world in spite of the widespread existence of socialist forms of economy and commitments to guaranteeing an adequate level of living.

Who Are the Poor?

One of the striking features of those who comprise the poor is the similarity between the groups in the historical case (England) and those in the contemporary developing nations. Among the poor we find those who are unable to work because of physical incapacity or lack of opportunity resulting from the state of the economy, as well as those who do work in marginal occupations but remain in the poverty segment because of the low-level and instability of rewards. Patterns of poverty-level employment appear to be quite similar when comparing Western development with that of the contemporary world. Some common occupations are those of pre-mechanized and unorganized construction worker, dockworker, porter, messenger, domestic worker, peddler, scavenger, and street artisan. These occupations are characterized by high energy or high time inputs with low wages per energy or time unit. Even at the present time, some occupations exist in advanced industrial society which are characterized by low wages per energy or time unit. These occupations are also characterized by extreme insecurity. Most of the occupations listed above have attributes like sporadic demand leading to intermittent employment in conjunction with an over-supply of potential laborers in these residual jobs.

Another set of occupations frequently associated with poverty conditions can be characterized as illicit. For Mayhew's England we find the activities of prostitution, thievery and begging associated with the London poor. The same is true in the developing nations today. In both cases, a distinction can be made between the amateur and the professional practitioner. Professional practitioners can hardly be classified as poor in either case. Amateurs, on the other hand, frequently use these activities to supplement other sources of income. Even when engaged in such activities for long periods of time, the amateur is not protected by the group structure and does not obtain enough cash to move away from a poverty level.

For those who obtain their incomes from the marginal occupations listed above, opportunities for upward mobility and the accumulation of resources are very limited; frequently such jobs are "dead-end" jobs. Careers may be characterized by horizontal movement from one marginal activity to another. The jobs may be viewed as alternative sources of cash used sequentially or even simultaneously by the poor individual or members of his household unit. However, this horizontal mobility can in no way be construed as upward mobility.

In the West, some of the previously mentioned occupations have become highly organized. With control of the labor supply through unionization and control of working conditions, workers in these occupations have actually moved up in the social stratification system. A primary example of this phenomenon is construction work.

Both in the West and in other areas of the world, it is possible to be recruited from amateur status into the organized group of illicit practitioners. This means entering a group in which the supply of labor is partially controlled, protection from authorities is insured and income becomes larger and more secure.

In still other cases, particularly in petty trade, it is possible to acquire enough capital to move into larger-scale operations. Attempts at such mobility are very frequent. However, the incidence of success is probably low. Finally, for those who sell their skills in the market as opposed to those who sell goods, one avenue of mobility is the acquisition of more highly prized skills.

Social Views of Poverty

The technological and ideological changes which accompany the transition to urban industrial society lead to great modification in the social perception of poverty, the evaluation of the poor and the actual behavioral responses of the poor themselves.

One of the basic shifts which has taken place in the West is the belief that poverty is *not* inevitable or necessary for system maintenance. The divine ordination of poverty and its blessedness as a state disappear as anti-materialism declines in the face of increasing productivity.

In the Western transition, as exemplified in the British case, poverty becomes viewed as the result of either economic conditions or individual flaws and is not considered a virtuous state. Economic conditions are still believed to be beyond the direct control of man and thus the elimination of poverty through intervention in the production or distribution system is not conceived as possible or desirable. This view persists throughout the nineteenth century. Much of the emphasis on the inevitability of poverty which remained during this transitional period is derived from the notion that the productive system has to be fed by cheap labor in order to allow the amassing of the large-scale capital needed for further economic growth. This produces a moralistic emphasis on a work ethic to support the perpetuation of a menial but willing work force. It is only in the twentieth century that a view emerges that stresses the possibility of eliminating poverty and views the existence of poverty as an anomaly in an affluent society.

In the non-Western world which is currently experiencing a parallel transition from traditional agrarian to urban industrial society, some of these same beliefs can be seen although they are not derived from the same economic processes as those in the Western case. What occurred over a two- to three-hundred-year period is now expected to occur over a two to three decade period. The capital intensive alternative (as opposed to labor intensive alternative) and advanced automation are available choices at an earlier phase in development. Thus, lags and overlaps between traditional and modern behavior and attitudes can be expected. To a certain extent, older beliefs about the blessedness of poverty and the fatalistic acceptance of it are carry-overs of traditional beliefs. In another way they are realistic perceptions of a very difficult and perhaps forever forestalled transition. The persistence of these traditional beliefs in *popular* thought can be expected for a long time. The excessive work ethic which developed in the West because of the need for labor has no direct analogue in the developing world.

Although popular belief may still emphasize the blessed and inevitable nature of poverty, official policy as formulated by governments receives a heavy input from twentieth-century Western thinking. At the nation-state level, poverty is viewed as an economic problem which can be eliminated through expanded production and intervention in the distributive system. This position is explicit in the social welfare programs developed by Third World governments. While the transition to this new policy view is in many ways easier in the non-Western world than it was in the historical Western case, the implementation of these policies is much more difficult. The limited productive capacity and the primacy given to governmental support of the development process itself restricts the resources available to governments which have officially adopted programs of social welfare. The persistence of traditional ideas of stratification and fatalism among the old elites and lay population reinforce the disjunction between official policy and achieved distribution.

The Evaluation of the Poor

As materialism comes to the fore and the basis for evaluating an individual is related more strongly to money, the "poor" begin to emerge as a social unit defined on the basis of material deprivation. In the West, where the belief in an expanding productive system permeated much of the thought of both the lay and intellectual communities, the poor began to be blamed for their own condition. It was an alleged weakness in their character and motivational structure as well as their immorality which made them poor. The previous distinction between such amorphous "poor" as those deprived through divine intervention (maimed, orphaned), the temporarily dislocated and the spiritually defiled underclass are blurred under the conditions of expansion. They are blurred empirically as well as conceptually. The newly conceived categories, the unemployed and the underemployed, become the new underclass and they are considered to have the immoral behavioral attributes of the previous underclasses.

Two related shifts which reinforced these negative evaluations of the poor in the West were the intensification of the work ethic and the developing belief in an open system in which an individual is responsible for his own social position. Work was considered to be the solution to all problems. Work was thus a solution to poverty during the early development of the Elizabethan Poor Laws. Later developments in the eighteenth and nineteenth centuries intensified the emphasis on work but did not offer employment opportunities within the community. Thus one had an obligation not only to work but to create the opportunity to work as well. Failure to obtain work was viewed as evidence of individual weakness and inadequacy.

The focus of society simultaneously shifted from the stable corporate group (guilds, kin groups and corporate villages) to the individual family unit. With the supposed increase in economic opportunity and the emphasis on productivity, upward mobility through individual achievement was emphasized over ascribed social position. The inability to take advantage of these opportunities was viewed as the fault of those who did not rise. This view of the poor was further reinforced by the growing belief that man could harness and control the forces of the universe and that the individual could control his own destiny.

Many of the materialistic aspects which characterize the West are developing in the non-Western world through diffusion as well as through spin-offs from the development process itself. Despite the fact that many world leaders state a preference for Western production techniques *without* Western materialism, the tendency for one to follow the other is pronounced. This can clearly be seen in the evaluation of the poor. To a certain extent, the poor are beginning to be viewed as a single unit characterized primarily by economic deprivation and they are beginning to lose their blessedness and gain a negative evaluation. However, some notions of the poor as spiritually superior survive.

The distinctions between the underclass and the "poor" is becoming somewhat blurred, but not to the extent that this happened in the West. One of the reasons that the distinction does become blurred is that the behavioral adaptations of the poor are confused with the immoral and defiling lifestyles of the former underclasses whose place the "poor" now occupy.

One of the basic differences in the evaluation of the poor in the West as opposed to the developing areas is that the latter have not generated an overemphasized work ethic. Work is still viewed as an instrumental activity, a means to an end, rather than an end in itself. Since the phase of labor intensive early capitalism which occurred in the West is not being recapitulated in the same way in the contemporary telescoped development process, the need for the glorification of work is not as great. A belief in the individual's responsibility for his own position seems to be growing as industrialism develops although it has not taken on the all pervasive role it assumed in the West. To a certain extent, the societal view of poverty in many developing nations is ambiguous. This is a result of the emerging emphasis on individualism which conflicts with older ascriptive notions about the causes of collective social position. Social mobility is emphasized and the individual is believed to be able to achieve a higher position than that ascribed by birth, but by no means is this belief as strong as it was in the historical Western development. Fatalism has not given way entirely to the belief in individual control of destiny. The assumption that the introduction of

Western technology will undermine all of the traditional belief systems which are *assumed* to be in conflict with such technological changes is not validated by actual events. It would seem that the position taken by nationalists in many of the underdeveloped areas of the world who want the benefits of industrial production without any basic shifts in belief and the position of many Westerners who see the introduction of technology as destroying traditional beliefs and creating a mirror image of the West are both invalid. What we, as anthropologists, see happening is a series of changes in traditional ideology which will facilitate the introduction of technology and the emergence of a new ideological amalgamation of traditional and modern motifs. This synthesis can be seen in the emergent views toward the poor. In the analysis of what is presently occurring in many of the developing nations, it is possible to see a direct shift from a supernatural explanation based upon divine prescription to an explanation based upon the nature of the economic system without the intervening excessive blame on the individual's character or morality. The creation of interventionist social welfare schemes which manipulate distribution in many underdeveloped areas (where scarce resources are making implementation difficult) can be seen as a result of the avoidance of an emphasis upon individual blame. However, it must be emphasized that, while avoiding the contemporary Western view of poverty, many of these societies have retained the traditional view of the poor as an inherently inferior defiled class of individuals who must be "cared for."

Behavioral Responses of the Poor

As the material definition of social class becomes the norm and the "poor" become a specific social category, behavioral attributes which had never been associated with economic factors in agrarian society become associated with material deprivation. As the cash economy becomes important, people are faced with surviving on a subsistence wage, an intermittent wage or sometimes no wage at all. Having no traditional corporate group or patron–client ties to provide psychological and economic support, alternative lifestyles and social structures have to be adopted to conserve the minimal resources available.

Thus flexible household structure, marital ties, child care arrangements, child scavenging and child recruitment to illicit activities, resorting to begging or petty theft for supplemental income, markets for stolen goods, and so on, develop in response to low income conditions. Related to these responses specifically and to the generally negative social evaluation of the poor, they become viewed as a source of anti-social behavior, that is, crime, juvenile delinquency, sexual immorality, excessive procreation, drunkenness and laziness.

In many discussions of the lifestyles of the poor in transitional societies, certain behavioral characteristics are singled out which may be considered typical of many people living in material deprivation. Among these, one cluster which stands out is that related to marriage and family patterns. In the description of the transition which occurred in the West and is occurring elsewhere today, frequent references have been made to the tendency to avoid formal marital arrangements. For the costermongers in England, the ragpickers in Japan and the residents of the *vecindades* in Mexico City or the *callejones* in Lima, consensual unions and sporadic mating patterns are both widespread and viewed as adaptive by both the poor and many social scientists. Although the members of the dominant classes in the societies in question view such patterns as immoral and anti-social (in that they cause excessive procreation and serve as poor influences on the moral standards of the system) it would seem that a more objective evaluation of this behavioral response would focus on its adaptability. Avoidance of costly ceremonies is one way of conserving resources. Flexibility in household structure, by permitting people to attach themselves to households when it is economically rational and to detach themselves when it is not, is another. Rather than viewing these patterns as deviant they should be viewed as promoting flexibility and expanding economic choices.

Different patterns of child care can be viewed in much the same way. Where children may become economic resources at an early age and where a mother's employment precludes her maintenance of a separate household, or the performance of full-time child care functions, the care of children may be turned over to other members of the mother's network for varying periods of time. Where such responses occur, they are patterned and shared by groups which accept them as normatively approved alternatives.

A number of other response patterns to conditions of material deprivation can be seen as more directly related to survival. These would include mechanisms for the pooling of resources, the creation of networks for informal borrowing, the use of second-hand and stolen goods, pawning, use of loansharks and patterns of frequent miniscule purchases. The *ooi* or auctioned cash pools in Hong Kong, the rotating cash pools in South Africa, the *tanda* or lottery drawn cash pool in Mexico, the raffles and funeral pools in Mayhew's London are all examples of slightly different ways of pooling cash and enforcing slight savings within marginal budgets to create relatively large sums for emergencies and/or occasional but necessary large purchases.

Mechanisms for redistributing second-hand and stolen goods, pawning devices and loansharking are found in all cases as well. One particular aspect of maximization responses which has been looked upon with disfavor by the dominant classes is the pattern of frequent small purchases, especially of snack foods. These appear to be wasteful of resources. However, in the context of the lives of the materially deprived with their intermittent cash income, time-extensive work activities and lack of cooking or storage facilities, such behavior appears to be a realistic response to the situation.

Analysis of the behavior of the poor usually focuses upon two mutually contradictory modes of behavior in the area of relationships to the larger society. On the one hand, much is made of the apathy, isolation and withdrawal of the poor; on the other hand, emphasis is placed on their hostility, aggression and violence. This seeming contradiction, a source of great controversy in the literature, can most easily be explained through the recognition that there are many other intervening variables which come between the interaction of material deprivation and attitudes toward the larger society, producing many types of behavioral responses.

One of the important intervening variables is the nature of the community of residence. Where communities are highly organized and stable, with a high degree of identity and solidarity, or when there is occupational and class heterogeneity (both incidentally related to the squatting pattern), a developing integration with the larger society is more likely to occur. Where such attributes are lacking, as in transient high rent slums with high rates of marginal employment or unemployment, one finds more apathy, withdrawal and/or aggression.

Another important intervening variable is the age-graded lifestyle groups which exist side by side in the same community and are not necessarily related to economic success. Surprisingly it has been found that the young, more trouble-prone unmarried migrant, is usually the individual with the greatest economic success potential and a history of job stability. It is the young tough lifestyle, rather than material deprivation, which is related to antisocial aggressive acts. Conversely, the temperance-oriented member of a fundamental religious sect might be isolated and withdrawn from participation in larger social institutions, but this would not merely be the result of material deprivation. To a certain extent, attempts to develop a coherent and cohesive cluster of behavioral responses typical of the poor founder upon the lack of recognition given to the diverse lifestyle patterns generated by age grading and other social phenomena.

Although we have not emphasized certain behavioral responses which *are* in fact maladaptive, they do exist. Many patterns of violent crime and mental illness are found to occur with greater frequency among the poor. Lack of monetary resources in a society which emphasizes material values does lead to a constraining milieu and a high potential for stress. However, before we even begin to assess the degree to which this occurs, we must identify the adaptive and normatively accepted alternative behaviors of the poor in order to define the truly deviant. Obviously a woman who abandons her children or who physically abuses them under stress is different from the woman who makes alternative child care arrangements within acceptable community norms. One major goal of the comparative and historical approach toward poverty is to distinguish between the adaptive alternative and the truly deviant behavior pattern. An additional implication of the comparative approach is that other forms of deviant behavior are characteristic of other segments of society, that is, the dominant classes. These patterns of deviance probably have greater impact on the system and should also be studied. The poor have no monopoly on deviance.

Poverty in an Advanced Industrial Society (United States)

One inevitable conclusion about poverty in advanced industrial society is that it is not as widespread when compared with transitional societies. However, increased technological capacity has not succeeded in eradicating deprivation. In addition, the bulk of the poor in such societies is drawn from different segments of the population than in transitional societies. There is, however, one group of poor in advanced industrial society which is similar to the materially deprived in transitional societies, that is, those who move from agrarian rural systems into urban industrial settings. This significant group consists of those who have most recently entered the new system, the rural Southern black, the Mexican American, the Indian and the Puerto Rican.

Although some technological unemployment can be seen in the early stages of industrial development (displaced artisans) the kind of technological unemployment which confronts the new poor in the United States is the replacement of men by machines which do not require much human supervision.

In the contemporary United States, the aged also comprise a significant proportion of the poor. With medical and health care advances, the life span has been significantly increased and many of those who were gainfully employed during their productive years fall into the poverty segment when they retire or are forced out of the labor market.

One would expect a similar pattern of behavioral responses by the poor, and ideological beliefs about the poor, only when one focuses upon that limited segment of the poor characterized by marginal activities. Thus, recent urban migrants and their first and second generation offspring might be expected to assume behavioral responses similar to those we have been discussing for transitional societies. Furthermore, complicating factors which intercede are the influence of advanced technological displacement which lowers opportunity and the pervasiveness of racism and racial discrimination as it affects employment. Communication media which promulgate an ideal middle-class lifestyle also intervene between status and behavior. While marital and household patterns, as well as mechanisms to maximize limited cash resources, may be similar, repressive racism and the resurgence of political ethnicism in the United States will have a great effect on the way in which the poor relate to the larger society.

One major distinction in the analysis of poverty in the West and in the developing world is in the area of attitudes toward the poor. The cognitive coalescence of the poor and the disreputable underclasses and the moralism engendered seems to have had particular significance in the West. The overriding emphasis on individual responsibility and blame for life chances reinforces the view of the poor as immoral. The development of the work ethic with its concomitant devaluation of non-productive activities are further inputs into an ideology which suggests that the poor are worthless. These views which might have been important in the development of Western capitalism are impeding welfare in the United States today.

A further point is that material deprivation must be viewed in an international perspective if meaningful eradication is to take place. We in the United States who cannot even develop new mechanisms for the redistribution of wealth in our own system must begin to see that redistribution must occur on a worldwide scale. Otherwise, poverty will remain a pressing problem. The relationship between poverty and personal and/or political violence is by no means clearcut. However, the relationship between poverty, lack of social justice and the inefficient use of manpower resources is well established at the present time. Although the prescription for a "cure" is simple to state, the implementation of any meaningful program either nationally or internationally is almost impossible to envision in light of recent experiences in the United States and the rest of the world.

SOME UNRESOLVED ISSUES

Although we have not labeled it as such, there is a basic division in the anthropological community based upon different views of poverty. Two groups exist which can be referred to as the structuralists and the culturalists. Structuralists see the basic causes of poverty in the capitalist industrial system. They suggest that as long as this system exists in the United States and other major nation-states poverty will continue. Some structuralists suggest that poverty can be eliminated through a modification of the capitalist system while others hold to the idea that the capitalist modes of production and distribution must be eliminated before poverty will disappear. The culturalists see poverty as a condition which is perpetuated by the poor and suggest that it can be eliminated by changing that cultural or subcultural system. Although we have subscribed to the structuralist position we have not been willing to accept the extreme position which states that it is only through the destruction of capitalism that poverty can be eliminated. Capitalism, like every other major economic and social ideology, has had to make compromises with reality. Although the ideological underpinnings may have remained static, the way the ideology is carried out in the maintenance of an actual economic system has changed in the Western world. In the United States the intervention of government in business and the organization of labor have introduced conditions which have been accommodated by the ideology. It is important to note that capitalism in the United States in the 1970s is a far cry from that of the nineteenth or even early twentieth centuries.

We believe the capitalist system can and must be further modified, particularly when some recognition is given to the dysfunctional attributes of maintaining a materially deprived segment of the population. We have also stressed the analysis of the behavioral responses to poverty, rather than writing a political polemic, because we believe that there are patterned responses to this condition which should be recognized and described by social scientists just as any other area should be. Many of these behavioral patterns are realistic adaptations to a real, although externally imposed, set of conditions. Understanding their genesis and maintenance would provide a major contribution to social science.

Aside from these considerations, the most important question revolves around the issue of the elimination of poverty. Whether this will happen or not is, of course, a fundamental issue of our time.

The Effects of Current Ideological Movements

There are several new ideological developments generated in the United States which have direct implications for societal attitudes toward poverty. One minor but intriguing trend is the re-emergence of anti-materialism, asceticism and the positive evaluation of voluntary poverty. To a great extent these trends are based on a negative feeling about the importance of material evaluations in the social system. The Hippies, and religious sects like Hari Krishna, are social movements based upon this trend. These groups have ideologies reminiscent of traditional agrarian societies and are, in some cases, patterned on agrarian sects. They are romantic attempts to return to what is perceived as a better way of life. Such romantic movements are analogous to those of the early periods of industrialism in the United States and England. Early utopian movements, the writings of the Lake poets in England and the Transcendentalists in New England as exemplified by Thoreau reflect these beliefs. Such movements, while serving a function of continually rehumanizing the system, did not have a permanent impact on the ideological direction of modern society and it is assumed that the contemporary romantic movements will not have a sustained effect either.

A second and perhaps more significant development is the current emphasis on ecology and conservation. At first glance, this movement seems to be an attempt to undermine the emphasis on productivity in the economy. To a small extent, the anti-technological aspects of ecology feed into some of the more blatant anti-materialist activities of the commune movement. However, the larger impact of the ecology movement is an extension of the value of man's ability to control the environment. The leaders of this movement are scientists rather than romanticists. They fear a situation in which uncontrolled production will lead to a destruction of resources and eventually the entire system. The questioning of unrestricted economic expansion leads people to interpret the movement as ascetic. However, it is really just an anti-hedonistic movement advocating a longer time perspective and the marshalling of current resources to take care of future needs. Thus, increased production is not in itself viewed as evil; only the needless destruction of future resources is viewed this way.

If this movement does capture the imagination of the larger society and productivity decreases, it would probably lead to a decline in the comfort level for the whole society. However, unless distribution changed, the gap between the poor and the middle class will remain the same. Since the movement itself should logically view the waste of human resources (unemployment, underemployment) as negatively as the waste of any other resources, it is likely that when this implication is recognized change in distribution would take place. In fact, the ecology movement itself points to many areas of our economy where large-scale labor inputs can be used to revitalize the environment and provide jobs. Cleaning up waterways, air purification and reforestation projects are all activities which require the utilization of large numbers of workers.

An additional element in ecology is the focus on restricting population growth. Unrestricted population growth is seen as a basic threat to the maintenance of a viable resource base. If ever we achieve zero population growth on a worldwide scale, in conjunction with increased productivity and a more equitable distribution system then poverty as a widespread condition can be more easily eliminated through conscious planning.

Despite these new movements, the modal trend in American society appears to be an unquestioning commitment to the unhampered growth of productivity and the increased utilization of resources to achieve higher levels of material comfort. Movement in the direction of an emphasis on "immediate gratification" appears to be built into our consumption-oriented economy. Cash on hand as a basic medium of exchange for the individual consumer is giving way to facilitated credit. Material consumption as the basis for evaluating social worth still reigns supreme.

As one consequence of the all-consuming emphasis upon the possession of material goods, programs developed to aid the poor are coming under greater criticism. Where narrow self-interest is concerned, it seems that arguments which focus upon aiding the poor because of social inequality or wasted human potential are considered irrelevant. As Americans become more encapsulated in a value system which is ethnocentrically focused upon their own society at the present time, the lessons of history and a broader perspective of man become even more essential.

References

ABRAMS, C.
1964 *Housing in the Modern World*. London: Faber and Faber.
ABU-LUGHOD, JANET
1969 "Migrant Adjustment to City Life: The Egyptian Case," in G. Breese (ed.), *The City in Newly Developing Countries: Readings on Urbanism and Urbanization*. Englewood Cliffs, N.J.: Prentice-Hall, Inc., pp. 376–388.
1969 "Varieties of Urban Experience," in I. Lapidus (ed.), *Middle Eastern Cities*, Berkeley: University of California Press.
ADAMS, R. N.
1970 *Crucifixion by Power*. Austin: University of Texas Press.
AERNI, MARY JANE
1967 "Contributions to Lewis Review Article," *Current Anthropology*, vol. 8, pp. 492–493.
ALA-I-LINA, VAIAO and FAY
1965 "Samoan Values and Economic Development," *The East-West Center Review*, vol. 1, pp. 3–18.
ARMSTRONG, R.
1967 "The Nightwatchman of Kano," *Middle Eastern Studies*, vol. 3.
BANFIELD, EDWARD
1970 *The Unheavenly City*. Boston: Little, Brown and Company.
BARNSBY, GEORGE
1970 "Attitudes to the Poor Law in the Nineteenth Century as Exemplified in the Black Country." Unpublished paper.
BASHAM, A. L.
1954 *The Wonder That Was India*. New York: Grove Press, Inc.

BECKER, DOROTHY
  1961 "The Visitor to the New York City Poor, 1843–1920," *Social Service Review,* vol. 35, pp. 382–396.
BELLAH, R. N.
  1957 *Tokugawa Religion: The Values of Preindustrial Japan.* New York: The Free Press.
BELSHAW, C. S.
  1963 "Pacific Island Towns and the Theory of Growth," in A. Spoehr (ed.), *Pacific Port Towns and Cities.* Honolulu: University of Hawaii Press, pp. 17–24.
BHARAT SEVAK SAMAJ
  1958 *Slums of Old Delhi.* New Delhi: Atma Ram & Sons.
BLOOMBERG, W. JR. and H. SCHMANDT (eds.)
  1970 *Power, Poverty and Urban Policy.* Urban Affairs Annual Review, vol. 42.
BLUESTONE, BARRY
  1955 "Lower-Income Workers and Marginal Industries," in Louis Ferman et al. (eds.), *Poverty in America.* Ann Arbor: University of Michigan Press, pp. 273–303.
BOGUE, DONALD and K. C. ZACHARIAH
  1962 "Urbanization and Migration in India," in R. Turner (ed.), *India's Urban Future.* Berkeley: University of California Press.
BOHANNON, P. and G. DALTON (eds.)
  1965 *Markets in Africa.* Garden City: Doubleday & Company, Inc.
BOOTH, CHARLES et al.
  1902 *Life and Labour of the People in London.* New York: Macmillan.
BOTT, ELIZABETH
  1957 *Family and Social Network.* London: Tavistock Press.
BREESE, G. (ed.)
  1969 *The City in Newly Developing Countries: Readings on Urbanism and Urbanization.* Englewood Cliffs, N.J.: Prentice-Hall, Inc.
BRYCE-LAPORTE, ROY
  1970 "Urban Relocation and Family Adaptation in Puerto Rico: A Case Study of Urban Ethnography," in William Mangin (ed.), *Peasants in Cities.* Boston: Houghton Mifflin Company, pp. 98–113.
BUTTERWORTH, DONALD S.
  1970 "A Study of the Urbanization Process Among Mixtec Migrants from Tilantongo in Mexico City," in William Mangin, *Peasants in Cities.* Boston: Houghton Mifflin Company, pp. 98–113.
BYRNE, M. S.
  1961 *Elizabethan Life in Town and Country.* London: University Paperbacks.

CAINE, TERRY A.

1971 "Class, Culture and Ethnicity in a Northern Mexican-American Community." Paper delivered at the 1971 meetings of the Society for Applied Anthropology.

CALDAROLA, CARLO

1968 "The Doya-Gai: A Japanese Version of Skid Row," *Pacific Affairs,* vol. 41, pp. 511–525.

CALLEY, M.

1956 "Economic Life in Mixed Blood Communities in New South Wales," *Oceania,* vol. 26, pp. 200–213.

CANCIAN, FRANCIS

1965 *Economics and Prestige in a Maya Community.* Stanford: Stanford University Press.

CAPLOVITZ, DAVID

1963 *The Poor Pay More.* New York: The Free Press.

CHAPEKAR, L. N.

1958 "Community Development Blocks in Badlapur," *Sociological Bulletin,* vol. 7, pp. 111–122.

CH'U, T'UNG-TSU

1957 "Chinese Class Structure and Its Ideology," in J. Fairbank (ed.) *Chinese Thought and Institutions.* Chicago: University of Chicago Press.

CLOWARD, RICHARD A. and LLOYD OHLIN

1960 *Delinquency and Opportunity.* New York: The Free Press.

COON, C. (ed.)

1948 *A Reader in General Anthropology.* New York: Henry Holt and Co.

CRAGG, K.

1964 *The Call of the Minaret.* New York: Oxford University Press, Inc.

CREVENNA, THOMAS (ed.)

1950 *Materiales para el estudio de la clase media en la America Latina.* Washington: Panamerican Union.

Current Anthropology

1967 Review of Lewis's work, vol. 8, pp. 480–500.

Current Anthropology

1969 Review article of Valentine, vol. 10, pp. 181–201.

DAVIS, ALLISON

1952 *Social Class Influences Upon Learning.* Cambridge: Harvard University Press.

DAVIS, KINGSLEY

1965 "The Urbanization of the Human Population," *Scientific American,* pp. 41–53.

DAVIS, K. and H. GOLDEN
1954 "Urbanization and the Development of Preindustrial Areas," *Economic Development and Cultural Change*, vol. 3, pp. 6–26.

DE JESUS, CAROLINA MARIA
1962 *Child of the Dark: The Diary of Carolina Maria de Jesus*. New York: The New American Library, Inc.

DEUTSCHER, I. and E. THOMPSON (eds.)
1969 *Among the People: Encounters with the Poor*. New York: Basic Books, Inc., Publishers.

DE VOS, G. and H. WAGATSUMA
1966 "The Ecology of a Special Buraku," in De Vos and Wagatsuma (eds.), *Japan's Invisible Race*. Berkeley and Los Angeles: University of California Press.
1966 *Japan's Invisible Race, ibid.*

DIETZ, HENRY
1969 "Urban Squatter Settlements in Peru," *Journal of Inter-American Studies*, vol. 11, pp. 353–370.

DOTSON, FLOYD
1953 "A Note on Participation in Voluntary Associations in a Mexican City," *American Sociological Review*, vol. 18, pp. 380–386.

EAMES, EDWIN
1953 "Some Aspects of Rural Migration from a North Indian Village," *Eastern Anthropologist*, vol. 7, pp. 13–26.
1954 "Population and Economic Structure of an Indian Rural Community," *Eastern Anthropologist*, vol. 8, pp. 173–181.

EAMES and W. SCHWAB
1964 "Urban Migration in India and Africa," *Human Organization*, vol. 23.

ELLIS, H. C. and S. M. NEWMAN
1971 " 'Gowster,' 'Ivy-Leaguer,' 'Hustler,' 'Conservative,' 'Mackman' and 'Continental': A Functional Analysis of Six Ghetto Roles," in E. B. Leacock (ed.), *Culture of Poverty*. New York: Simon & Schuster, Inc., pp. 299–315.

ERASMUS, CHARLES
1965 "The Occurrence and Disappearance of Reciprocal Farm Labor in Latin America," in D. Heath and R. Adams (eds.), *Contemporary Cultures and Societies of Latin America*. New York: Random House, Inc., pp. 189–193.

FABREGA, HORACIO, JR.
1971 "Begging in a Southeastern Mexican City," *Human Organization*, vol. 30, pp. 277–287.

FAIRBANK, J. (ed.)
1957 *Chinese Thought and Institutions*. Chicago: University of Chicago Press.

FAVA, S. (ed.)
1968 *Urbanism in World Perspective.* New York: Crowell Company.

FERMAN, LOUIS et al. (eds.)
1965 *Poverty in America.* Ann Arbor: University of Michigan Press.

FOSTER, GEORGE
1962 *Traditional Cultures and the Impact of Technological Change.* New York: Harper & Row, Publishers.

FOX, ROBIN
1967 *Kinship and Marriage.* Harmondsworth, Middlesex, England: Penguin Books, Ltd.

FRANK, ANDREW
1966 "Urban Poverty in Latin America," *Studies in Comparative International Development,* vol. 2, pp. 75–84.

FRANKEL, BARBARA
1969 "When Systems Collide: Ambiguous Marital Status Reporting Among Low Income Negroes in Philadelphia." Unpublished paper.

GANS, H.
1968 "Culture and Class in the Study of Poverty," in Daniel Moynihan (ed.), *On Understanding Poverty.* New York: Basic Books, Inc., Publishers.

GEERTZ, C.
1963 *Peddlers and Princes.* Chicago: University of Chicago Press.

GEORGE, DOROTHY
1953 *England in Transition.* Baltimore: Penguin Books, Inc.

GERMANI, GINO
1961 "Inquiry into the Social Effects of Urbanization in a Working-class Sector of Buenos Aires," in Philip Hauser (ed.), *Urbanization in Latin America.* New York: UNESCO, pp. 206–233.

GLADWIN, THOMAS
1961 "The Anthropologist's View of Poverty," in *The Social Welfare Forum.* New York: Columbia University Press.

GOLDRICH, D. et al.
1967 "The Political Integration of Lower-Class Urban Settlements in Chile and Peru," *Studies in International Development,* vol. 3.

GONZALEZ, NANCIE L. S.
1969 *Black Carib Household Structure.* Seattle: University of Washington Press.

GORDON, MARGARET S. (ed.)
1965 *Poverty in America.* San Francisco: Chandler.

GORE, M. S.
1958 "Society and the Begger," *Sociological Bulletin,* vol. 7, pp. 23–48.

GULICK, JOHN
1967 *Tripoli: A Modern Arab City.* Cambridge: Harvard University Press.

1969 "Village and City: Cultural Continuities in Twentieth Century Middle Eastern Cultures," in Ira Lapidus (ed.), *Middle Ea* ' *Cities*. Berkeley: University of California Press.

GUTKIND, P. C. W.

1967 "The Energy of Despair: Social Organization of the Unemployed in Two African Cities: Lagos and Nairobi," *Civilizations*, vol. 17, pp. 186–211.

1968 "African Responses to Urban Wage Employment," *International Labour Review*, vol. 97, pp. 135–167.

1970 "The Poor in Urban Africa: A Prologue to Modernization, Conflict and the Unfinished Revolution," in W. Bloomberg and H. J. Schmandt (eds.), *Power, Poverty and Urban Policy*, Urban Affairs Annual Review, vol. 2.

HAGEN, E.

1962 *On The Theory of Social Change*. Homewood, Illinois: Dorsey Press.

HALLIDAY, ANDREW

1861 "Beggars," in Henry Mayhew, *London Labour and the London Poor*, vol. 4. London: Frank Cass and Company, Ltd.

HALPERN, JOEL

1967 *The Changing Village Community*. Englewood Cliffs, N.J.: Prentice-Hall, Inc.

HAMMEL, E. A.

1961 "The Family Cycle in a Coastal Peruvian Slum and Village," *American Anthropologist*, vol. 63, pp. 346–354.

1964 "Some Characteristics of Rural Village and Urban Slum Population on the Coast of Peru," *Southwestern Journal of Anthropology*, vol. 20, pp. 346–358.

1969 *Power in Ica*. Boston: Little, Brown and Company.

HANNERZ, ULF

1970 *Soulside*. New York: Columbia University Press.

HANSON, ROBERT C. and O. G. SIMMONS

1969 "Differential Experience Paths of Rural Migrants to the City," *American Behavioral Scientist*, vol. 13, pp. 14–35.

HARA, KIMI

1968 "Problems Related to One-Parent (mother) Families in Miraka City," *Journal of Social Science*, vol. 7, pp. 347–348.

HARRINGTON, MICHAEL

1962 *The Other America: Poverty in the United States*. Baltimore: Penguin Books, Inc.

HARRIS, M.

1971 *Culture, Nature and Man*. New York: Crowell.

HARRISON, R. S.

1967 "Migrants in the City of Tripoli, Libya," *Geographical Review,* vol. 57, pp. 397–423.

HAUSER, PHILIP

1961 *Urbanization in Latin America.* New York: UNESCO.

HEATH, D. and R. ADAMS (eds.)

1965 *Contemporary Cultures and Societies of Latin America.* New York: Random House.

HENRIQUES, FERNANDO

1951 "West Indian Family Organization," *Caribbean Quarterly,* vol. 2, pp. 16–24.

HILL, POLLY

1956 *The Gold Coast Cocoa Farmer.* London: Oxford University Press.

1963 *The Migrant Cocoa Farmers of South Ghana: A Study of Rural Capitalism.* Cambridge, England: Cambridge University Press.

HODGSON, M. G. S.

1958 *Introduction to Islamic Civilization.* Chicago: University of Chicago Press.

HOEBEL, E. A.

1966 *Anthropology: The Study of Man.* New York: McGraw-Hill, Inc.

HOLMBERG, ALAN

1950 *Nomads of the Long Bow,* Institute of Social Anthropology, Publication no. 10, Smithsonian Institution, Washington.

HOWE, MARVINE

1970 "Under Apartheid It Is the Black Women Who Suffer Most," *The New York Times,* October 20.

HUNTER, M.

1956 "An Urban Community in East London," in UNESCO, *Social Implications of Industrialization and Urbanization in Africa South of the Sahara.* Geneva.

IRELAN, LOLA et al.

1969 "Ethnicity, Poverty and Selected Attitudes: A Test of the Culture of Poverty Hypotheses," *Social Forces,* vol. 47, pp. 405–443.

ISAACS, H.

1968 "India's Ex-Untouchables," in Sylvia Fava (ed.), *Urbanism in World Perspective.* New York: Thomas Y. Crowell Company, pp. 350–352.

JAYAKER, S.

1952 *Rural Sweepers in the City.* Mysore City: Wesley Press and Publishing Co.

JOHNSON, JOHN J.

1958 *Political Change in Latin America: The Emergence of the Middle Sectors.* Stanford: Stanford University Press.

JOHNSON, N. and P. SANDAY
1971 "Subcultural Variations in an Urban Poor Population," *American Anthropologist*, vol. 73, pp. 128–144.

JONES, STANLEY
1970 Report of paper delivered at the 55th Annual Meeting of the American Speech Association.

JORDAN, W. K.
1959 *Philanthropy in England 1480–1660*. New York: Russell Sage Foundation.

Journal of the Hong Kong Institute of Social Research
1965 "Report on Making Ends Meet," vol. 1, pp. 1–126.

JUSSERAND, J. J.
1950 *English Wayfaring Life in the Middle Ages*. London: Ernest Benn Ltd. (first published 1889).

KAY, P.
1963 "Aspects of Social Structure in a Tahitian Urban Neighborhood," *Journal of the Polynesian Society*, vol. 72.
1963 "Urbanization in the Tahitian Household," in A. Spoehr (ed.), *Pacific Port Towns and Cities*. Honolulu: University of Hawaii Press, pp. 65–74.

KAYE, BARRINGTON
1966 *Upper Nankin Street Singapore*. Singapore: University of Malaya Press.

KHALAF, S.
1965 *Prostitution in a Changing Society*. Beirut: Khayats.

KLUCKHOHN, C. and W. KELLY
1945 "The Concept of Culture," in R. Linton (ed.), *The Science of Man in the World Crisis*. New York: Columbia University Press, pp. 78–103.

KURODA, TOSHIO
1965 "Occupational Mobility," *Journal of Social and Political Ideas in Japan*, vol. 3, pp. 36–44.

LABINI, P.
1968 "Precarious Employment in Sicily," *International Labor Review*, vol. 89.

LAPIDUS, I. (ed.)
1969 *Middle Eastern Cities*. Berkeley: University of California Press.

LAQUIAN, A.
1968 *Slums are for People*. Phillipines: Bustamante Press.

LATHBRIDGE, H.
1966 "Girls in Danger: On Prostitution," *Far Eastern Economic Review*, vol. 53, pp. 583–587.

LEACOCK, E. B. (ed.)

1971 *Culture of Poverty: A Critique.* New York: Simon & Schuster, Inc.

LEEDS, ANTHONY

1970 "The Significant Variables Determining the Characteristics of Squatter Settlements," *America Latina,* vol. 12.

1971 "The Concept of the 'Culture of Poverty': Conceptual, Logical and Empirical Problems with Perspectives from Brazil and Peru," in E. Leacock (ed.) *op. cit.*

LELYVELD, JOSEPH

1970 "Kishan Babu," in William Mangin (ed.), *Peasants in Cities.* Boston: Houghton Mifflin Company, pp. 135–137.

LERNER, DANIEL

1958 *The Passing of Traditional Society: Modernizing the Middle East.* New York: The Free Press.

LEVINE, R., N. KLEIN and C. OWEN

1967 "Father-Child Relations and Changing Life Styles in Ibadan Nigeria," in H. Miner (ed.), *The City in Modern Africa.* New York: Praeger Publishers, Inc., pp. 215–257.

LEWIS, HYLAN

1968 *Culture, Class and Poverty: Three Papers for the Child Rearing Study of Low Income District of Columbia Families.* Washington, D.C.: Cross-Tell.

LEWIS, OSCAR

1951 *Life in a Mexican Village: Tepoztlan Revisited.* Urbana: University of Illinois Press.

1955 *Life in a Mexican Village.* Urbana: University of Illinois Press.

1958 *Village Life in Northern India.* Urbana: University of Illinois Press.

1959 *Five Families: Mexican Studies in the Culture of Poverty.* New York: Basic Books, Inc., Publishers.

1961 *Children of Sanchez.* New York: Random House, Inc.

1965 *La Vida: A Puerto Rican Family in the Culture of Poverty.* New York: Random House, Inc.

1965 "The Culture of Poverty," in J. TePaske and S. Fischer (eds.), *Explosive Forces in Latin America.* Columbus: Ohio State University Press.

1966 "The Culture of Poverty," *Scientific American,* vol. 215.

1969 "The Possessions of the Poor," *Scientific American,* vol. 221, pp. 114–124.

LEONARD, F.

1966 "Helping the Unemployed in the 19th Century: The Case of the American Tramp," *Social Service Review,* vol. 40, pp. 429–434.

LERNER, DANIEL
  1958   *The Passing of Traditional Society.* New York: The Free Press.
LIEBOW, ELLIOT
  1967   *Tally's Corner.* Boston: Little, Brown and Company.
  1970   "No Man Can Live with the Terrible Knowledge that He Is Not Needed," *New York Times Magazine,* pp. 28–29, 129–133.
LINTON, RALPH
  1936   *The Study of Man.* New York: Appleton-Century-Crofts.
LINTON, R. (ed.)
  1945   *The Science of Man in the World Crisis.* New York: Columbia University Press.
LOEWE, MICHAEL
  1966   *Imperial China.* New York: Praeger Publishers, Inc.
  1968   *Everyday Life in Imperial China.* New York: Harper & Row, Publishers.
LOPREATO, JOSEPH
  1967   *Peasants No More.* San Francisco: Chandler Publishing Co.
LYNCH, OWEN
  1969   *The Politics of Untouchability.* New York: Columbia University Press.
MALTHUS, T.
  1914   *An Essay on the Principle of Population.* New York: E. P. Dutton & Co., Inc. (first published 1798).
MANGIN, WILLIAM
  1967   "Latin American Squatter Settlements: A Problem and a Solution," *Latin American Research Review,* vol. 2, pp. 65–98.
  1970   *Peasants in Cities.* Boston: Houghton Mifflin Company.
  1970   "Poverty and Politics in the Latin American City," in Bloomberg and Schmandt (eds.), *op. cit.*
MARRIS, PETER
  1961   *Family and Social Change in an African City.* London: Routledge and Kegan Paul.
  1967   "Methods and Motives," in Horace Miner (ed.), *The City in Modern Africa.* New York: Praeger Publishers, Inc.
MARX, KARL
  1906   *Capital: A Critique of Political Economy.* Chicago: C. H. Kerr and Co.
MATOS MAR, JOSÉ
  1961   "Migration and Urbanization: the Barriadas of Lima," in Hauser (ed.), *op. cit.,* pp. 170–190.
MAYER, PHILLIP
  1961   *Townsmen or Tribesmen: Conservatism and the Process of Urbanization in a South African City.* Capetown: Oxford University Press.

MAYHEW, HENRY
1967 *London Labour and the London Poor*, vols. 1–4. London: Frank Cass and Co., Ltd. (first published 1861–62).

McGEE, T. G.
1967 *The Southeast Asian City*. New York: Praeger Publishers, Inc.

McNEILL, WILLIAM
1969 *History of Western Civilization*. Chicago: University of Chicago Press.

MILLER, H.
1965 "Poverty and the Negro" in Ferman et al. (eds.), *op. cit.*, pp. 160–175.

MILLER, S. M.
1964 "The American Lower Class: A Typological Approach," *Social Research*, vol. 31, pp. 416–432.

MILLER, S. M., F. REISSMAN and A. SEAGULL
1968 "Poverty and Self-Indulgence: A Critique of the Non-Deferred Gratification Pattern," in Ferman et al. (eds.), *op. cit.*, pp. 416–432.

MILLER, WALTER B.
1958 "Implications of Urban Lower Class Culture for Social Work," *The Social Service Review*, vol. 33.

1959 "Lower Class Culture as a Generating Milieu of Gang Delinquency," *The Journal of Social Issues*, vol. 14.

1966 "Violent Crime in City Gangs," *The Annals*, vol. 365.

1968 "The Elimination of the American Lower Class as National Policy: A Critique of the Ideology of the Poverty Movement of the 1960's," in Moynihan (ed.), *On Understanding Poverty*. New York: Basic Books, Inc., Publishers.

1971 "Subculture, Social Reform and the 'Culture of Poverty,' " *Human Organization*, vol. 30, pp. 111–125.

MILLER, W. B. and WILLIAM KVARACEUS
1969 *Delinquent Behavior: Culture and the Individual*. National Education Association.

MILONE, PAULINE
1966 *Urban Areas in Indonesia*. University of California Institute of International Studies, Research Series no. 10.

MINER, H. (ed.)
1967 *The City in Modern Africa*. New York: Praeger Publishers, Inc.

MINTZ, S. W.
1956 "Cañelmar: The Subculture of a Rural Sugar Plantation Proletariat," in Julian H. Steward (ed.), *The People of Puerto Rico*. Urbana: University of Illinois Press, pp. 314–417.

MOONEY, J. D.
1967 "Urban Poverty and Labor Force Participation," *American Economic Review*, vol. 57, pp. 104–119.

MOORE, WILBERT
1965 *The Impact of Industry.* Englewood Cliffs, N.J.: Prentice-Hall, Inc.

MORAES, DOM
1970 "Bombay: Wealth, Shanty-towns, Speakeasies, Intellectual Ad Men and Death on the Train," *New York Times Magazine*, Oct. 11.

MOYNIHAN, D.
1965 *The Negro Family: The Case for National Action.* Washington: United States Department of Labor.
1968 *On Understanding Poverty.* New York: Basic Books, Inc., Publishers.

MYRDAL, GUNNAR
1957 *Rich Lands and Poor: The Road to World Prosperity.* New York: Harper & Row, Publishers.
1963 *Challenge to Affluence.* New York: Pantheon Books, Inc.
1970 *The Challenge of World Poverty: A World Anti-Poverty Program in Outline.* New York: Pantheon Books, Inc.

NELSON, JOAN
1970 "Urban Poor: Disruption or Political Integration in Third World Cities," *World Politics*, vol. 22, pp. 393–414.

New York Magazine, May 1, 1972, vol. 5, no. 18.

New York Times, April 17, 1969.

New York Times, Dec. 20, 1970.

O'BRIEN, HUGH P.
1968 Preliminary findings of research at the Center for the Study of Man in Contemporary Society of the University of Notre Dame, as reported in *The Catholic Virginian*, April 12.

OFFENBACHER, DEBORAH B.
1968 "Cultures in Conflict: Home and School as Seen Through the Eyes of Lower Class Students," *The Urban Review*, vol. 2.

OKA, TAKASHI
1971 "Tokyo Housing Shortage Persists Amid Affluence," *The New York Times*, Jan. 5, p. 8.

ORSHANSKY, MOLLIE
1965 "Counting the Poor, Another Look at the Poverty Profile," *Social Security Bulletin.*

PATCH, RICHARD
1967 "La Parada: Lima's Market," *American Universities Field Staff Report*, West Coast of South America, vol. 14.

PAUW, B.

1963 *The Second Generation.* Capetown: University Press.

PEACOCK, JAMES and THOMAS KIRSCH

1970 *The Human Direction.* New York: Appleton-Century-Crofts.

PEARSE, ANDREW

1961 "Some Characteristics of Urbanization in the City of Rio de Janeiro," in Hauser (ed.), *Urbanization in Latin America,* pp. 191–205.

PEATTIE, L. R.

1968 *The View from the Barrio.* Ann Arbor: University of Michigan Press.

PETAL, A.

1959 "Some Reflections on the Beggar Problem in Ahmedabad," *Sociological Bulletin,* vol. 8, pp. 5–15.

PHILLIPS, R. E.

1956 "The Bantu in the City: A Study of Cultural Adjustment on the Witwatersrand," in UNESCO, *Social Implications of Industrialization and Urbanization in Africa South of the Sahara.* Geneva.

PICKTHALL, M. M.

1961 *The Meaning of the Glorious Koran.* New York: The New American Library, Inc.

PIVEN, FRANCES FOX and RICHARD A. CLOWARD

1971 "The Relief of Welfare," *Transaction,* vol. 8, pp. 31–39, 52–53.

PLOTNICOV, LEONARD

1970 "Nigerians: The Dream is Unfulfilled," in Mangin (ed.), *Peasants in Cities,* pp. 170–174.

POLYANI, KARL

1944 *The Great Transformation.* Boston: Beacon Press.

PRICE, J.

1966 "A History of the Outcast: Untouchability in Japan," in G. De Vos and H. Wagatsuma (eds.), *op. cit.*

1968 "The Economic Organization of the Outcasts of Feudal Tokyo," *Anthropological Quarterly,* vol. 41, pp. 209–217.

RAINWATER, LEE

1968 "Problem of Lower-Class Culture and Poverty-War Strategy," in Moynihan (ed.), *On Understanding Poverty.*

RAO, B. L.

1966 *Community and Development: A Study of Two Indian Villages.* Minneapolis: University of Minnesota Press.

RAUM, O. F.

1969 "Self-Help Associations," *African Studies,* vol. 28, pp. 119–141.

RAY, T.

1969 *The Politics of Venezualan Barrios.* Berkeley: University of California Press.

RAZVI, N. A.
1965 "Extent and Avenues of Prostitution," *Pakistani Review*, vol. 13, pp. 6–7.
REDFIELD, R.
1965 *Peasant Society and Culture.* Chicago: University of Chicago Press (Phoenix edition).
REISSMAN, FRANK, JEROME COHEN and ARTHUR PEARL
1964 *Mental Health of the Poor.* New York: The Free Press.
RICHARDSON, MILES
1970 *San Pedro, Colombia: Small Town in a Developing Society.* New York: Holt, Rinehart & Winston, Inc.
ROACH, JAMES and O. GURSSLIN
1967 "An Evaluation of the Concept of Culture of Poverty," *Social Forces*, vol. 45, pp. 383–391.
ROBERTS, BRYAN
1970 "The Social Organization of Low Income Families," in R. N. Adams, *Crucifixion by Power.* Austin: University of Texas Press, pp. 479–515.
1970 "Urban Poverty and Political Behavior in Guatemala," *Human Organization*, vol. 29, pp. 20–29.
RODMAN, HYMAN
1963 "The Lower Class Value Stretch," *Social Forces*, vol. 42, pp. 205–215.
1969 "Lower Class Attitudes toward Deviant Family Patterns: A Cross-Cultural Study," *Journal of Marriage and the Family*, vol. 31, pp, 325–331.
ROGLER, LLOYD
1967 "Slums in Latin America," *Journal of Inter-American Studies*, vol. 9, pp. 507–528.
ROHRLICH, G. F.
1964 "Social Security in World-Wide Perspective," *Social Service Review*, vol. 38.
ROSS, ARTHUR
1964 *Unemployment and the American Economy.* New York: John Wiley Inc.
ROWNTREE, B. S.
1902 *Poverty: A Study of Town Life.* London: Macmillan and Co., Ltd.
SAFA, HELEN I.
1964 "From Shanty Town to Public Housing," *Caribbean Studies*, vol. 4, pp. 2–12.
1965 "The Female-Based Household in Public Housing," *Human Organization*, vol. 24, pp. 135–140.
1968 "The Social Isolation of the Urban Poor: Life in a Puerto Rican Shanty Town," in Isaac Deutscher and E. Thompson (eds.),

Among the People: Encounters with the Poor. New York: Basic Books, Inc., Publishers, pp. 335–351.

SALUSBURY, G. T.

1948 *Street Life in Medieval England.* Oxford: Pen-in-Hand.

SALZ, B.

1955 *The Human Element in Industrialization.* American Anthropological Association Memoir 85.

SCHEIDERMAN, L.

1963 *The Culture of Poverty: A Study of the Value-Orientation Preferences of the Chronically Inpoverished.* Unpublished doctoral dissertation, University of Minnesota.

SELIGMAN, BEN B. (ed.)

1965 *Poverty as a Public Issue.* New York: The Free Press.

SEN, S. N.

1960 *City of Calcutta: A Socio-economic Survey.* Calcutta: Firma Mukhopadhyan.

SHANNON, L. W.

1968 "The Economic Absorption and Cultural Integration of Immigrant Workers," *American Behavioral Scientist,* vol. 14.

SHEPPARD, HAROLD L.

1968 "The Poverty of Aging," in Ferman et al. (eds.), *op. cit.,* pp. 176–189.

SIDDIQUI, M. K.

1968 "The Slums of Calcutta: A Problem and Its Solution," *Indian Journal of Social Work,* vol. 29, pp. 173–182.

SIMPSON, DAVID

1968 "The Dimensions of World Poverty," *Scientific American,* vol. 219, pp. 27–35.

SINGER, M. (ed.)

1959 *Traditional India.* Philadelphia: American Folklore Society.

SOUTHALL, AIDAN

1970 "Urban Migration and the Residence of Children in Kampala," in Mangin (ed.), *Peasants in Cities,* pp. 150–159.

SOVANI, N. V.

1964 "The Analysis of Overurbanization," *Economic Development and Cultural Change,* vol. 12, pp. 113–132.

SPENCER, H.

1965 "Poverty Purifies Society," in Robert E. Will and H. G. Vatter (eds.), *Poverty in Affluence.* New York: Harcourt, Brace & World, Inc., p. 581.

SPOEHR, A. (ed.)

1963 *Pacific Port Towns and Cities.* Honolulu: University of Hawaii Press.

STENTON, D. M.
> 1951   *English Society in the Early Middle Ages* (*1066–1307*). Harmondsworth, Middlesex, England: Penguin Books, Ltd.

STENTON, F.
> 1961   *The First Century of English Feudalism.* Oxford: Clarendon Press.

STEWARD, JULIAN H.
> 1955   *Theory of Culture Change: The Methodology of Multilinear Evolution.* Urbana: University of Illinois Press.

STEWARD, J. (ed.)
> 1956   *The People of Puerto Rico.* Urbana: University of Illinois Press.

STOKES, R.
> 1962   "A Theory of Slums," *Land Economics,* vol. 38, pp. 187–197.

SUMNER, WILLIAM
> 1965   "Survival of the Unfittest," in Will and Vatter (eds.), *op. cit.*

SUNDQUIST, JAMES
> 1969   "Origins of the War on Poverty," in Sundquist (ed.), *On Fighting Poverty.* New York: Basic Books, Inc., Publishers.

SUZUKI, P.
> 1967   "Encounters with Istanbul: Urban Peasants and Village Peasants," *International Journal of Comparative Sociology,* vol. 8, pp. 208–215.

TAIRA, KOJI
> 1967   "Public Assistance in Japan: Developments and Trends," *Journal of Asian Studies,* vol. 27, pp. 95–109.
> 1968   "Ragpickers and Community Development: Ant's Villa in Tokyo," *Industrial and Labor Relations Review,* vol. 22, pp. 3–19.

TAYLOR, LEE
> 1968   *Occupational Sociology.* New York: Oxford University Press.

TEN BROEK, JACOBUS (ed.)
> 1966   *The Law of the Poor.* San Francisco: Chandler Press.

TE PASKE, J. and FISCHER, S. (eds.)
> 1964   *Explosive Forces in Latin America.* Columbus: Ohio State University Press.

TEXTOR, ROBERT
> 1961   *From Peasant to Pedicab Driver.* Southeast Asia Studies Cultural Report Series no. 9, Yale University Press, New Haven.

TITMUSS, R. M.
> 1963   "The Welfare State: Images and Realities," *Social Service Review,* vol. 37, pp. 1–11.

TROELTSCH, E.
> 1960   *The Social Teaching of the Christian Churches.* New York: Harper & Row, Publishers, vol. 1.

TURNER, ROY (ed.)

1962 *India's Urban Future*. Berkeley: University of California Press.

UNESCO

1956 *Social Implications of Industrialization and Urbanization in Africa South of the Sahara*. Geneva.

VALENTINE, CHARLES

1968 *Culture and Poverty: A Critique and Counterproposals*. Chicago: University of Chicago Press.

VALENTINE, C. and B. L. VALENTINE

1969 "Ethnography and Large-Scale Complex Sociocultural Systems" (mimeo).

1970 "Making the Scene, Digging the Action and Telling it Like it Is: Anthropologists at Work in a Dark Ghetto," in N. Whitten and J. Szwed (eds.), *Afro-American Anthropology: Contemporary Perspectives*. New York: The Free Press, pp. 403–429.

VEBLEN, THORSTEN

1945 *The Theory of the Leisure Class*. New York: The Viking Press, Inc. (first published in 1899).

VERSTER, JOAN

1967 "Social Survey of Western Township, 1964," *African Studies*, vol. 26, pp. 175–246.

VIDYARTHI, L. P.

1970 *Sociocultural Implications of Industrialization in India: A Case Study of Tribal Bihar*. Delhi: N. S. Saxena.

Viewpoints

1967 "Shoeshine Boys in North Africa: Horatio Alger Again."

VOGT, EVON T.

1970 *Zinacantan*. Cambridge: Harvard University Press.

VON GRUNEBAUM, G. E.

1953 *Medieval Islam*. Chicago: University of Chicago Press.

WEBER, MAX

1930 *Protestant Ethic and the Spirit of Capitalism*. London: Allen and Unwin.

WIENER, M. (ed.)

1957 *Introduction to the Civilization of India: Changing Dimensions of Indian Society and Culture*. Chicago: University of Chicago Press.

WEISBROD, BURTON (ed.)

1965 *The Economics of Poverty: An American Paradox*. Englewood Cliffs, N.J.: Prentice-Hall, Inc.

WHITE, L.

1949 *The Science of Culture*. New York: Grove Press, Inc.

WHITEFORD, ANDREW

1964 *Two Cities in Latin America*. Garden City: Doubleday & Company, Inc.

WHITTEN, N. and J. SZWED (eds.)

1970   *Afro-American Anthropology: Contemporary Perspectives.* New York: The Free Press.

WILL, R. and H. G. VATTER (eds.)

1965   *Poverty in Affluence.* New York: Harcourt, Brace & World, Inc.

WILLARD, W. and H. PADFIELD (eds.)

1970   "Poverty and Social Disorder," *Human Organization,* vol. 29.

WILLIAMS, J. A.

1962   *Islam.* New York: George Brazillier, Inc.

WINTER, J.

1971   *The Poor: Culture of Poverty or Poverty of Culture.* Grand Rapids: Eardman.

WOLF, ERIC R.

1955   "Types of Latin American Peasantry," *American Anthropologist,* vol. 57, pp. 452–471.

1956   "San Jose: Subcultures of a Traditional Coffee Municipality," in Julian H. Steward (ed.), *The People of Puerto Rico.* Urbana: University of Illinois Press, pp. 171–264.

1957   "The Closed Corporate Community in Mesoamerica and Central Java," *Southwestern Journal of Anthropology,* vol. 13.

YANG, C. K.

"The Functional Relationship between Confucian Thought and Chinese Religion," in Fairbanks, *op. cit.,* pp. 269–290.

YARMOLINSKY, ADAM

1969   "The Beginnings of the OEO," in J. Sundquist (ed.), *op. cit.*

ZACHARIAH, K. C.

1969   "Bombay Migration Study: A Pilot Analysis of Migration to an Asian Metropolis," in G. Breese (ed.), *op. cit.,* pp. 36–75.

Index